Vicious and Immoral

Vicious and Immoral

HOMOSEXUALITY, THE AMERICAN REVOLUTION, AND THE TRIALS OF ROBERT NEWBURGH

JOHN GILBERT MCCURDY

JOHNS HOPKINS UNIVERSITY PRESS BALTIMORE

© 2024 Johns Hopkins University Press
All rights reserved. Published 2024
Printed in the United States of America on
acid-free paper
2 4 6 8 9 7 5 3 1

Johns Hopkins University Press
2715 North Charles Street
Baltimore, Maryland 21218
www.press.jhu.edu

Cataloging-in-Publication data is available
from the Library of Congress
A catalog record for this book is available
from the British Library.

ISBN: 978-1-4214-4853-4 (hardcover)
ISBN: 978-1-4214-4854-1 (ebook)

*Special discounts are available for bulk purchases
of this book. For more information, please contact
Special Sales at specialsales@jh.edu.*

CONTENTS

ILLUSTRATIONS

DRAMATIS PERSONAE

*

PRINCIPAL

The Reverend Robert Newburgh,
chaplain to the Eighteenth (Royal Irish)
Regiment of Foot

COMMANDING OFFICERS

Lieutenant General Thomas Gage,
commander in chief of the British army in North America

Major General Frederick Haldimand,
acting commander in chief

Lieutenant General Sir John Sebright,
colonel of the Eighteenth Regiment

Lieutenant Colonel John Wilkins,
Eighteenth Regiment

Major Isaac Hamilton,
Eighteenth Regiment

Lieutenant Colonel William Nesbitt,
Forty-Seventh Regiment of Foot

THE CAPTAINS
(EIGHTEENTH REGIMENT)

Captain Thomas Batt (Retired)

Captain Benjamin Chapman

Captain Benjamin Charnock Payne

Captain John Mawby Sr.,
adjutant and acting quartermaster

Captain John Shee

THE SUBALTERNS

Lieutenant Alexander Fowler,
Eighteenth Regiment

Ensign Nicholas Trist,
Eighteenth Regiment

Lieutenant Robert Collins,
Fourth Battalion, Royal Artillery

ENLISTED MEN OF THE
EIGHTEENTH REGIMENT

Sergeant Joseph Pyrah, quartermaster sergeant

Private John Green, tailor

Private Nicholas Gaffney

Private Robert Jeff, tailor

Privates Isaac Hudson and William Osborne,
Newburgh's servants

CHRONOLOGY

𝓔

December 18, 1742 ❖ Robert Newburgh baptized at St. Mary's, Donnybrook, Ireland

October 8, 1769 ❖ Newburgh ordained a priest in the Church of Ireland, County Galway

November 18, 1772 ❖ Newburgh commissioned chaplain to the Eighteenth (Royal Irish) Regiment
July–December 1772 ❖ Eighteenth Regiment rotates from Illinois to Philadelphia

May 4, 1773 ❖ Newburgh is accused of having sex with his servant by Thomas Batt
August–September 1773 ❖ Newburgh arrives in Philadelphia
October 4–16, 1773 ❖ McDermott's general court-martial, New Brunswick
December 1773 ❖ Newburgh files a civil suit against Batt
December 1773 ❖ Newburgh moves into the Philadelphia barracks

April 5, 1774 ❖ Tailors' regimental court-martial, Philadelphia
April 8, 1774 ❖ Officers' meeting at Hamilton's room, Philadelphia
April 12–21, 1774 ❖ Newburgh's court of enquiry, Philadelphia

May 24–25, 1774 ❖ Green's general court-martial, Perth Amboy

May 26–27, 1774 ❖ Mawby's general court-martial, Perth Amboy

May 27, 1774 ❖ Jeff accuses Newburgh of buggery

May 28–June 3, 1774 ❖ Gaffney's general court-martial, Perth Amboy

May 28, 1774 ❖ Hamilton accuses Newburgh of perjury, prevarication, falsehood, and vicious and ungentlemanlike behavior (Mawby later adds insolence to his commanding officer)

June 1, 1774 ❖ Newburgh is arrested and confined to barracks

July 13, 1774 ❖ Gage orders a general court-martial for Newburgh

August 8–27, 1774 ❖ Newburgh's general court-martial, New York

September–October 1774 ❖ Eighteenth Regiment rotates from Philadelphia to New Jersey, New York, and Boston

April 19, 1775 ❖ Eighteenth Regiment suffers casualties at the Battles of Lexington and Concord

May 13, 1775 ❖ Newburgh leaves New York for London

June 6, 1775 ❖ Eighteenth Regiment withdraws from New York

June 17, 1775 ❖ Eighteenth Regiment suffers casualties at the Battle of Bunker Hill

July 28–August 18, 1775 ❖ Payne's general court-martial, Boston

August–September 1775 ❖ Fowler's general court-martial, Boston

December 1775–March 1776 ❖ Eighteenth Regiment rotates from North America to England

April 23, 1776 ❖ Newburgh transfers to the Fifteenth Regiment

July 9, 1779 ❖ Newburgh retires from the British army on half-pay

December 31, 1825 ❖ Robert Newburgh dies, chaplain to Belleisle Garrison, France

NOTE TO THE READER

ℰ

WHAT SHOULD WE CALL MEN WHO HAVE SEX WITH MEN? Or those who desire sex with men or who are believed to have such desires? In modern parlance, we term them *homosexuals*, but since this label was not introduced until the nineteenth century, should we apply it to earlier eras?

David Halperin, Rictor Norton, and Michael Bronski have answered this question in the affirmative. Deploying the term *homosexual* across time demonstrates the long history of same-sex love and the resiliency of an identity so long denied. Although writing about an eighteenth-century homosexual is anachronistic, it is no different from using African American or Latino to describe people who lived long before these terms were widely used.

William Benemenn, Thomas Foster, and Richard Godbeer are more skeptical. Given shifting notions of sexuality and identity, mislabeling historical figures can obscure our understanding of the past and even impose present-day ideas where they do not belong. For this reason, these and other historians prefer broader term like male-male intimacy and homoeroticism.

For the most part, I have chosen to use the language of the time. In the eighteenth century, *sodomite* and *catamite* were occasionally employed to label men who had sex with men, but at Newburgh's trials, the most common demonym was *buggerer*. Yet I also want to acknowledge the transhistorical potential of

Newburgh's experience, so I also employ *homosexual* and *homo-sexuality* where I believe these terms to be appropriate.

I have made every effort to transcribe the exact words and spellings as they are rendered in the original documents. All emphasis is in the original, although I have italicized words underlined in the original court documents.

Vicious and Immoral

PROLOGUE

The Parson Is a Buggerer

ON AUGUST 8, 1774, TWO DOZEN BRITISH OFFICERS and soldiers gathered in New York City to judge the Reverend Robert Newburgh. Newburgh was chaplain to the Eighteenth Regiment of Foot, also known as the Royal Irish, and he faced a general court-martial for "Vicious and Immorral Behaviour." For two years, Newburgh had been dogged by claims that he had had sex with another man, and these rumors were fanned by his appearance and actions. He dressed in flamboyant clothes, helped a private slander his captain, and claimed equal rights. Such poor character seemed proof enough that the parson was a buggerer.[1]

Prosecuting the case was Captain Benjamin Chapman. Chapman had heard allegations of Newburgh's buggery from the other officers had personally observed his inappropriate attire. Such evidence led the captain to believe that the chaplain was inclined to commit other crimes. As he made his case before the court, Chapman charged Newburgh with disobeying his commanding officer and arousing mutiny among the enlisted men. Such actions were particularly consequential at a time of gathering colonial rebellion. Newburgh was guilty of upending the social order and for that reason should be expelled from the British army, Chapman argued.

But Newburgh also had defenders. Lieutenant Alexander Fowler testified that the chaplain was a man of impeccable

1

character. He had seen letters from prominent men testifying to Newburgh's good morals, and he believed that his aid of enlisted men was motivated by Christian duty, not prurient interest. Fowler was less concerned about colonial unrest than Chapman was. He had grown disenchanted with the British army and had befriended Americans who supported the nascent revolution. Fowler believed that Newburgh should be cleared of all charges, concluding that a suspicion of buggery was no reason to expel a man from the army.

For three weeks in August 1774, the British army paused to consider if Robert Newburgh was a buggerer. As they pondered the case, the officers involved explored contemporary perceptions of male-male intimacy and asked what a man's sexual partners revealed about his character. The American Revolution cast a shadow over the trials as the impending rebellion shaped understandings of sexual acts and identity. By hearing testimony from Newburgh, Chapman, Fowler, and others, the court raised questions about whether sexual liberalism had inspired rebellion or whether a nation conceived in liberty could include men with same-sex desires.

❖ ❖ ❖

I first discovered the trials of Robert Newburgh in July 2011. At the time, I was at the William L. Clements Library of the University of Michigan in Ann Arbor, researching the British army and the coming of the American Revolution. While reading through the correspondence of General Thomas Gage, I came across the transcript of a case involving buggery. Although I was curious about the trial, it didn't seem relevant to my investigation of quartering, so I set it aside.

Years later I returned to the Clements and the curious transcript. I wanted to know more about what went on in the barracks, and I thought that this case might make a good article or a useful footnote for future scholars. Once I started reading the transcript in depth, however, I realized that I had located only the tip of the iceberg. The transcript in Ann Arbor was but one of several legal actions involving Robert Newburgh. At the UK National Archives at Kew, I discovered six more trials related to Newburgh, including his August 1774 court-martial. I had unearthed hundreds of pages of transcripts, affidavits, and correspondence that were too complicated—and too interesting—for an article.

I am both an early American historian and a gay man, and as such, I know that there are few good sources on homosexuality from before the twentieth century. When I teach courses on the American Revolution and LGBTQ+ history, I am often embarrassed by how little I have to share with my students about same-sex sex in eighteenth-century America. To my delight, I discovered an amazing level of detail in Newburgh's cases, involving people and topics directly related to the American War of Independence. I had discovered a way to situate homosexuality at the creation of the United States.

❖ ❖ ❖

Sex between men is simultaneously timeless and timely. People of the same sex have always been intimate, but the understanding of such intimacies has changed considerably over time. An evolving terminology is indicative of this instability. Medieval clerics denounced *sodomy*, while the English parliament promulgated a law against *buggery* in the sixteenth century. Both terms bore the mark of divine disapproval, as evidenced by the destruction of Sodom in Genesis 19 and the heretical Bogomils, respectively. Yet as Western cultures became more permissive, the labels changed again. In 1868, the Hungarian writer Karl-Maria Kertbeny coined the term *homosexual* as part of a campaign to decriminalize male-male sex. A century later, liberation movements trumpeted *gay* as a less clinical and more joyous term. In the twenty-first century, *LGBTQ+* has gained popularity, even though the number of letters in this acronym is hardly a settled matter.[2]

Exploring male-male intimacy in the past requires that we not project our own expectations and identities back in time. We should be attuned to language and culture, listening both for what was said and for what was heard. The trials of Robert Newburgh allow an unparalleled opportunity to do just that. The August 1774 court-martial was the culmination of lawsuits, trials, and conflicts that lasted for more than a year, and that preserved a detailed portrait of how people in Great Britain and its transatlantic empire viewed men who had sex with men. Historians have overlooked these trials; when they are mentioned at all, Newburgh has been assigned to the wrong regiment or dismissed as a troublemaker. No one has bothered to ask what his experience might tell us about homosexuality in Revolutionary America.[3]

In the eighteenth century, people living in Great Britain, Ireland, and the American colonies (here termed the Anglo Atlantic) understood that men who had sex with other men were different. To the extent that these men were labeled, the most common demonym was *buggerer*. Buggerer was not a sexual identity per se, but it marked one who desired sex with men. A buggerer had inner qualities that could be observed through external displays of colorful clothes and effeminate actions; in effect, it was part of a man's character. Some joked about buggerers, although such jokes had a blue humor. In the eyes of many, buggerers were immoral and threatened the divine order. They failed to marry and father children, preying instead on men who were their social inferiors. Buggerers tempted others into depravity, not necessarily for sex, but as pawns whom they could manipulate to ruin society.

Yet not everyone feared the buggerer. Some were reluctant to label men based on nothing but appearance, and they questioned the motives of those who persecuted men who had sex with men. Others chose to ignore certain stories, and some even wondered out loud whether society might be more tolerant. The eighteenth century was the age of Enlightenment, an intellectual and philosophical movement that promoted ideals of liberty and equality. Historian Charles Upchurch has argued that the Enlightenment's emphasis on individual rights and sensibility contained the seeds of sexual liberalism. To wit, the first defense of homosexuality in English was composed by Jeremy Bentham in 1774, the same year as Newburgh's court-martial.[4]

The trials of Robert Newburgh also shine a spotlight on LGBTQ+ people at the founding of the United States. Despite the wealth of information on the American Revolution and generations of debates over its meaning, sexual minorities and gender nonconformists are still notably absent from the historical record. Nearly all accounts of the creation of the republic avoid same-sex intimacy; likewise, histories of sexuality ignore the Revolution. For this reason, any reading of the American Revolution leaves the impression that everyone involved was straight.[5]

Newburgh's cases are an opportunity to rectify this omission. Occurring only eight months before the Revolutionary War began, the court-martial is populated with individuals and ideas that shaped American independence. Captain Chapman remained loyal to King George III, and many of the Royal Irish officers who accused Newburgh of buggery contested America's struggle for independence at Lexington-Concord and Bunker Hill. Conversely, Lieutenant Fowler left the British army to become a US citizen, while the lawyers and judges to whom Newburgh looked for legal advice were instrumental in forming the Commonwealth of Pennsylvania. The Eighteenth Regiment ruptured over the case of Robert Newburgh, and this division anticipated the Revolution.

Moreover, the same words that were used to prosecute Newburgh were used to discourage American independence. Chapman denounced both sodomy and rebellion in the same breath as contrary to the values of order and loyalty. Conversely, the rhetoric of the Revolution, like that of the Enlightenment, contained an implicit toleration of homosexuality, and Newburgh defended himself by proclaiming his liberties. He never argued that he had the right to have sex with a man, but he pleaded his case for personal preference, rights, and liberalism in terms that evoked the language of the Declaration of Independence. The creation of the United States did not give rise to a land of sexual liberty, but the trials of Robert Newburgh reveal that the language of the Revolution was used to defend buggerers.

❖   ❖   ❖

In truth, Robert Newburgh is a terrible subject for a book on homosexuality in Revolutionary America. First, it is not clear that he ever had sex with a man. Throughout his trials, Newburgh insisted that he was not a buggerer, yet this might have been a legal strategy like the libel prosecution employed by Oscar Wilde to rebut the Marquis of Queensberry's accusation of sodomy. Regardless of whether Newburgh was a liar or merely wrongly accused, his trials were built on the assumption that he had had sex with a man, and he defended himself accordingly. Second, Robert Newburgh was not an American. Unlike his supporters and his lawyers, he never renounced the authority of King George III but remained a loyal British subject until the end of his life. While he spoke the same language as the American revolutionaries, he was nonetheless on the opposing side.[6]

Newburgh's trials are also an imperfect dataset. The transcripts and other documents cover a small number of people over a relatively short period. Historians have criticized such accounts of sex trials as sensational and revealing of only one form of knowledge. These cases exclusively entail male-male intimacy; they are silent on lesbianism, bisexuality, and transgender issues. Although women and African Americans appear occasionally, nearly every voice recorded is white and male. Yet if we wait for the perfect person, case, and source, we will miss a golden opportunity to situate LGBTQ+ issues at the nation's founding; it is better to acknowledge the imperfections and ask what this one story can tell us.[7]

This book is a close reading of Newburgh's story and his trials as they relate to homosexuality and the American Revolution. Such an approach is necessary to unpack the subtle nuances in eighteenth-century language and insinuations that might not be evident to modern readers. Context for the issues discussed here is derived from contemporary sources, but this is a work of depth rather than breadth.

For the most part, this book follows the chronology of the accusation and trials, although for the purpose of clarity, I have taken some of the material out of sequence for thematic analysis. Newburgh's story began with sexual acts, but when his accusers could not prove that he was guilty of buggery, they attacked his character. The label of buggerer was so hard to shake that Newburgh resorted to insisting that a man's sexual reputation was irrelevant to his position and his rights.

What happened to one man at one moment in time defines neither the LGBTQ+ experience nor the American Revolution. We may extrapolate from it, but it cannot answer all our questions. Nevertheless, the trials of Robert Newburgh can help us understand homosexuality in an era that is both similar to and different from our own, and it can help us appreciate the potential for sexual revolution that was present at the very creation of the United States.

CHAPTER ONE

A Native of Ireland

THERE MAY HAVE BEEN SOME CONCERN about Robert Newburgh's character when he was a boy. In 1769, his uncle Thomas
Newburgh published a collection of poems drawn from a life-
time of observations, including "On a young BOY's being dress'd
in Girl's Cloathes":

> See how the jealous Fair repine
> To think the *Boy's, their* Charms outshine,
> And that in him, the Misses Dress
> Shou'd more than female Charms express.
> Console yourselves ye Fair.—the Boy
> Is but a living Baby-toy:
> And tho' his Face the Eye may charm
> 'Tis you alone, the Heart can warm.

The poem is playful and innocent, perhaps describing a scene
inside a nursery where children try on different outfits and
identities. It assures girls that no matter how alluring a boy
may appear in a dress, only a woman can attract a man.[1]

Although the inspiration of the poem is not stated, Thomas
Newburgh often based works on his extended family. The same
1769 collection included verses about another nephew and two
relatives of Robert's mother. Thomas also had sufficient opportunity to observe his nephew as a cousin later wrote that his
house "was always filled with . . . Broghill, Arthur, Thomas,

and Robert Newburgh." Many years later, captains in the Eighteenth Regiment would cite Robert's flamboyant dress as proof of his predilection for sex with men. Perhaps Thomas saw a hint of this when his nephew was still a boy.[2]

The poem is not an admonishment against crossdressing; rather, it dismisses outward appearances as irrelevant. To some extent, this was a condition of childhood; in the eighteenth century, boys under the age of six were often dressed in gowns. Yet there was also a nascent liberalism in the ode that paralleled Thomas's other poems such as "Every Man to his Liking, &c." In 1769, the Anglo Atlantic was being reshaped by the Enlightenment, and this reflection on a boy in girl's clothes pointed to a link between personal freedoms and gender nonconformity. Whether Robert Newburgh was the subject of the poem or not, he certainly agreed with such enlightened thinking. When he later defended himself against charges of buggery, he argued that a man's clothes had no effect on his ability to do his duty.[3]

"I am a Native of Ireland," Robert Newburgh proclaimed at his court-martial. Born and raised on the Emerald Isle, Newburgh's life exemplified the conditions and contradictions of that particular corner of the Anglo Atlantic. A Protestant descended from a line of wealthy planters, he was unquestionably loyal to the British Empire, attaching himself to its two greatest institutions: the Anglican Church and His Majesty's Army. Yet his early years were indicative of more than colonialism. Like England's American colonies, Ireland was roiled by political and cultural upheaval in the eighteenth century. Same-sex intimacy had long been part of Irish history, but buggery came to be seen as a threat to the moral order as Newburgh grew into manhood. Even before he left Ireland, rumors circulated that his actions and appearance threatened the very institutions that supported English power in Ireland and America.[4]

❖ ❖ ❖

Those who knew Robert Newburgh well reported that he prided "himself upon his family character." He had much to be proud of. On his father's side, Newburgh could trace his lineage to Henry de Beaumont, who helped William I conquer England, and who was created the first Earl of Warwick. Beaumont hailed from a town in Normandy named Le Neubourg (literally, "the new town"), and his son Roger took the surname de Neubourg when he settled at Dorset in southwest England. For the next six hundred years, the family altered the spelling of its name several times (Neufbourg, Newborough, Newburg, Newberry) before settling on Newburgh in the early seventeenth century. An unrelated Scottish peer pronounced it "*New*-bruh" and this may have been true of the Dorset Newburghs as well.[5]

Thomas Newburgh was the first in the family to settle in Ireland, acquiring estates in Donegal, Fermanagh, and Tyrone. He arrived to help suppress the rebellion of 1641, and his wealth came from dispossessing Catholic Gaels of their property. His son, also named Thomas, relocated to County Cavan in north central Ireland, where he became one of the most powerful men in the county, serving as high sheriff, militia colonel, and member of the Irish parliament. Thomas married Mary Taylor, the granddaughter of another wealthy planter who held 1,500 acres near the newly established village of Ballyhaise. Thomas and Mary's eldest son, Brockhill, inherited these fruits of conquest and was truly to the manor born.[6]

The Irish Newburghs were part of a group known as the Protestant Ascendancy. Following the failed rebellion of 1641 and a second uprising fifty years later, English soldiers and settlers drove the native Irish from their lands, remaking the country into an English colony. Power in the Parliament of Ireland shifted decisively to the Protestant landholders, while the Church of Ireland seized Roman Catholic parishes and in-

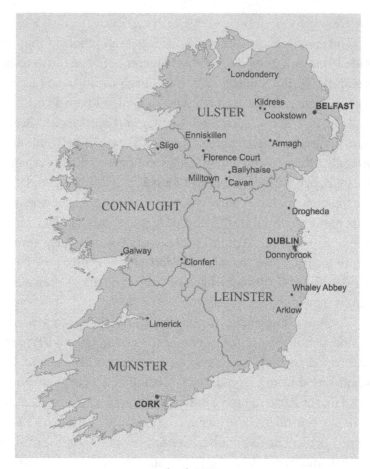

Ireland, 1773

Source: Jacqueline Alessi (2022)

stalled Anglican priests in them. Penal laws and test acts followed, which further impoverished the Gaelic population and
voided their political rights. The settlement of Scottish Presbyterians, mostly in Ulster, also marginalized the native population, although the Scots were often left out of power as well.
The English planters were a distinct minority, with Protestants
constituting less than thirty percent of Ireland's 2.5 million
people. But they controlled the country.[7]

The British army supported the Protestant Ascendancy with twelve thousand regular soldiers. Europe's largest barracks rose in Dublin in 1702, and by midcentury, British redcoats were quartered in more than fifty towns across Ireland. Funded by Irish taxpayers, the soldiers collected taxes, supported English justice, and suppressed rebellion. At times, the Irish parliament balked at the cost, but the gentry had no objection to a standing army in Ireland.[8]

Brockhill Newburgh embodied the Protestant Ascendancy. Born with "that truly protestant zeal, which he had inherited from his *English* ancestors," Brockhill recruited soldiers to fight for the English king William III against Catholic Gaels in 1691. He succeeded his father as high sheriff of Cavan and served a dozen years in the Parliament of Ireland. Brockhill also funded construction of the Castleterra Church so that his family might enjoy regular Anglican worship.[9]

In 1705, Brockhill Newburgh built Ballyhaise House on the River Annalee five miles northeast of Cavan Town. He enlarged it thirty years later in the Palladian style popularized at the time by Richard Castle. Ballyhaise outshone every other house in the county, with an oval salon, brick arches, and stucco walls. Jonathan Swift praised Ballyhaise House as "not only the best, but the *only* house he had seen in *Ireland*," although a later observer dismissed it as "the indulgence of feudal vanity." The Ballyhaise estate cultivated flax for the burgeoning linen market, and the lands were worked by men dispossessed by Brockhill's ancestors. Once, when he attempted to evict a man for overdue rent, Newburgh was stabbed by a tenant, who inflicted "a dangerous wound" that almost proved fatal.[10]

Brockhill Newburgh had at least six children, none of whom could quite match their father's prominence. Two sons took turns as high sheriff of Cavan, while two daughters married members of parliament. Brockhill's eldest son, Thomas, inherited Ballyhaise House, but he had little interest in being

Ballyhaise House
Source: Padriac Colum, *My Irish Year* (New York: Pott, 1912), 53.
Library of Congress, 12029128.

a lord of the manor. Instead, he studied law at Oxford before he took to writing poetry about his family. The youngest son, Arthur, received neither a large inheritance nor a college education but set to work in linen manufacturing, leaving Ballyhaise for Dublin.[11]

In the early 1730s, Arthur Newburgh married Florence Cole. Like Arthur, Florence descended from wealthy English planters. Her great-grandfather founded Enniskillen in County Fermanagh, and both of her grandfathers served in the Irish parliament. Florence's brother, John Cole, achieved a level of prominence that Brockhill Newburgh could only dream of when he was created Baron Mountflorence in 1760. The baron built Florence Court, a Palladian manor house with baroque plasterwork that made Ballyhaise House look plain by comparison. The eminence of the Coles continued into the next generation when the baron's son became Earl of Enniskillen. Robert

Newburgh was proud of his aristocratic connections, bragging to intimates of "walking with his uncle, Lord Mount florence." His maternal relations also provided inspiration for a career. Florence's younger brother Henry Cole attended Trinity College and became a priest.[12]

Robert Newburgh was born in late 1742 in Donnybrook, a suburb south of Dublin. On December 18, he was baptized at St. Mary's Anglican parish. He was not the eldest son but was preceded by at least three brothers and an untold number of sisters. At the time of Robert's birth, the Newburghs were probably living at Ballinguile, a rented estate less than a thousand feet from the site of his baptism, yet the family moved about the Dublin area. Robert's brother Arthur was christened the year before at a different Church of Ireland parish, and Arthur and Florence were living north of the River Liffey twenty years later. Robert and his brothers regularly visited Ballyhaise House where their uncle Thomas took note.[13]

Newburgh's family included at least one foster son who was approximately Robert's age. Fosterage was a common practice in Ireland whereby a child was adopted by another family. Traditionally, a child paid to be fostered, as the adoptive family was expected to provide an education for him. The Newburghs' foster son was tasked with being Robert's personal servant, and the two men grew quite close.[14]

Robert's closeness with his servant was in part a condition of his chronic illness. He was a sickly child, and poor health plagued him well into adulthood. For this reason, he often had "a Servant to sleep in the Room with him." Such intimacy was common at the time, and Robert insisted that his brother Broghill followed the same practice. Yet the illness and remedy would later raise eyebrows; that he slept in the same bed as his servant well into his twenties was the basis for the charge that he was a buggerer.[15]

In addition to being surrounded by servants, Newburgh grew up with other trappings of the Protestant Ascendancy. Testimony from the court-martial indicates that he was skilled at riding and that he spoke Latin. He also studied with a private tutor, which was a mark of privilege during an era when most elite families sent their sons to royal or diocesan schools.[16]

Newburgh also inherited the responsibilities of his imperial upbringing. Two winters before his birth, a great frost destroyed crops and livestock, leaving many Catholic Gaels to suffer starvation, disease, and death in what was termed *bliain an áir*, or the year of slaughter. The experience was made worse by English colonialism. The army put down food riots, while the Royal Navy prevented grain shipments from reaching Ireland due to an ongoing war with Spain. In place of state action, the Protestant Ascendancy sought to alleviate Irish suffering. The gentry distributed food to the countryside, and the widow of an Irish politician employed men to build an obelisk known as Conolly's Folly. Priests from the Church of Ireland distributed alms, while bishops reminded landlords of their Christian duty not to evict their tenants. Although these efforts did not prevent up to a fifth of the Irish population from dying, they were indicative of the noblesse oblige and cultural blind spots that Robert Newburgh carried with him into the chaplaincy.[17]

❖ ❖ ❖

Robert Newburgh was born at a dynamic time in Irish history. *Bliain an áir* exposed the human cost of the island's colonial arrangement and prompted change. After 1740, mixed farming expanded as did grain production; consequently, health improved, and Ireland's population doubled over the next fifty years. A rising bourgeoisie sought fortunes in Dublin, as linen production sparked a market revolution. Hemp, linen, and flax grew as a percentage of the total value of Irish exports, from less than ten percent in 1700 to fifty percent in 1750. Arthur Newburgh was at the forefront of this change, serving as secretary to the powerful Linen Board. This enhanced the family's prominence and enabled their son to excel in his vocational pursuits.[18]

Growing up in Dublin, Robert Newburgh was exposed to a world of wealth and influence. With about 130,000 inhabitants at midcentury, Dublin was Ireland's largest city and a world away from Ballyhaise's feudal pretensions. In addition to being a manufacturing center, it was the capital, and the British king appointed a lord lieutenant who held court at Dublin Castle every other year. The Parliament of Ireland sat regularly, although the day-to-day management of the colony devolved to the Undertaker, a quasi–prime minister. It does not appear that Arthur and Florence Newburgh had access to this uppermost stratum of Protestant Irish society, but they put their son in contact with powerful men. Throughout his life, Robert would know the right person to contact for a recommendation or an inside advantage.[19]

Dublin was also part of the Anglo Atlantic. The Protestant Ascendancy remained culturally tied to London, and they recreated the British capital in Dublin. Coffeehouses and taverns nurtured a secular public sphere, while a growing number of bookshops and newspapers brought fresh ideas to the city. Dublin's appearance underwent a transformation as well, as new buildings gave the Irish capital a decidedly Georgian order. A visitor reported three theaters at midcentury, and the premiere of Handel's *Messiah* took place at the Great Music Hall in April 1742. Robert Newburgh imbibed this culture, joining the Freemasons, a fraternal organization in which ambitious men demonstrated their commitment to moral improvement. He also acquired an appreciation for the theater that would persist for many years.[20]

Dublin was full of British soldiers. The massive Royal Barracks towered over the city, and men in bright red uniforms
stood for regular spring and summer reviews in Phoenix Park.
The British army was particularly conspicuous during the lord
lieutenant's biennial visits, filling Dublin Castle with military
pageantry, and chaplains were part of the performance of regal
power.[21]

On February 27, 1759, Robert Newburgh entered Trinity
College. He was sixteen at the time, not an unusual age to
embark on higher education in the eighteenth century. The
alumni record notes that he was a pensioner, meaning that he
paid tuition, and that he became a bachelor of arts in spring
term 1763. Other than that, Trinity reports "N.F.P.": no further particulars.[22]

If Newburgh did not make an impression on Trinity, Trinity
certainly made an impression on him. The Dublin college was
rapidly improving in the middle of the eighteenth century, adding several stately Palladian buildings and reforming its curriculum. Long known as "the sleeping sister" of the more rigorous
English universities, Trinity added professorships in mathematics, modern history, and oriental languages when Newburgh
was a student. A copy of the diploma that he produced during
his trial indicates that he continued his studies at Trinity for a
year after he took his degree. Similarly, testimony from the
court-martial recorded that he "read a good deal in Divinity
Physick & History" and took "great Plesure and Satisfaction"
from "talking on those subjects."[23]

It was at Trinity that Newburgh encountered the Irish Enlightenment. In the 1690s, Anglican thinkers in Ireland began
to promote empirical methodology, arguing that knowledge
was best obtained through verifiable evidence such as direct
observation or the scientific method. In its early stages, such
enlightened thinking did not question the existence of God or
the truth of divine revelation; it was not deistic but emphasized

a common humanity and the Christian responsibility to alleviate suffering. Trinity was hardly radical, but a new way of thinking was entering the curriculum.[24]

Professor of oratory John Lawson promoted skilled rhetoric
as a way of enabling men to refine themselves. Lawson told his
students that "the orator, who employs his talents aright, is one
of the most useful members of the community," so long as he
infused his words with "religion, humanity, and virtuous industry." It was a lesson that Newburgh took to heart and that
would animate his performance at his court-martial. In his closing arguments, he invoked the highest principles of the Enlightenment and Christian compassion.[25]

The spirit of the Irish Enlightenment spread throughout
Dublin. Sympathy was a principal value of the enlightened person, leading Dubliners to organize charitable societies and
erect hospitals. It encouraged tolerance both as a personal at-
tribute and as a prerequisite for sociability. As men and women
gathered in coffeehouses and fraternal organizations like the
Freemasons, they overlooked the religious differences that divided Ireland. By the 1760s, some descendants of the Protestant Ascendancy questioned the disfranchisement of Catholics.
Some even called themselves *Irish* and plotted to end English
control of the island. Although independence did not arrive
until 1922, similar ideals of liberty and self-determination that
gave rise to the United States were present in eighteenth-
century Ireland.[26]

Newburgh's time at Trinity also introduced him to classical
depictions of homosexuality. During Hilary Term, sophomores
read *The Iliad* with its depiction of the love between Achilles and
Patroclus, as well as works by the Roman poet Juvenal, who sa-
tirically asked why a man should marry a woman when he could
have sex with a boy. Students connected these stories to their
own lives, and we know that avowed homosexuals like Anne
Lister and Lord Byron saw reflections of their desires in the

classics. For some, same-sex love coincided with a spirit of reform. In the 1790s, Trinity student Thomas Moore translated
homoerotic verses by the ancient Greek poet Anacreon while
promoting Catholic Emancipation and Irish independence. Such
ideas shaped Newburgh's character and, like his rhetorical skills,
surfaced at his trials.[27]

Before Newburgh finished college, his family fell apart. In
a scandal that foreshadowed his son's fall from grace, Arthur
Newburgh was accused of misappropriation of funds at the
Linen Board. The details are uncertain, but a parliamentary inquiry followed, and Arthur was compelled to borrow money
from a Dublin merchant to correct the imbalance. Then, in
March 1762, Arthur suddenly died "at his house on Finglas-
road." His wife, Florence, followed him to the grave two months
later. Abruptly, both of Robert's parents were gone. Arthur's
eldest son, Broghill, took his father's place as secretary to the
Linen Board and married, while Arthur junior became a flax
grower in County Donegal. It is unclear what happened to the
other members of the Newburgh household, such as Robert's
foster brother, once Arthur and Florence died.[28]

Upon his father's death, Robert Newburgh was appointed
"clerk-assistant to the trustees of the linen manufacture," working under his brother Broghill. But he had no intention of following in his father's footsteps. His true inheritance was his
college education, and he used it to pursue a profession. In this,
he was part of the Irish "middle layer" in seeking a livelihood
based not on land or name but on intelligence and training.[29]

It would be shortsighted to speculate that Newburgh's
career trajectory was entirely due to material concerns. He was
different from the rest of his family and imbued with wander-
lust. He was the only son to attend college, and the only sibling not to marry. Instead, he found his place in a homosocial
world. He drank alcohol often enough to know how to make a
toddy, and he took tobacco often enough to own a snuff box.

He spent his youth in all-male institutions like Trinity College and the Freemasons, and then joined the sex-segregated professions of the church and the army. At the age of twenty-two, Robert Newburgh left Dublin and embarked upon a new adventure that forever set him apart from the Ireland he had grown up in.[30]

❖ ❖ ❖

In the fifth century, a sixteen-year-old Roman Briton named Patrick was captured by pirates and taken to Ireland as a slave. According to his *Confession*, Patrick was held in bondage for six years and only escaped when he located a ship sailing back to Britain. On the voyage home, the sailors solicited Patrick for sexual favors, but he was unwilling to provide them. "And on that day, to be sure, I refused to suck their nipples on account of the fear of God." The sailors ferried him back to Britain anyway. The young man later returned to Ireland to Christianize the island, and he became Ireland's beloved Saint Patrick.[31]

Homoerotic stories are woven throughout the history of Robert Newburgh's homeland. According to medieval hagiography, the seventh-century saint Mo Ling was visited by Jesus Christ in the form a seven-year-old boy, and the saint took to "fondling Him till the hour of the rising on the morrow." Artwork suggestive of male-male intimacy appears in the Book of Kells, and archaeologists have discovered two adult male skeletons buried with their arms entwined in County Sligo. Around 1610, Eochaidh Ó hÉoghusa wrote odes of love to men from an estate near Enniskillen. One of Ó hÉoghusa's last poems was addressed to Myles O'Reilly, a young man in County Cavan, placing both the poet and the object of his affection in the vicinity of Newburgh's paternal and maternal estates.[32]

To be sure, there was a cultural taboo against male-male sex in Ireland. Ecclesiastical texts specified punishments for a variety of sexual activities between men. The Penitential of Columban, a sixth-century Irish saint, prescribed abstention from meat and wine for seven years for any layman who "commits fornication according to the sodomic rite." However, for a thousand years after Saint Patrick, homosexuality was not against the law in Ireland.[33]

English colonization changed that. Like Ireland, England also had a long history of tender monks and kings with male favorites; unlike Ireland, however, England criminalized the act of two men having sex. Sodomy was prohibited under English law as early as 1290. The Parliament of England increased the penalties in 1533 when lawmakers made "the detestable and abominable Vice of Buggery committed with Mankind or Beast" punishable by death and loss of estates. The buggery law was part of King Henry VIII's campaign to reform the English Church, and it echoed Protestant suspicions of monastic immorality. The law was reaffirmed in 1563, and two centuries later, jurist William Blackstone reported that it remained in force. Proof of buggery required evidence of both penetration and emission, and although the law also forbad bestiality, Blackstone spoke only of human intercourse when he prescribed the same punishment for buggerers "if both are arrived at years of discretion."[34]

The English banned homosexuality in Ireland following the highly publicized trial of Mervyn Touchet, second earl of Castlehaven. In 1630, Castlehaven was accused of raping his wife and sodomizing two servants, and a trial followed a year later that resulted in his execution. Although the earl was an Englishman, his title and wealth derived from his father's Irish estates; he also preferred Irish servants, including one whom he was ultimately convicted of buggering. Castlehaven's case drew attention to the lack of a sodomy law in Ireland and proved to the Protestant Ascendancy that Ireland was a wild place in need of correction. In 1634, the Irish parliament made buggery a capital crime.[35]

Like the Anglican Church and the British army, the buggery law was part of the English conquest of Ireland. In fact, as the British Empire expanded throughout the world, colonizers repeatedly made the same arguments they had made in Ireland: that because indigenous cultures did not do enough to punish perverse acts, English laws against sodomy had to be imposed on them. Advocates of Irish independence reversed this logic and insisted that buggery was a vice introduced to the island by the English. This inaccuracy spoke to a larger truth. As Ireland integrated into the Anglo Atlantic, its permissive approach to homosexuality disappeared.[36]

Although conviction for buggery carried the death penalty, sex between men was rarely prosecuted in either England or Ireland. Between 1731 and 1750, twenty-two accused sodomites appeared before the Central Criminal Court (also known as the Old Bailey), but none were hanged. In the forty years that followed, only a few men were executed for buggery in the British Isles. Observing this evidence, at least one historian has suggested there was a tolerance of male-male intimacy in the first part of the eighteenth century.[37]

In the 1720s, a homosexual subculture appeared for the first time in England. Mollies, as they were known, filled the pages of British newspapers, as did the "molly houses," where men engaged other men for romantic and sexual purposes. "I found between 40 and 50 Men making Love to one another," reported an informant who visited Mother Clap's infamous establishment. He observed men mimicking the appearance of women and dancing with one another before they adjourned "by Couples into another Room on the same Floor, to be marry'd, as they call'd it."[38]

The liberality of the age also created a backlash. Much of what we know about the molly houses comes from the Society for the Reformation of Manners, whose members infiltrated the establishments, seeking evidence against their clientele. After three mollies were hanged in 1726, their houses disappeared, and men who sought sex with other men were driven underground.[39]

The condemnation of homosexuality grew more pronounced over the course of the eighteenth century. Around 1750, sermons and moral tracts decried the effects of sodomy on British society. *Satan's Harvest Home* lamented men "who, unable to please the Women, chuse rather to run into unnatural Vices with one another." The tract's author blamed the coddling of schoolboys, the effeminacy of men's clothes, and the popularity of opera for the epidemic of buggery. Like Irish nationalists, he insisted that sodomy was a foreign import (from Italy: "the Mother and Nurse of Sodomy"), and like English colonizers, he demanded harsh penalties. "Instead of the Pillory, I would have the Stake be the Punishment of those, who . . . preposterously burn for each other."[40]

As British authors grew hostile toward same-sex intimacy, the public was encouraged to participate in punishing sodomites. A common penalty for buggery was a stint in the pillory. With his hands and feet locked in the wooden stocks, a convicted man was subjected to verbal taunts and physical abuse. On multiple occasions, pilloried sodomites were killed by onlookers who hurled rocks at them. Edmund Burke decried the cruelty of such deaths in the British parliament, but others worried that such public punishment only made buggerers shameless.[41]

The sodomite also emerged as a literary character as authors mocked men who had sex with men or who looked like they might want to. Tobias Smollett's 1748 novel *The Adventures of Roderick Random* features a minor character, Captain Whiffle, who dresses in flamboyant clothes and maintains "a correspondence with the surgeon, not fit to be named." Although authors like Smollett were no more tolerant of sodomy than moralists, their tone was more humorous. The buggerer was not a subject of fear but something to laugh at.[42]

The eighteenth century was also an age of scandal. Both England and Ireland produced tales of upstanding men who gave in to their base desires and fell from grace. Men of the highest rank, from the military and the church, were discovered soliciting sex from younger men. Captain Edward Rigby, Oxford don Robert Thistlethwayte, and Archbishop of Armagh George Stone were each humiliated in the press and forced into exile in France. Even rumor could be a lethal weapon; it brought down these men and even implicated the British monarchy. Interest in such scandals grew in the 1770s, ensnaring lowlier men. Former royal artilleryman Robert Jones, Irish playwright Isaac Bickerstaff, and West End actor Samuel Foote were each ruined by accusations of buggery between 1772 and 1775.[43]

For Irish Protestants, probably no scandal was as poignant as that of John Atherton. Born and educated in England, Atherton belonged to the first generation of the Protestant Ascendancy, emigrating to Ireland around 1630 to minister to an Anglican church in Dublin. He was a leading voice of reform and one of the staunchest supporters of Ireland's 1634 buggery law. Under the patronage of the lord lieutenant, Atherton became bishop of Waterford and Lismore, and he entered Ireland's House of Lords. But his ambition attracted powerful enemies. Despite being a husband and father, Atherton was accused of a host of sexual crimes including buggery, and in 1640, he was hanged under the very law he helped enact. The tale of Bishop Atherton was reprinted widely after his death and remained a cultural touchstone a century later.[44]

For a young Irish Protestant like Robert Newburgh, such stories were cautionary tales. He was living in world that condemned homosexuality, and he knew that any man accused of being a buggerer could become the object of public scorn, the butt of jokes, and the target of character assassination.

❖ ❖ ❖

After graduating from Trinity College, Robert Newburgh embarked on his career. While the Irish Enlightenment prompted some men to turn a wary eye toward the British empire, he embraced the two institutions that helped to create and expand English power across the globe: the Anglican Church and the British army. Both allowed him to take advantage of British imperialism and traverse the Atlantic.

Around 1766, Newburgh was ordained a deacon in the Church of Ireland. This was the first of a two-step process toward becoming an Anglican priest. The details of his entrance into the ministry are sketchy. Trinity College had a professor of divinity, but most men learned the trade by studying with a local clergyman. Newburgh likely apprenticed with his uncle Henry Cole, who was rector at Derryloran Parish in Cookstown, County Tyrone.[45]

After his first ordination, Newburgh became a curate at Drumlane Parish near Milltown, County Cavan. A curacy was a temporary appointment that paid little, but at least Drumlane came with a vicarage. It also put him closer to his relatives, as Milltown was only ten miles from Ballyhaise House and twenty miles from Florence Court. But he failed to advance in the diocese of Kilmore. Archdeacon William Cradock reported that Newburgh "behaved with all possible propriety" at Drumlane, but the young man was not one to be patient with the world. He asked the bishop of Clonfert and Kilmacduagh to be transferred to his diocese.[46]

On October 8, 1769, Newburgh was admitted "to the Holy order of Priest or Presbyter, according to the Rite and Custom of the Church in Ireland." The site of his second ordination was

Cathedral Church of St. Brendan, a twelfth-century castle with heads carved in stone over the doorway and a narrow nave. Draped in brilliantly colored flowing robes, he took his holy orders. In many ways, the site foreshadowed his future. Clonfert Cathedral was founded by St. Brendan the Navigator, a man who crossed the Atlantic in the sixth century and saw a variety of historical and mythical sites. He spied an iceberg that reminded him of the Holy City and discovered Judas Iscariot on a deserted island being tormented daily for his treachery. St. Brendan revealed that lands to the west were filled with promises and damnation.[47]

There were many reasons why Newburgh wanted to be a clergyman. For an aspiring professional, the ministry could provide access to economic and social prestige. There were many vacant Anglican parishes throughout Ireland, and the Irish parliament had recently passed a law increasing rectors' salaries. Some achieved notoriety, like Jonathan Swift, the dean of St. Patrick's Cathedral, while Robert's uncle Henry earned a respectable £300 per year.[48]

The church also might have fit Newburgh's temperament. He was "blessed with so much Christian meekness," a friend later remarked, even if he did not demonstrate this at trial. A religious appointment also offered the opportunity to enact the enlightened ideals of Christian charity. His ancestry and education had taught him the importance of noblesse oblige, and he later sought to help the less fortunate in America.[49]

As a clergyman in the Church of Ireland, Newburgh joined one of the king's four churches, which included worshippers in England, Scotland, and America. Anglican worship was more ceremonial than the Puritan meeting. Doctrinally, the church aspired to *via media*, meaning a latitudinarian approach that sought to include as many people as possible by not haggling over the finer points of theology. Such leniency befitted a state church whose clergy were supported by the taxes of members and nonmembers alike.[50]

In 1769, Reverend Newburgh became a traveling priest. To assist him in this endeavor, he looked to "Persons of Rank and distinction in that Kingdom" to promote his interests. His uncle Thomas may have helped him obtain the curacy at Drumlane as his family was friendly with the archdeacon of Kilmore. When the Reverend William Tisdall at Kildress in County Tyrone died in 1769, Newburgh headed north. Kildress was only three miles west of his uncle's parish at Cookstown. When Henry Cole died a few months later, Newburgh took over his uncle's parish at Derryloran as well. In 1771, Henry Cottingham of Whaley Abbey arranged for Newburgh to minister to "the United Parishes" in County Wicklow.[51]

There is no reason to think that Robert Newburgh was anything other than a good priest. "I officiated in the public Office of a Curate," he later recalled, "and discharged my Duty to the Satisfaction of my Parishoners that I lived in intimacy with." We might speculate about how intimate he was with his congregations, especially given an account of his ministry. Cookstown parishioner Thomas Patten testified that the curate "Visited William Sewart Esqrs. Famely of Killymoon and was Visited by the Young Gentelmen of that Famely sometimes." Perhaps this was innocent pastoral work, or perhaps it was something more.[52]

Indeed, it was during Newburgh's curacy that rumors first arose about his sexual behavior. Around 1769, he spent a month in Sligo and took his foster brother with him as a servant. Rumors began to spread thereafter about their sleeping arrangements. The story reached Drogheda, and in the summer of 1772, a minister in Arklow was heard gossiping about Newburgh's impropriety with his servant. Newburgh would later claim that he had never heard these stories. It was only when he reached America that allegations about his sexual activities were recorded, but the rumors indicate that people across Ireland had been aware of his buggery for three years.[53]

In the fall of 1772, Newburgh applied to become a chaplain in the British army. At the time he was a curate in the diocese of Dublin, a disappointing return home for an aspiring professional. Work as a religious journeyman was unsatisfying and paid little. Curates were guaranteed only £60 per year by law, or a fifth of what Uncle Henry earned as a rector. The army provided better opportunities for advancement. British officers had a place in polite society, and senior officers enjoyed great privilege and influence. Military life also carried with it the opportunity to tour the empire, and this appealed to him.[54]

"Having an Inclination to go abroad I determined to procure the Place of Chaplain to a Regiment," Newburgh later recalled. He first approached the Forty-Seventh Regiment but settled on the Eighteenth, also known as the Royal Irish Regiment. He wrote to the colonel of the regiment, Lieutenant General Sir John Saunders Sebright. Sebright was a man of considerable prominence: a baronet and member of the British parliament. He alone admitted officers to the Eighteenth Regiment, so Newburgh had to apply to Sebright for a chaplaincy.[55]

To support his application, Newburgh solicited testimonials from prominent men in Britain and Ireland, and he forwarded them to Sebright at Beechwood Park in Hertfordshire, England. The most impressive recommendation came from Irish privy councilor Sir Henry Cavendish who offered "Testimony to Mr. Newburgh's good Character." This impressed Sebright who wrote, "I Cannot receive a better than the recommendation of So respectable a Gentleman." On November 18, 1772, Robert Newburgh was commissioned a chaplain in the Royal Irish Regiment.[56]

Newburgh had to pay to join the Eighteenth Regiment. The purchase system was time-honored tradition in the British army that required a considerable investment. No record remains of

the transaction, but a chaplaincy typically cost £500. Once purchased, it was his to profit from through salary, favors, or graft,
and he could sell it when he left the service. In fact, Newburgh
did not purchase his commission from Sebright, but from Daniel Thomas, the regiment's current chaplain.[57]

British army regulations required every regiment to employ
an ordained Anglican clergyman, but most did not. Regimental returns from 1766 indicate that only four of the fifteen
regiments in North America were served by a chaplain or deputy. This culture of absenteeism was due primarily to the chaplains' low pay. At midcentury, a chaplain received six shillings
eight pence per day plus five shillings for subsistence. However, he also was expected to pay for his own food, clothes,
and personal effects, meaning that there was often very little
left over at the end of one's tour of duty. For this reason, many
treated chaplaincies as sinecures and hired deputies to march
with the army while they remained at an English or Irish parish. The previous two chaplains in the Royal Irish had drawn
pay for nearly three decades without ever joining the army in
theater. Sebright was adamant that "the regt has been much
too Long without the assistance of a Clergyman," and he allowed Newburgh to purchase the chaplaincy only on the condition that by May 1, 1773, he would "Embark for America, to
Join the regt at Philadelphia."[58]

In many respects, Newburgh was like other Anglican clergymen who entered the chaplaincy. Another priest who traveled
to North America cited his "Duty as an English Protestant" to
serve in a land of heretics and hedonism. The Reverend Thomas
Charles Heslop Scott joined the Thirty-Fourth Regiment in
Canada to instruct soldiers on "attending their duty to their *Cre-
ator*, & to learn their proper subordination." Chaplains regularly
delivered sermons to soldiers and counseled those wounded in
battle or awaiting the sentence of a court-martial.[59]

Chaplains were not field officers but were part of the army's support staff like surgeons. They maintained a distance from the soldiery and often ministered to civilians. In addition to his regimental duties, the Reverend John Stuart was a missionary to the Mohawks and helped establish the first grammar school in Upper Canada. But taking an interest in civilians could rankle the officers. When Reverend Scott observed soldiers stealing colonists' livestock, he was outraged by "the depredations upon the Habitants" and helped arrest ten culprits. For this act, he was ordered out of garrison and defamed by General Barry St. Leger. Scott responded by demanding a court of enquiry, citing his "Civil rights" and the "priviledges of the Clergy."[60]

Many chaplains brought their wives and children to America. The Reverend John Bryan complained bitterly about how warfare in North America compromised his ability to support his family, while Reverend Stuart thought the army should provide transport and supplies for his family, which "consists of 8 Persons." As a bachelor, Robert Newburgh was unusual as a British army chaplain, although some men joined the army seeking opportunities denied them at home. He may have hoped to find a wife through the service, or maybe the army appealed to him for the opposite reason.[61]

At least one person found Newburgh's change of career unusual. Among the letters of support was one from Colonel Eyre Massey of the Twenty-Seventh Regiment. Massey had come to know Newburgh when the young man was a curate near his villa in Dublin, and he spoke highly of the "worthy Jolly Parson" who "has the good Wishes of all his parishoners." But the colonel also qualified his support: "I would rather Chose him for a Captain of Grenadiers, than for a Chaplain." Massey did not elaborate on this point, but it alluded to Newburgh's appearance. Grenadiers wore tall miter-shaped hats

Colonel Eyre Massey

Source: Ignatius Joseph van den Berghe [after Richard Bull], *General Massey*
(London, 1800). British Museum, Prints and Drawings, 1612920821.

and flashy clothes. Nevertheless, Massey recommended Newburgh for service, informing Sebright that "a good man, always
makes a good Officer in any Station."[62]

Upon being commissioned, Newburgh headed to Cork on
the southern coast of Ireland to await passage to America.
Cork was Ireland's second-largest city, and although it lacked
Dublin's Georgian refinement, its coffeehouses and newspapers connected it to the Anglo Atlantic. Cork was the primary
port for the British army in Ireland, and thousands of soldiers
resided in the city as they awaited departure to distant lands.
To serve the redcoats, public houses and brothels opened
around the city and the nearby towns.[63]

❖ ❖ ❖

In early May 1773, Robert Newburgh received a most disquieting letter. "I am unfortunately acquainted with Some parts of your Character," the letter began, "which render you a very Improper person to act as Chaplain to a regiment I highly honour." According to the letter, several former and current British army officers had attested that Newburgh was "guilty of a most Horrid and *unnatural Crime* particularly with your own Man Servant, whom you slept with." He had no choice but to delay joining the Eighteenth Regiment until he cleared his name.[64]

The author of the letter was Thomas Batt. In some ways, Batt was like Newburgh; he was about thirty years old and a Protestant Irishman. Unlike Newburgh, however, Batt had been an officer in the Eighteenth Regiment for a decade, working his way up from ensign to captain. He had spent several years in America and had recently married a wealthy woman and fathered a son. In January 1773, Batt had sold his commission and left the army to become a wine merchant. He planned to ply his wares in Philadelphia and had returned home to procure a supply. It was in Ireland that Batt first heard rumors of Newburgh's relations with his servant.[65]

Thomas Batt was a careful observer of character. As a captain, he often found himself in the position of judging whether men were "fit for Service" and of making his opinions known. "I always consult my own feelings," he told a superior, adding "I am disinterested and write the truth." Batt was also a resolute pursuer of facts. When he first heard rumors of Newburgh's sexual acts, he interviewed two British officers and "Several other Gentlemen," who confirmed the story. Such evidence convinced him that the new chaplain had committed buggery, and for that reason, he believed that Newburgh did not belong in the Royal Irish Regiment.[66]

Batt's revelations were a complete shock to Newburgh. He had not even assumed his new position but already his career was in jeopardy. He later claimed that he took the news calmly, but he must have been apoplectic. He concluded that he had "to face my Accusers, and to wipe off every Stain from my Character, before I left Ireland." He tracked down one of the men who had told Batt about his sleeping arrangements, and another man who had heard the story, taking written statements from both. He also sought assistance from powerful men in the Church of Ireland, but they were less helpful. The prebendary of St. Patrick's Cathedral, Fowler Comings, informed him that "my Power is very limited indeed," while the arrival of a formal statement of support from the diocese of Dublin was delayed.[67]

Two weeks after he received Batt's letter, Newburgh wrote to General Sebright. According to orders, he was supposed to depart for America by May 1, but it was now May 18. Not wanting to repeat Batt's accusations to the colonel of his regiment, he applied for a leave of absence on account of his "ill State of Health." In truth, he wanted to track down the second officer who had spread rumors of his affairs, but as that officer had gone to England, he sought to follow him there.[68]

Sebright was displeased with the delay. Upon receiving the letter, he admonished Newburgh that his "long absence" from the regiment made him "guilty of Disobedience" and "Contempt of your Colonel." Batt had also written to Sebright, informing him that he had seen Newburgh "in good health a few days before," and that he had proposed "to go on board that Ship with him, that was to sail in three days from Cork." This was an outright lie; Batt would later testify that he had no intention of sailing with an accused buggerer. Regardless, Sebright ordered Newburgh to "immediately repair to the Head

Quarters of the regt in America; & you will take the Consequence of your Disobedience."[69]

In late May or early June 1773, Robert Newburgh left Ireland for Philadelphia to begin work as a chaplain in the British army. By the time he landed in America, everyone in the Eighteenth Regiment had heard that he was a buggerer.

CHAPTER TWO

The Happy State of the Royal Irish

ON MARCH 16, 1772, Sergeant Martin Bell embarked on a mission of great importance. Bell was a member of the Eighteenth or Royal Irish Regiment, which was stationed at a small frontier outpost along the Mississippi River named Cahokia. As quartermaster sergeant, Bell was responsible for procuring supplies, including alcohol, so he headed "to a Spanish Settlemt. on the other side of the River to purchase some Spirits" as there was nothing to drink in Cahokia.[1]

Bell took a flat-bottomed boat across the Mississippi to the recently founded town of St. Louis. There, he purchased fifty gallons of ratafia, a sweet, flavored liqueur sometimes called taffee, and returned to Cahokia. The next day, Bell distributed the ratafia to the soldiers so that they could mark a day of particular importance to the Royal Irish. "It being the Custom of the Regiment to Celebrate St. Patrick's day," the men of the Eighteenth remembered Ireland at the western frontier of Britain's North American empire.[2]

Robert Newburgh was not the only native of Ireland. The Eighteenth Regiment was filled with Irish men who chose to serve a British king in America. Having much in common with the soldiers and officers of the regiment, Newburgh forged strong friendships with some of his compatriots. But the new chaplain also stood apart from the regiment. He possessed a pedigree and education that few in Ireland or the British army could rival, and his enlightened opinions turned friends into enemies. Reports of that he had had sex with a man only hardened these differences.

Yet Newburgh was not responsible for all the problems in the Eighteenth Regiment. Long before his arrival, the regiment was tinged with suspicion and fractured by deep divisions. On St. Patrick's Day 1772, Sergeant Bell sold the ratafia he had procured to the soldiers in the regiment. But several enlisted men complained about the cost of the taffee and speculated that their commanding officer was profiting from the sale. The Royal Irish was already primed with acrimony when Newburgh arrived; the accusation that he was a buggerer sparked an explosion.

❖ ❖ ❖

The Eighteenth Regiment of Foot was a product of English imperialism in Ireland. Following the Rebellion of 1641, the colonizers created independent companies of pikemen and musketeers who were decidedly Protestant and loyal to England. King Charles II consolidated these companies following his restoration to the throne and later folded them into the English establishment. In 1684, the king named this loyal troop the Irish Regiment of Foot.

The Irish Regiment was effective during the Williamite War of 1689–91 and helped to defeat the Jacobite uprising. Thereafter, the soldiers saw little of Ireland. The regiment was dispatched to the Continent, where the men fought with distinction in the 1695 siege of Namur, earning the regimental motto *Virtutis Namurcensis Præmium* ("reward for valor at Namur") and a majestic new moniker. Henceforth, the unit would be known as the *Royal* Irish Regiment.

The Royal Irish fought in Europe during the War of Spanish Succession and spent the next twenty years at Minorca. In 1742, the unit returned to the British Isles to defend England

and Ireland during the War of Austrian Succession and the Seven Years' War. As part of the reorganization of the British army in 1751, the regiment was numbered along with all other units and subsequently became known as the Eighteenth Regiment of Foot.[3]

In the spring of 1767, the Royal Irish headed to North America as part of the army's elaborate rotation system. After its defeat in the Seven Years' War, France surrendered nearly all of its territories in North America, and Great Britain claimed everything from the Atlantic to the Mississippi. To occupy the new lands, Britain deployed fifteen regiments over an area extending from Quebec to Illinois. Commanded by General Thomas Gage, the North American Establishment sought to impose British rule on French colonists and Native Americans, and, if necessary, maintain order in the American colonies as well. In 1767, Gage ordered the Eighteenth to rotate from Ireland to America in order to relieve the Thirty-Fourth Regiment in Illinois.

On July 10, 1767, the Royal Irish landed at Philadelphia. It was in exceptional shape. Commanding the regiment was Lieutenant Colonel John Wilkins, an English-born career officer with extensive battlefield experience in North America. Wilkins oversaw nine companies, each of which was headed by a captain, and each captain was assisted by a lieutenant or an ensign, who were known as subalterns. Each company also included sergeants and corporals (noncommissioned officers), a drummer, and approximately forty privates. A regimental adjutant took care of the paperwork, a quartermaster found housing, and a surgeon provided medical care. Wives and children also accompanied the men. All told, there were nearly five hundred members of the Eighteenth when it arrived in America. But there was no chaplain.[4]

The Royal Irish quartered in Philadelphia for ten months, and in the spring of 1768, Colonel Wilkins led seven companies west. Marching overland, the regiment caused a stir before it left Pennsylvania. In Lancaster, soldiers impressed wagons and horses as was their right under Britain's Quartering Act, but this sat poorly with the Pennsylvania farmers. At Carlisle, the townspeople hid their cartage and livestock in an effort to keep them from being taken by the army. Outraged, Wilkins forced soldiers into the colonists' homes and took "what we want." It was an ugly scene that left these Americans with bad feelings about the British army.[5]

North America, 1774

Source: Jacqueline Alessi (2022)

The seven companies marched to Pittsburgh and divided again. While two remained at Fort Pitt, the other five sailed down the Ohio River and then up the Mississippi to Fort Chartres, where they relieved the Thirty-Fourth Regiment. The companies spread across the region, with some men relocating to Kaskaskia twenty miles downriver and others to Cahokia fifty miles upriver. The flat river plain and humid weather of Illinois was foreign to men who had grown up in the British Isles. Disease and depravation hit the regiment hard that first winter, killing three officers, forty enlisted men, and several members of the soldiers' families.[6]

Upon reaching Illinois, the troops discovered that they were surrounded by people unlike themselves. Francophone colonists farmed in Kaskaskia and Cahokia, while the Indigenous Illiniwek peoples, such as the Tamaroa, Peoria, and Michigamea, also called the region home. The groups mostly coexisted without incident, but unexpected Chickasaw and Kickapoo raids kept tensions high. At times, soldiers were caught in the crossfire, such as when an unidentified Native killed Private John Knight near Cahokia. The French colonists helped the army by serving as interpreters and organizing a militia, while Colonel Wilkins tried to regulate trade and administer justice among the colonists. Nevertheless, the men of the Eighteenth had a poor opinion of life on the Mississippi. Years later, a soldier feared that his captain "would send him to Senegal or back again to the Illinois among the Savages."[7]

The Royal Irish remained in Illinois until 1772. It was a hard four years. Regular patrols were interspersed with irregular repairs to the fort and work on the garrison farm, but everyone had too much time on his hands. Alcohol was plentiful, and although this improved a diet of salted pork, venison, and bear, it also led to drunkenness on duty, disrespect for authority, and fistfights. Some soldiers earned extra cash by carrying hogwash, husking corn, and "Weeding & Cutting pickets" on an officer's farm, but they spent these extra wages on more alcohol. According to Sergeant Bell, "the men were always Murmuring."[8]

❖ ❖ ❖

Lieutenant Colonel John Wilkins had a side hustle. Before he left Philadelphia, the commanding officer of the Eighteenth Regiment signed a contract with the trading firm of Baynton, Wharton, and Morgan whereby he would provide military protection for the company's agents and merchandise in exchange for five percent of the company's profits from the Illinois trade. But the deal was not entirely proper. Part of the reason why the British government had stationed five companies in Illinois was to encourage trade in the region, meaning that Wilkins was profiting from simply doing his duty. When revenues came in lower than anticipated, Baynton, Wharton, and Morgan reduced Wilkins's share, citing ethical concerns. In return, Wilkins arrested firm partner George Morgan and imprisoned him at Fort Chartres.[9]

Wilkins's highhanded actions attracted the attention of the regiment's officers. They began murmuring about Wilkins, especially after an engineer accused him of corruption. Various captains, lieutenants, and ensigns lined up against Wilkins, later filing a formal complaint with the British army. Because of his "Crimes of the most serious, not to say attrocious nature," thirteen officers declared that it would be inconsistent "with our Notions of the Honor of the King's Service" to "ever think of *doing Duty* with Lieut. Colonel Wilkins."[10]

Having lost the confidence of his officers, Wilkins's command became precarious. In late 1771, he requested leave from General Gage to return to England and clear his name. He also contemplated selling his commission and retiring from the service entirely. In May 1772, Wilkins left Fort Chartres, never to return to America or resume his command of the Royal Irish. He had been toppled by a cabal of his own officers.[11]

Captain Benjamin Chapman appears to have been at the heart of the action against Wilkins. Chapman was an Irishman who had joined the British army when he was only sixteen. He journeyed to Illinois with the Eighteenth as a lieutenant, and he commanded the garrison at Kaskaskia before being promoted to captain. Chapman was ambitious and impatient. He took on additional assignments, serving as regimental paymaster and searching for deserters. He also maintained a special closeness with Wilkins, serving directly under him; indeed, he may have manipulated this intimacy to bring down the colonel. It was Chapman who reported the discrepancies in Wilkins's accounts to Gage. An officer later described the action against Wilkins as "a difference between him and Lieut.— now Captain—Chapman."[12]

To be sure, Chapman's ambition could exceed his ability. His education was rudimentary, and this showed up in his work. Gage often found irregularities in his accounts, and his writings evince few classical references. This lack of refinement, at times, hindered his ambition. Unmarried during his time in America, Chapman attracted attention when he propositioned a soldier's wife for sex, and when she refused his advances, he ordered her out of the barracks. Yet for all his faults, he was loyal to king and country, and genuinely relished "the happy state of the Royal Irish."[13]

Chapman had much in common with Robert Newburgh's accuser, Thomas Batt. The two were about the same age, and both had entered the army as young men. In 1767, they joined the Eighteenth Regiment on its march to Illinois and there became steadfast friends. The two men were promoted to captaincies within a day of each other, and it appears that Batt was as ambitious as Chapman, at least until he married and left the army. Yet even after he became a wine merchant, Batt remained close to Chapman.

Before the two captains left Illinois, Chapman and Batt were joined by a third man of similar opinions: Benjamin Charnock Payne. Payne was a decade older and more cultured than

An Officer of the Eighteenth Regiment

Source: Jacques Brouillet, "18th Foot," in *British and Egyptian Troops in Egypt* (1798–1800). Prints, Drawings and Watercolors from the Anne S. K. Brown Military Collection, Brown Digital Repository, Brown University Library.

either of the other two. But he also had a penchant for violence that unnerved the men who served under him. Like Chapman, Payne also ordered soldiers' wives out of the barracks, although this was for selling illicit alcohol, not because they spurned his sexual advances.[14]

The captains also shared a dislike of Robert Newburgh. Following Batt's initial accusation, Chapman and Payne carried on the case against him. In many ways, the captains offered a preview of their campaign against the chaplain in their treatment of Wilkins. Having successfully proved "Colonel Wilkins guilty of scandalous Practices unbecoming an Officer and a Gentleman," Chapman, Batt, and Payne used the same language to try to force Newburgh out of the Royal Irish Regiment.[15]

❖ ❖ ❖

Not all officers in the Eighteenth Regiment thought that Colonel Wilkins deserved to lose his command. The names of one captain and three ensigns were conspicuously absent from the formal complaint filed against the commanding officer. Others who initially sided with Chapman later regretted their decision and even sought forgiveness from Wilkins. Lieutenant Alexander Fowler was one such man.

Fowler was about the same age as Chapman, and like him, he entered the British army as a teenager. As an ensign in the Seventy-Fourth Regiment, he took part in Britain's 1762 assault on Havana. When that regiment disbanded at the end of the Seven Years' War, he purchased a lieutenancy with the Eighteenth in 1768, which was already in Illinois.[16]

According to Fowler, by "the time I joined the Royal Irish at Fort Chartres, the whole Regiment was in a Flame against Colonel Wilkins." He quickly came under the influence of Chapman. "I hear'd Colonel Wilkin's Character Traduced, and I weakly Joined in the Traduction," he remembered. Thereafter, Fowler helped Chapman build a case against Wilkins. "He has become altogether hardened & callous to any Sensations of Shame," Fowler wrote, adding "We must *Detest* Him more than ever." When Wilkins was struck with "a severe Inflammation in his Bowels," Fowler took delight in nature's judgment on the colonel.[17]

Fowler's comment about Wilkins's poor health would come to haunt him. While serving in Illinois, he was "seized with this excruciating disorder, which has rendered me a Cripple." Fowler described his condition as "A Violent Rheumatism in my Limbs," which led to "Scarbutick Ulcers." Chapman confirmed that Fowler was "almost entirely deprived of the Use of his Limbs," and another officer testified that other subalterns had to perform his chores. Thereafter, Fowler often found himself confined to the barracks, and he sought cures like taking mercury. In time, he considered retiring, but for a man who was barely thirty, this was a difficult decision, so he delayed resigning his commission.[18]

Fowler's disability changed his perspective on life. Although he described himself as "by nature Cholerick and Warm in my Resentments," he came to regret his actions against Wilkins as motivated by "more Zeal than Prudence." He corresponded with the former commanding officer and, in time, "we found we had been in some degree both to blame, and made such Mutual & Manly Concessions to each other." As Fowler grew more sanguine in his opinion of Wilkins, his friendship with Chapman deteriorated.[19]

Perhaps because of his disability, Fowler built a life outside of the army. Unlike Chapman, Fowler was married, and he brought his wife, Frances, with him to Illinois. It is possible that Fowler's affection for Wilkins originated from a promise of land, which would have allowed him to become a farmer and provide for his family.[20]

As Fowler fell out with Chapman, he grew closer to another subaltern: Ensign Nicholas Trist. Trist was an Englishman who came from a more elite background than most officers in the regiment, and he was educated. He purchased his commission at the relatively advanced age of twenty-seven, and this gave him a different perspective on army life. Unlike most soldiers,

Trist "did not like Madeira, and very seldom drank any thing in a morning." Although he joined the officers in deposing Wilkins, Trist subsequently became a supporter of the colonel. In time, Fowler and Trist became fast friends.[21]

While the captains led the campaign against Robert Newburgh, Fowler and Trist defended the chaplain. Maybe because they were less ambitious or maybe because they were less committed to the British army, the subalterns were sympathetic to Newburgh's plight and became his closest companions. Fowler and Trist also remembered the move against Wilkins and took lessons from it. When the captains announced that they would not serve with a man of Newburgh's character, the subalterns implored the chaplain to stay and fight for his reputation. They had seen that a man who left the Royal Irish in disgrace did not return.

❖ ❖ ❖

Even before the Eighteenth Regiment marched to Illinois, imperial planners were having second thoughts about stationing the army along the Mississippi River. At the end of the last war, King George III proclaimed all land west of the Appalachians to be reserved for Indigenous peoples, but white settlers headed west anyway. Conflicts between Native Americans and European Americans became common thereafter. Although the British army tried to maintain the peace, the backcountry was too vast for a few regiments to patrol. Worse, both Natives and newcomers looked on the redcoats with suspicion, and when British soldiers attempted to impose order, they were attacked. As a result, in December 1771, the king ordered "a Reduction of all the Establishments" on the frontier, and General Gage began the process of withdrawing the army from Illinois.[22]

The task of leading the Royal Irish out of the backcountry fell to Major Isaac Hamilton. Hamilton had remained in Philadelphia with two companies while the rest of the regiment marched west, but with Wilkins's departure, he became the highest-ranking member of the unit and thus its commanding officer. In early 1772, he headed to Illinois, where he found the five companies still riled up by the Wilkins affair.[23]

Hamilton's arrival brought calm to the regiment. A generation older than the captains and subalterns, he had a long but undistinguished career in the British army, and this had taught him the importance of unit cohesion. However, Hamilton also suffered from chronic illness, and this hindered his leadership. Upon reaching Illinois, he acquiesced to more ambitious men like Chapman. Although Hamilton was the commanding officer, it was the captains who took control.[24]

In July 1772, the Eighteenth Regiment prepared to leave Illinois. Captain John Shee sold off his store of spirits to the enlisted men and allowed them to toast Fort Chartres before destroying it. The soldiers abandoned Cahokia to the Francophone colonists and Native Americans, although fifty unfortunate men were ordered to remain behind at a hastily assembled Fort Gage in Kaskaskia. The rest of the troops sailed up the Ohio River to Pittsburgh, where they reunited with the two companies that they had left behind four years earlier. As part of the drawdown of forces in the backcountry, Fort Pitt was deemed unnecessary, so the soldiers razed it as well.[25]

By December 1772, almost all of the Royal Irish had reunited in Philadelphia. The time in Illinois had changed the unit but not for the better. Desertion, death, and disability had reduced the number of privates from nearly four hundred to less than two hundred. The officers were divided, with a sickly major in charge. Yet there was hope for a reversal of fortunes. Being stationed in Philadelphia gave the regiment an opportunity to enlist new recruits, while on the other side of the Atlantic, General Sebright had hired a new chaplain.[26]

In 1772, Philadelphia was the largest city in British North America, with a population approaching thirty thousand. Nearly a century had passed since William Penn founded the city for

the Society of Friends (Quakers), and since then, it had attracted
a variety of ethnicities and religious denominations. Like Dublin
and Cork, Philadelphia aspired to cosmopolitanism. A visitor
noted that the city's buildings were "mostly all brick, and very
neat, three and four stories high, well furnished within, and well
lighted." The city also had a burgeoning public sphere, much of
which was attributable to Benjamin Franklin. Franklin ran the
city's most successful newspaper, organized its first library,
and helped found a college. Philadelphia was also the capital of
Pennsylvania, with an impressive statehouse rising at Fifth and
Chestnut.[27]

The Philadelphia barracks stood apart from the city's refinement. Located in the suburb of Northern Liberties, the barracks occupied one of the poorest and most violent areas in
the region. The records of the Overseers of the Poor contain
many names from the Northern Liberties, while a newspaper
report from 1769 told of a fatal skirmish between a butcher,
who was "going to his slaughter-house near the barracks" and
a drunken tanner. As the occupations of the men involved indicate, Northern Liberties was filled with meat processors.
Blood ran in the streets, and a foul stench hung in the air.[28]

The barracks were massive. Built in 1756–57 at the cost of
£10,000, they consisted of two parallel buildings, each a block
in length, and capable of housing "17 or 1800 men." The barracks initially only accommodated enlisted men, but when the
Eighteenth first quartered in the city, Colonel Wilkins asked
the assembly to add apartments for officers. In response, the
province spent £1,600 to construct an officers' quarters that
transformed the edifice into a single U-shaped building. A civilian carpenter named Joseph Fox served as barrackmaster,
and he kept the structure in good repair and procured "Fire-
Wood, Candles, Small-Beer, &c." for the inhabitants. Major
Hamilton was particularly impressed with Fox's work, declaring
that "no Troops have been better supplied, nor any Applica-

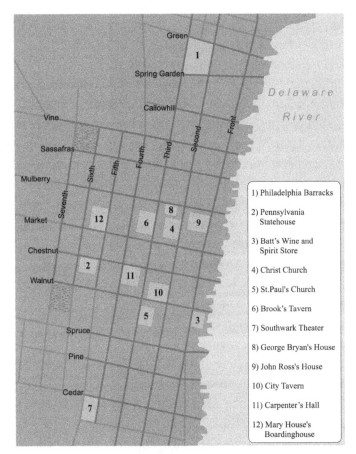

Philadelphia, 1774
Source: Jacqueline Alessi (2022)

tions from Commanding Officers more politely attended to, than here."[29]

Life at the barracks had a certain routine. The day began at sunrise with morning roll call. Privates and noncommissioned officers shared rooms, but each commissioned officer had a room to himself, sometimes more. The men had to cook meals for themselves, and they seem to have taken turns doing so. The food was mostly bread and beef, the quality of which was immeasurably better than in Illinois, although they still over-salted the meat. Privates took turns mounting guard. Soldiers were forbidden from taking employment in the city, so they worked for the regiment, some repairing shoes and others sewing uniforms. Evenings in the barracks were boisterous. Wives and children joined the men, making the regiment a family. The day ended promptly at 9:00 p.m., when the drummers beat tattoo, after which everyone was supposed to be in bed and quiet.[30]

As had been the case in Illinois, the men quickly grew bored in Philadelphia and sought unhealthy diversions. "The Barracks of Philadelphia was surrounded with Tippling Houses," recalled Captain Payne who fretted over how "the Morals of the Men were so much debauched" by their "constant frequenting" of the taverns. Local women could also be had, either as girlfriends or prostitutes. For some, the temptation of freedom was too great. An advertisement in the *Pennsylvania Gazette* reported how Mark Wiley had left his unit: "It is reported he is a deserter from the Royal Irish regiment, and has a wife near Wilmington." Wiley changed his name to John May and ran away with "a mulatto wench" instead of his wife.[31]

It did not take long for regimental tensions to resurface, but unlike in Illinois, the divisions now reached beyond the officers' corps. First, there was a complaint about how much enlisted men should be paid for extra work. Upon returning to Philadelphia, Major Hamilton observed that the soldiers' "accoutrements were rendered bad & unserviceable," so he ordered the men to make new pouches, shoulder belts, and waist belts. According to one private, the soldiers were paid for the initial leatherwork, but later, when Hamilton "thought proper to make an Alteration in the Waist-belts," he offered no "pay or Satisfaction for the same."[32]

The loudest critic of the officers was Private Nicholas Gaffney. Gaffney was an Irishman who had trained as shoemaker. He had served in the Eighteenth Regiment for more than a decade and marched to Illinois as a member of Captain Shee's company.

While serving at Cahokia, Gaffney was promoted to the rank of corporal, but he did not live up to his new position. Two years later, he was "reduced" to private, and thereafter, he nursed a grudge against Shee.[33] Upon reaching Philadelphia, Gaffney filed formal charges against his captain, including an allegation that Shee sold poor-quality goods to the soldiers for a profit. The same method of accusation and rumor that Chapman had used to topple Wilkins now appealed to privates like Gaffney.

Rebellion was in the air. By 1773, Philadelphians had grown uneasy with British military power in their city and royal rule in general. Colonial distrust of the empire began in earnest in 1765, when the British Parliament passed a stamp tax and riots broke out across the continent. The presence of British troops in American cities further irritated the colonists, especially after members of the Twenty-Ninth Regiment massacred five Bostonians in 1770. Thereafter, committees of correspondence formed to monitor the movements of redcoats.

The Royal Irish witnessed the changing colonial attitude firsthand. When the regiment marched east from Illinois, General Gage asked that the Philadelphia barracks be fitted up for the soldiers' arrival. The quarters were "in very bad Order" with much of the "Bedding, Barrack Furniture, &c." missing, so he asked the provincial assembly to fund repairs. Pennsylvania usually responded to such requests without complaint, but the ongoing dispute over taxes and the Boston Massacre had soured colonial lawmakers on the British army. The assembly agreed to appropriate £4,000 to repair the Philadelphia barracks, but the money came with conditions: legislators wanted answers about the Eighteenth's seizure of wagons and horses when it had marched through Carlisle three years earlier.[34]

❖ ❖ ❖

In late July 1773, Thomas Batt arrived in Philadelphia. Departing Cork in May, the former captain of the Eighteenth Regiment sailed aboard the *Penn*, a snow or square-rigged vessel captained by John McCaddon.[35] In Ireland, Batt had procured a supply of madeira, rum, and brandy for his new business, and by August 20, advertisements appeared in the Philadelphia newspapers for "Batt's Wine and Spirits Store" on Walnut Street.[36]

Batt wasted no time reuniting with Benjamin Chapman and the other captains of the Royal Irish. Batt brought news from the British Isles, including politics and gossip. He revealed that a new chaplain would soon be joining their regiment, and that he had heard from numerous sources—including Captain McCaddon—that the priest was a buggerer. Batt believed that a man known for having sex other men should be disqualified from military service. He was hardly alone in this opinion.

Since the rise of the standing army, English politicians and moralists had fretted that sodomy infected the nation's defense. In the late seventeenth century, England adopted a permanent and professional military—or, in the parlance of the day—a standing army. Although common throughout Western Europe, the institution was controversial in England because the country had long relied on a civilian militia for its defense. Whig politicians like John Trenchard and Thomas Gordon bemoaned standing armies as "threatening and pernicious, and the ready instruments of certain ruin" to individual liberties. The militia was supposed to be composed of men who fought for their families and property, but a standing army was filled with bachelors and foreigners who supported absolutism and had no regard for English morals. Among the other vices that professional troops were supposedly prone to was buggery.[37]

Shortly after the rise of the standing army, a homosexual scandal rocked the military. In 1698, Captain Edward Rigby was court-martialed for buggery. When a military trial cleared Rigby, a member of the Society for Reformation of Manners devised a plan to entrap him. A nineteen-year-old man was sent to seduce the captain who responded by kissing him and asking: "if he should F— him." When the young man objected, Rigby claimed it was "no more than was done in our Fore fathers time" and added that "he had seen the Czar of Muscovy through a hole at Sea, lye with Prince Alexander." Rigby was arrested and pilloried. In a broadside intended to be distributed during Rigby's time in the stocks, an unnamed author lamented:

> The Souldiers, whom next we put trust in,
> > No widdow can tame
> > Or virgin reclaim
> But at the wrong Place will be thrusting.

For some, Captain Rigby proved the corruption of a standing army.[38]

Incidents like Rigby's case embarrassed military leaders. Although the British army and Royal Navy achieved momentous victories in North America, Europe, and Asia throughout the eighteenth century, the military continued to attract critics. In response, young and ambitious officers campaigned against immorality in the ranks. There was no official prohibition on same-sex relations in the armed forces, so men anxious about their own advancement called on lawmakers to remedy this.

Change began in the Royal Navy. Upon revising the Naval Act in 1749, Parliament declared "the unnatural and detestable Sin of Buggery or Sodomy with Man or Beast" to be a crime punishable by death upon the sentence of a court-martial. Thereafter, the Navy began enforcing the statute with regularity. Between 1756 and 1806, thirty-three sailors were convicted of buggery, and nineteen were sentenced to hang. Records for the British army are less complete, but soldiers were also punished. During the Seven Years' War, Private Charles McHoennan was court-martialed for attempted sodomy and sentenced to a thousand lashes. Punishments increased thereafter, especially during the Napoleonic Wars.[39]

Thomas Batt's assault on Robert Newburgh was consistent with the military's fear that it had become a refuge for sodomites. Although Batt had resigned his commission, his status was still tied to the army; he was thus deeply concerned that a man reputed to be a buggerer would impugn his former regiment. Captains Chapman and Payne felt the same way. For men loyal to King George, the character of the Royal Irish stood above all else, and they worried deeply about how tales of Newburgh's sexual relations with his servant might affect their reputations.

When he was in Ireland buying wine, Batt may have come across the story of Isaac Bickerstaff. Bickerstaff was an Anglo-Irish man whose ambition had led him to enlist in the British army. He served as a lieutenant in the Fifth Regiment of Foot for a decade and joined the Royal Marines during the Seven Years' War. Upon retiring from service, he headed to London, where he joined the theater and began writing comic operas like *Thomas and Sally* and *Love in a Village*. In 1772, at the height of his success, newspapers reported that Bickerstaff "grew enamoured, the other Night at Whitehall with one of the Centinels and made Love to him." Apparently, the former lieutenant never strayed from the army as his paramour was "a Soldier being of that rough cast."[40]

If Batt heard about Bickerstaff's case, he would have understood its gravity. It was not just that a former officer had committed buggery, but that he had made the army an object of ridicule. Circulating along with Bickerstaff's case was an amusing piece of English doggerel that mocked "these enlighten'd times" in which an Irish playwright did "for grenadiers imprudent burn."

> Of manly love, ah! why are men asham'd?
> A new red coat, fierce cock and killing air
> Will captivate the most obdurate fair;

Perhaps in Batt's mind, Newburgh's flamboyant appearance conjured an image like the grenadier who drew Bickerstaff's lust. Certainly, the former captain loathed people laughing at the Eighteenth Regiment.[41]

❖ ❖ ❖

The Reverend Robert Newburgh left Ireland later than Batt, trailing his accuser by about a month. He had to pay for his own "Voyage from Europe," which he would later claim was quite costly. As typical of a man of means, he brought several trunks of clothes with him. Presumably, these clothes included the type of ostentatious attire that Colonel Massey had claimed made him look like a grenadier.[42]

Aboard the ship from Cork, Newburgh was popular among the passengers. He traveled with Thomas Exshaw, a man whom he had met during his curacy in County Wicklow. Exshaw reported that Newburgh "discharg'd the Duty of a Clergyman" while on board, and that he forged a "Friendship and intimacy" with the ship's captain and his wife. Fellow traveler Marcus Weekes testified that "Mr. Newburgh Visited and prayed by the Sick passengers at the Manifest Peril of his Own Health." But the ocean voyage aggravated Newburgh's chronic illness, so he took to his cabin for the remainder of the journey.[43]

Newburgh's poor health continued after he reached America. He disembarked at New Castle, Delaware, where he "was confined some time by Sickness." Weekes remained with him "as long as his Business could permit," and during that time, the two men attended church where Newburgh partook "of the Holy Sacrament with piety and Devotion." Yet it took some time to recover from the voyage. It was September before he reached Philadelphia.[44]

Upon joining up with the Royal Irish, Robert Newburgh began his duties as chaplain. For more than a year, the regiment had looked to Anglican clergymen in the city to deliver Sunday sermons, but now the chaplain could take over such

A Grenadier

Source: P. H. Smitherman [after David Morier], *Grenadier, 27th Foot, 1751*
(London, 1965). © Hugh Evelyn Prints.

responsibilities. He led morning and evening prayer, adminis-
tered the Lord's Supper, and visited men in the infirmary. He
was also tasked with marrying soldiers in the regiment, baptiz-
ing their children, and "Reading the funeral Service" when they
died.[45]

He forged collegial relationships with the Anglican clergy-men in Philadelphia. Subsequent testimony suggests that he had connections with the Reverend Jacob Duché of Christ Church and the Reverend William Stringer of St. Paul's. The two priests' congregations were theologically opposed: St. Paul's was evangelical, while Christ Church was liturgical. Newburgh's association with both men suggests that he was neutral in doctrine and liturgy.[46]

He also hired a servant. It was customary for a well-to-do man in the British army to hire an enlisted man to clean his uniform, dress his hair or wig, and shave him. Newburgh was accustomed to such service, although he had been without a personal valet since he parted with his foster brother in Ireland. His first servant in America was Private Isaac Hudson. Hudson helped procure his food rations and later helped him find quarters. The private had no complaints about the chaplain, and he profited from the extra income. It cost Newburgh one shilling per week for Hudson's services. For a man accustomed to being tended by a servant, such an expense was a necessity.[47]

Curiously, Newburgh did not quarter in the barracks when he arrived in Philadelphia. Instead, he rented a room from Mr. Brooks, possibly the Brooks who ran a tavern at Third and Market, nearly a mile from the Northern Liberties. Choosing to live apart from the regiment was an unconventional decision and reflected a lack of experience with army protocol. Although officers were free to pay for their own lodgings, few did so. Poor health may have kept him away, or perhaps the gossip about his character made him feel unwelcome among the officers and enlisted men.[48]

Newburgh later claimed that by the time he reached Philadelphia, reports that he had slept with his servant "had been carried to the Officers." Initially, however, such stories did not prevent the captains and subalterns from helping him become acquainted with military life. In fact, Captain Payne recommended Isaac Hudson as a servant. Grateful for the help, Newburgh sent Payne "trivial Compliments" including a bottle of syrup and a pineapple.[49]

Newburgh also befriended Ensign Nicholas Trist. The two men shared a formal education, and this gave them something in common that the rest of regiment did not share. "They have had a Club amoungst themselves on every Monday night," Trist later recalled, at which "they used to entertain themselves in talking on" religion, science, and history. Soon after, Trist introduced Newburgh to Lieutenant Alexander Fowler and the three men became "Constant Companions." Such closeness with the subalterns caught the attention of the captains, and soon the regimental divisions that had appeared in Illinois took on a new dimension. However, in the fall of 1773, the chaplain remained blissfully detached from such barrack politics.[50]

❖ ❖ ❖

Living apart from the regiment, Robert Newburgh had the opportunity to partake in urban entertainments. He attended the theater at least once, planting "himself in the front row of the Stage Box" at the Southwark Theater. In early November 1773, the American Company performed *School for Fathers* and *Lionel and Clarissa* in Philadelphia. Both plays were written by Isaac Bickerstaff, the former Irish officer who had been brought down the year before for buggering a soldier. As a fellow native of Ireland, Newburgh likely knew about the playwright's sexual acts and their consequences when he paid seven shillings six pence for a ticket.[51]

His urban entertainments may have included sex. Philadelphia hosted a greater variety of sexual expression than any other late colonial American city. Self-divorce, bastardy, and interracial sex were commonplace, and commercial sex increased as British troops poured into the city. If Newburgh wanted sexual

THE HAPPY STATE OF THE ROYAL IRISH · 59

intercourse with a woman, he could have found it. Sex with a man would have been harder to procure but not impossible.[52]

The British army was not opposed to its soldiers having sex. Many in the Eighteenth Regiment were married, even enlisted men. Wives lived in the barracks, sleeping with their husbands in berths and eating at the communal table. The army more than tolerated this, allotting rations for six women per company; it also tasked the wives with cooking and cleaning. Occasionally, couples fought. Captain Payne ordered a private's companion out of the barracks when "It was reported that his wife beat him." Children tagged along as well. Captain John Mawby brought at least two sons with him: John junior, who was commissioned a lieutenant in 1771, and a little boy of three or four whom he named Sebright in honor of the regiment's colonel.[53]

For bachelors, taverns around the barracks offered ample opportunity for companionship. Sexually transmitted infections plagued the regiment. Before he accused Captain Shee of corruption, Private Gaffney was reported to have "had a Clap" that kept him from doing his duties for about "nine weeks." But even if they could not have sex, men sought companionship. Private Thomas Maddison tried to bring a woman into the barracks, but "not from a lascivious motive, as he had then lost his private parts" to venereal disease.[54]

The army recognized that men's lusts could not be easily controlled, but the captains tired of enlisted men being unable to do their duty because of their wanton desires. A main reason why General Sebright wanted a chaplain to join the Eighteenth was to impress good morals and restraint upon the men. The captains no doubt saw the irony of a reputed buggerer serving in this role.

It is probable that there were homosexual liaisons in the Philadelphia barracks; perhaps there were bestial ones. Certainly, there was masturbation. But as long as these deviant activities did not disturb the social order, they were ignored. Counterintuitively for an institution that so emphatically denounced sodomy, the British army did very little to prosecute it. General Gage and Major Hamilton preferred that such acts not be spoken of, and many in the Royal Irish agreed. Newburgh could have engaged in buggery so long as it did not attract attention.[55]

But there were limits. A decade later, Spanish officials in St. Augustine, Florida, uncovered a sodomy ring in the barracks. Following rumors that soldiers were paying ten- and eleven-year-old boys for sex, seven privates and three corporals were arrested and court-martialed. A lurid investigation followed that included the examination of two boys' anuses; it also revealed that the houses of leading officials had been used for trysts. When buggery intersected with pederasty and prostitution, the army could not look the other way. Upon conviction, the soldiers in St. Augustine were sentenced to jail time and hard labor in Puerto Rico.[56]

The men of the Eighteenth did not need to look as far as Florida to see the destruction that sexual depravity inflicted on a soldier and his unit. In early October 1773, just as rumors of Newburgh's reputation began to swirl about the Philadelphia barracks, Captain Payne, Ensign Trist, and two other Royal Irish officers trekked sixty miles northeast to New Brunswick, New Jersey, to sit in judgment of Ensign William McDermott. McDermott faced a general court-martial for sexually assaulting the two little girls and infecting them with a sexually transmitted disease, probably syphilis. It was a heartbreaking story that ruined lives and reputations.

McDermott was a member of the Forty-Seventh Regiment, which had sailed from Cork to New York the previous May. Also on board was Lieutenant Robert Shaw as well as Shaw's wife and four children. According to testimony, six weeks into the voyage, the surgeon examined seven-year-old Kitty Shaw and "Confirm'd Clap on her." The surgeon "then ask'd the Child what Mr. McDermott had done to her, and she said that he had hurt her with his Cock." Upon examining Kitty's younger sister Jenny, the surgeon "found her in much the same state."[57]

At the court-martial, Kitty Shaw confirmed the surgeon's story. She stated that "Mr. McDermott took her into his bed, and made her feel his Backside before," meaning his genitals. She pulled her hand away, but he insisted she touch him. Her sister Jenny was in bed with them, and she asked for some food. "Mr. McDermott then took a small piece of Biscuit" and placed it in her "Backside before, and afterwards put his Tongue in her Mouth." He then had "put his backside before to her backside before, and kept going in and out, and when he took it away it was all Wet." After he finished the unspeakable act, McDermott gave Kitty some sugar and warned her not to tell anyone or "her Mama would flog her." The little girl's story had all the hallmark signs of child sexual abuse: an unsuspected man using persuasion and coercion, followed by intimidation and secrecy. Kitty also testified that "she felt something run out from her"; there had been penetration and the emission of semen.[58]

The idea of a man forcing himself on a little girl was repugnant to everyone, and the British army took the matter gravely. The North American deputy judge advocate, Captain Stephen Payne Adye, prosecuted McDermott personally. Adye called several witnesses who offered damning testimony against McDermott, including his captain, servants, and Kitty's father. However, Elizabeth Griffin, who worked as a nurse to the Shaw children, gave contrary evidence. Griffin testified that she had known the girls "to have been Disordered ever since she came to live with Mr. Shaw," and she claimed that the mother had passed venereal disease to her children through breastfeeding. Kitty's mother had coaxed the girls to blame McDermott in order to absolve herself of guilt, Griffin claimed.[59]

McDermott pleaded innocent, repeating the nurse's testimony as well as the surgeon's observation that neither girl exhibited "marks of Force or Violence." He admitted that he had contracted a sexually transmitted infection in Ireland, but he was hardly the only one. A lieutenant testified that "other Gentlemen" known "to have had the Venereal Disease lay in the Cabbin" with the Shaw children. McDermott ultimately pinned the guilt on Thomas Todd, the ship's steward, who was conveniently absent from the trial. Several witnesses confirmed that Todd had syphilis including one man who claimed that Todd had "shewed him his private parts which appeared to him to be in a Shocking Condition." In the end, the court found the ensign not guilty and acquitted him. Yet the stain on his character was indelible, and he left the service. The following May, William McDermott transferred to the Sixteenth Regiment, but a year later he retired from the British army and thereafter disappears from the historical record.[60]

McDermott's court-martial deeply affected the Royal Irish. Payne and Trist brought stories of the trial back to Philadelphia when they returned in late October. Thereafter, the case became a popular topic of conversation in the barracks among officers and enlisted men including the chaplain. The following spring, it was reported that Robert Newburgh had made light of McDermott's case, and according to Chapman, said "that if a man permitted a Child to play with his private parts, untill his Lust Should be raised, he saw no harm in his acting with it."[61]

Although Newburgh vigorously denied ever uttering such words, they fit a pattern. By November 1773, the captains in the Royal Irish began to connect the rumors of the chaplain's sexual activities in Ireland to his behavior in America. Shortly after McDermott's trial, Chapman was visiting Edmund Fanning, in nearby Bristol, Pennsylvania. Fanning was the personal secretary to the governor of New York, so Chapman was horrified when Newburgh suddenly passed by on horseback. As Chapman later told the story:

> as he was walking with Colonel Fanning, the Revd. Mr. Newburgh Galloped Close by them in a most unbecoming dress, and Col. Fanning asked him if he knew whose Groom that was, upon which he answered that he was sorry to Say that he was a Clergyman and Chaplain to the 18th regt. that he replied that he was also sorry to See it, for that he looked more Like a fashionable Groom or Jockey than one of that Sacred Function.

The incident infuriated Chapman, as Newburgh had embarrassed him in front of a powerful man. After that, he "determined within himself never to take any notice" of the chaplain "unless unavoidably Compelled to it." Chapman was the most powerful man in the barracks, so when he shunned Newburgh, the other officers and enlisted men knew to follow his lead.[62]

As the fall turned to winter in Philadelphia, Newburgh felt a new coolness among the Royal Irish. As the men turned their backs on him, he learned that he could not tend to their spiritual needs. He sought solace from Trist and Fowler, but this created other problems. The captains and subalterns were separated by ambition and experience, differences which had played out in their opinions of Colonel Wilkins. By the end of 1773, Wilkins was gone, but the regiment's rifts had mapped onto the officers' relationships with Robert Newburgh.

CHAPTER THREE

Mr. Newburgh Would Cruise up His Gut

THE EIGHTEENTH REGIMENT had been in Philadelphia for about a year when word arrived that the commander in chief was coming for an official inspection. By late 1773, Thomas Gage had departed for England, leaving Major General Frederick Haldimand in charge of the North American Establishment. Haldimand was a Swiss-born officer who corresponded only in French. In early November, the *New-York Gazette* announced that "his Excellency the General" would soon leave New York for Philadelphia "to review the Royal regiment of Ireland, commanded by Major Hamilton."[1]

On November 17, 1773, the officers and enlisted men of the regiment assembled on the parade ground in the center of the Philadelphia barracks. The infantrymen wore red coats, "faced, lapelled and lined blue," with blue breeches, long white gaiters, and "a mixed white and blue lace." The officers shone with metal badges bearing the insignia of the regiment: a Celtic harp and crown, encircled with the words *Virtutis Namurcensis Præmium*. Ornamented with lace of blue and yellow, hanging sleeves, chevrons, and tassels, drummers beat in time as the men lined up for review. It was a citywide spectacle. Philadelphian Sarah Eve journaled how she joined "people of all ranks and denominations" who watched the performance and was "as agreeably entertained as the smoke and noise of guns could afford."[2]

Standing with the troops were Captains Benjamin Chapman and Benjamin Charnock Payne, as well as subalterns Lieutenant Alexander Fowler and Ensign Nicholas Trist. The regimental chaplain, the Reverend Robert Newburgh, was also certainly in attendance, perhaps jealous of the regiment's grenadiers who wore blue and white tufts on their caps. Indeed, the only person missing was General Haldimand. Shortly before the commander in chief was set to depart from New York, it was announced that "his Excellency's Journey to Philadelphia is postponed." Lieutenant Colonel James Robertson arrived in his place, and the review continued as scheduled.[3]

Although the reason for Haldimand's absence was not revealed at the time, the growing unrest in the American colonies played a role. In May 1773, Parliament passed the Tea Act, and this angered the colonists as yet another instance of taxation without representation. In Philadelphia, mass meetings of thousands denounced the law, and on October 20, the *Pennsylvania Gazette* printed eight resolves that rebuked Parliament's actions as an attempt "to introduce arbitrary Government and Slavery" to America. A month after Colonel Robertson reviewed the Royal Irish, a group of colonists tossed tea into Boston Harbor.[4]

❖ ❖ ❖

In December 1773, Robert Newburgh filed a civil lawsuit against Thomas Batt. Since the chaplain had joined the regiment, there had been murmurings about his sexual past. His comments on the McDermott trial and his unusual appearance on horseback seemed to confirm that he was a man of poor character. After ministering to the Royal Irish for three months, it was apparent to Newburgh that he was no longer welcome in the regiment.

At this point, no one filed formal charges against Newburgh for sodomy. The British army was empowered to court-martial men for immoral acts, and Pennsylvania law prescribed death for men convicted "of sodomy or buggery," yet neither Batt nor anyone else pursued such a course. Instead, they hoped that simply embarrassing the chaplain would force him to voluntarily withdraw from the regiment and return to Ireland. But Newburgh had no intention of backing down. In order to save his career, he had to defend his reputation. He could not admit to any sexual acts but had to assert that he had not engaged in buggery. Yet it was not enough to simply deny that he had had sex with another man; he had to force Batt to retract his accusation in order to clear his character. For an heir to the Protestant Ascendancy, this meant a lawsuit.[5]

For this first case, Newburgh did not seek military justice but filed a civil suit in the Court of Common Pleas for Philadelphia County. It appears that he first went to his commanding officer and complained about Batt, but Major Isaac Hamilton discouraged him from involving the army as Batt was no longer an active officer. Moreover, by pursuing a civil action, Newburgh could collect monetary damages so long as he could prove that Batt's malicious gossip had ruined his good name.

In effect, Newburgh sued to prove that he had not had sex with a man. It was common in early modern England and colonial America for individuals to seek justice against unwarranted gossip and rumors. Women accused of witchcraft sued those who claimed that they were in league with the devil, and in so doing, used the law to force their accusers to recant. Such women knew that *not* seeking legal recourse to correct a spurious charge was a tacit admission of guilt.[6]

Sex was often at the center of slander suits. Unmarried women went to court to defend their chastity against untoward rumors, while men filed suits over accusations of interracial fornication and bestiality. Some men sued to tamp down rumors that they had had sex with another man. In 1756, Lawrence Pells of County Essex, England, "brought his Action" against Joseph Thorp for "calling him Buggerer." Pells's action was successful, so Thorp had to print an announcement in the local newspaper acknowledging that he had been wrong to state that Pells was "guilty of sodomitical Practices." Much like an accusation of witchcraft, an unanswered rumor of buggery implied guilt. Newburgh needed Batt to recant his words or else everyone would know that he had had sex with a man.[7]

On December 15, 1773, Robert Newburgh and Thomas Batt appeared at the office of the Honorable George Bryan, a justice for the Court of Common Pleas. In response to Newburgh's lawsuit, Batt insisted that he had not besmirched the chaplain's reputation. The best line of defense when facing a slander suit was to prove that the words spoken were truthful, and this was the course that Batt pursued. To extinguish the case against him, he gave evidence that Newburgh had buggered another man.

Also in attendance at Judge Bryan's office was Ensign Henry Hamilton of the Sixty-Fourth Regiment. Hamilton had known Newburgh in Ireland, and Batt brought him to give evidence of the chaplain's sexual activities. Swearing on a Bible, Hamilton testified that five years earlier in Sligo, he had rented a room in a house where Newburgh had also lodged. Hamilton reported that a separate bed had been placed in Newburgh's chambers for his "Servant Boy," but either the landlady or her maid did "Notice & remark that the said Pallet Bed was Unspoiled." Hamilton understood this to mean that the servant's bed was "Not used or Slept on."

The ensign's revelation was hardly conclusive, so Bryan pressed him for more information. Had he observed any "unusual Familiarities" between Newburgh and his servant? Hamilton did not answer the question directly but stated that he "did indeed think the Boy was very free," much more so that he "should have allowed a Servant to have been with him." "He

The Honorable George Bryan

Source: Burton Alva Konkle, *George Bryan and the Constitution of Pennsylvania* (Philadelphia: Campbell, 1922), preface. Library of Congress, 22007931.

hath often heard," he concluded, that Newburgh "was Suspect of Buggery, & that the same was commonly reported at Sligo & elsewhere in Ireland."[8]

Although the evidence was circumstantial and vague, Hamilton reasonably concluded that Newburgh and his servant had slept in the same bed, and he had confirmed this report by observing the two men's interactions and widespread rumors. Yet Hamilton did not state whether he suspected the two men of oral or anal intercourse; he had not even seen them hug or kiss. Further, it was unclear whether Newburgh's repeated buggery was confined to one servant or if it extended to other men.

Judge Bryan then allowed the chaplain to cross-examine the witness. Newburgh reminded Hamilton that when they had lived in the same house, they had once joined "in making an Entertainment." How, then, could the ensign claim that he avoided "my Company on knowing these Scandalous Reports?" Hamilton replied that he had not heard the rumors of buggery until after Newburgh had departed. But had he witnessed "any Immorality in my Conduct at Sligo," Newburgh asked, "or did I give you Cause to Suspect me of any"? On this point, Hamilton could offer no additional evidence, only that he "thought it Improper & Indecent" that a man's servant should sleep with him.[9]

Having sex with one's servant was a familiar trope in the eighteenth century. Sex typically occurred between people of unequal status, and it was typically deemed unnecessary for a man to receive the consent of his wife, servant, or slave for intercourse. Such patriarchal privilege could even apply to homosexual relations. Before 1700, many in Europe presumed that all men desired women *and* adolescent boys, and English courts rarely prosecuted men who had sex with their male servants. So common was the practice that the term *servant* became a euphemism for a prostitute. Robert Newburgh would hardly have been the first man to help himself to the body of a male hireling.[10]

But there were limits. The courts got involved when sexual relations between masters and servants turned violent. A century earlier in Connecticut, Nicholas Sension was prosecuted for sodomizing his servant after the young man reported that Sension's "attempts were so violent and constant" that he "found it difficult to keep" his master off of him. Yet Sension was a respected member of the community, and he was only fined for his crimes. Relations with servants below the age of criminal responsibility also attracted legal action. Although Hamilton referred to the chaplain's "Servant Boy," there was no suggestion that Newburgh's sexual partner was below the age of puberty.[11]

There was something untoward about men who had sex with their servants. Sir Francis Bacon was chided by his mother for allowing a servant to sleep in his room because it elevated the servant and lowered him. When the Earl of Castlehaven was convicted of sodomizing his servant, the English aristocracy condemned him for taking advantage of his dependents. A man who slept with his servant was unable to exercise the restraint required of manhood and was thus not a proper master. In Batt's opinion, such a man did not belong in His Majesty's army.[12]

After Ensign Hamilton's testimony on December 15, Robert Newburgh returned to his room at Mr. Brooks's. Although the evidence against him was unfortunate, it was not damning. Batt's aggressive response had surprised him, but he had faith in the Pennsylvania courts to render justice. But Batt did not share his patience. The next day, the former captain waited on the chaplain at his lodging. According to Newburgh, Batt "advised me as A Freind to cease" the lawsuit. In his version of events, Batt recalled telling Newburgh that he was being foolish and "advised him to drop the Suit as it would be attended with expense to both of them."

It was at this point that Batt might have offered Newburgh a sum of cash to drop the lawsuit. What was said between the two men was not recorded, but later that day, Newburgh met with Major Hamilton and told him that Batt "had been asking his forgiveness and making acknowledgements." Whether these acknowledgments included a payment of £300 would later be the subject of considerable contention, yet rumors swirled around the barracks that Batt offered an amount equivalent to a clergyman's annual salary to forget that he had ever accused the chaplain of buggery. That Newburgh was the source of these rumors enraged Batt.[13]

Newburgh then invited Batt to meet him "at Mr. Ross's my Lawyer," so the two men reconvened at Ross's house on December 16. This time, Batt brought his own counsel: "Mr. Campbell a Lawyer." Batt again implored Newburgh to drop the suit, but as the officers of the Eighteenth would soon learn, Newburgh was unwilling to back down. He would not be shamed for being a sodomite. "I also told you, no Reconciliation could take Place between you & me, until the Laws of my Country had determin'd the Affair."[14]

Batt erupted. He accused Newburgh of lying to Major Hamilton, and he called him "a worthless fellow, whose Character, he knew himself was not worth supporting." He dared the priest to continue the case against him, adding that if he did, he "would drag Anecdotes of him from the most hidden or remote parts of the earth and make him as black as Twelve o'Clock at night." With that, the negotiations ceased. Newburgh would continue his civil suit against the former captain, and Batt would continue to believe that the chaplain was guilty of buggery.[15]

Although neither Newburgh nor Batt involved themselves with colonial politics, the men whom they turned to fight the civil case were deeply implicated in the independence movement. Newburgh's lawyer was most likely John Ross, a Pennsylvania assemblyman and attorney general for Delaware. John Adams thought him "a great Tory," but shortly before his death two years later, he was converted to the Patriot cause. Ross's half-brother George signed the Declaration of Independence, and his nephew's wife, Elizabeth Griscom, earned immortality as American flag maker Betsy Ross. Batt's lawyer is harder to trace, but he was probably "George Campbell, Esq.," who later transported money for the Continental Congress. The judge in the suit, George Bryan, was an avowed Patriot. Five years after hearing Ensign Hamilton's testimony, the Irish-born Bryan became the chief executive of the independent Commonwealth of Pennsylvania.[16]

❖ ❖ ❖

In the initial phase of Robert Newburgh's trials, his accusers focused on what he had done. The story shared by Ensign Hamilton focused on specific actions that he had either witnessed or reasonably concluded to be true based on circumstantial evidence. While Newburgh's reputation was also in question, it was his sexual acts that Thomas Batt highlighted. In so doing, Batt followed the law. Whether termed sodomy or buggery, "the infamous *crime against nature*" was like any other illicit act that could be documented and punished.

As Batt indicated in his threat, he knew quite a bit more about Newburgh's sexual acts. Although the records of the civil case have been lost, Batt's words were preserved in subsequent military trials. He added considerable detail to Hamilton's initial observations, and although he never personally witnessed any acts of buggery, he insisted that several highly respected men knew about it. As with any crime, Batt worried about recidivism; it was not just that Newburgh had committed buggery, but that he intended to do so again. Batt's account of Newburgh's actions and the meaning that he derived from them comport with eighteenth-century perceptions of male-male intimacy and reveal how people in the Anglo Atlantic understood homosexual desire.

The first time that Batt learned that Newburgh was guilty of buggery was in January 1773, when the two men were still in Ireland. Thomas Batt was shopping for wine and spirits for his future shop when the topic of the Eighteenth Regiment's new chaplain came up. According to Batt:

A short time before I sold out of the Regiment, I was in Company with a Number of Gentlemen in Drogheda, who asked me if I knew Mr. N. who purchased the Chaplaincy of the Royal Irish? I told them, that untill I was informed He was Our Chaplain; I did not know there was such a Man living; they then laughed at Me a good deal, And said I should soon know him, for that the first Opportunity, he would be into my beef; in short Many told Me He was a Notorious buggerer, And some of the Gentlemen told me to give them as Authors, and that they would prove it was a common report.

The claim alarmed Batt. He was humiliated by the story of Newburgh's buggery and angered that it made him the object of ridicule. Mockery was at the core of attacks on men who had sex with men, although usually the buggerer was the object of ridicule, not the listener. Batt resolved to discover whether there was any truth to the rumors and inform the officers of the Royal Irish about what he had learned.

A few days later, Batt traveled from Drogheda to Cork, but "unfortunately Mr. N. took the same Route." Newburgh had also journeyed to Cork looking for passage to America. Hearing that another member of his regiment was in town, he called on Batt at his lodging and informed him that "he intended to Sail in the Vessel" with him to America. This created a dilemma for Batt. The possibility of spending four to six weeks on a ship with a man guilty of sodomy worried him, especially as he learned more about Newburgh's desires. While waiting in Cork, Batt overheard two captains discussing rumors of the chaplain's acts. Batt was horrified to learn that Newburgh intended to bugger again.

> **Q.** from the Court—Did He (Capt. Batt) ever hear Capt. Bailey of the 48th Regt. Make Use of any Expressions relative to Mr. Newburgh?

A. He did, at his own lodgings in Cork, hear Capt. Bailey say to Capt. McAddon, of the Snow, Penn, that if He (McAddon) took Mr. Newburgh to Sea with him, that Mr. Newburgh would cruise up his *Gut*; At the same time, Capt. McAddon said positively he would not take him, and observed, that he thought it was very extraordinary, Mr. Newburgh should want his Negro-Man to Sleep so nigh him.

Upon receiving this information, Batt refused "to go Passenger from Cork with Mr. Newburgh." He would not become the object of Newburgh's lust.[17]

Batt's language in these testimonials was far more explicit than anything Hamilton had revealed. It was not just that Newburgh had slept with his servant; rather, he was "a Notorious Buggerer" who might set his designs on any man, even Batt. By repeating phrases like "be into my beef" and "cruise up his Gut," Batt described Robert as a sexual predator. Nor was Batt alone in such fears. According to testimony, these phrases came from respectable gentlemen like Captains Bailey and McCaddon.

The descriptive phrases also indicate that Batt and the others believed Newburgh to be interested in anal sex. "Gut" was a euphemism for rectum, while "beef" referred to flesh, presumably the stocky part of a man's body such as his backside. Although eighteenth-century propriety kept Batt from being more explicit, these phrases indicate that it was not masturbation or oral sex that brought Batt's rebuke; it was the fear that Newburgh would penetrate him.

Batt and the other men were also revealingly specific in their accusations. Newburgh's lusts were confined to men. Like other acts of nonvaginal intercourse, sex between men was deemed unnatural by church and state. Yet his accusers did not suggest that he also sought to rape women or children; they did not confuse his desires with those of Ensign McDermott, who had been accused of sexually assaulting a seven-year-old girl. Nor did they imply that Newburgh was interested in buggering animals. Whether or not sodomy was a confused category in the eighteenth century, Batt only referred to a man who had sex with men when he repeated the charge that Newburgh was "A Notorious Buggerer."[18]

Batt's testimony also indicates that Newburgh was imagined as being the active partner in sexual intercourse. Because he was accused of having sex with a servant, he was perceived to be a top, not a bottom. During this era, the active partner in male-male relations was rarely deemed more acceptable, and in some locales, he received harsher penalties for sodomy than the submissive one. That Newburgh was a top also suggests that there was no gender confusion in Batt's accusations. Neither he nor the other gentlemen thought that Newburgh was a woman trapped in a man's body.[19]

Batt also included a curious detail about the race of Newburgh's servant, claiming that McCaddon described him as "his Negro-Man." This point is not repeated anywhere else in Newburgh's trials, and it was most likely incorrect. The African population in eighteenth-century Ireland was miniscule; only a few thousand out of a population of four million. McCaddon and Batt were probably conflating status and race such that *negro* in this context was synonymous with *servant*. Or maybe this was an intentionally racist attack on Newburgh's character. If sex with a male servant was worthy of rebuke, then sex with a Black male servant only compounded his depravity.[20]

Batt's account recalls other eighteenth-century accounts of men who had sex with men. Having grown up in Ireland, both Newburgh and Batt would have known the story of George Stone. An Englishman by birth, Stone was an Anglican clergyman who rose quickly in the Church of Ireland, becoming the archbishop of Armagh and Primate of All Ireland in 1747.

Stone's ambition also included politics, and by the 1750s, he represented the interests of the lord lieutenant against the Irish parliament. However, this made him an enemy of parliamentary leaders like Speaker of the House of Commons Henry Boyle. In 1754, Boyle and others brought down the archbishop by accusing him of buggery.[21]

At the height of Stone's power, a pamphlet appeared that purported to be the love letters between "G—— S—-" and his young male lover. An obvious forgery, the correspondence was intended to embarrass the archbishop by making it look like he lusted after his "Dear Cunny." "I Hate Women," the fictitious Stone exclaimed; "there is no Love equal to that of Man and Man." He cared not which sexual position he assumed and told the story of three men who had sex, concluding, "oh! How happy was the Man in the Middle, for he was both Agent and Patient, Giver and Receiver, active and passive."

The pamphlet put biblical and classical allusions in Stone's mouth. He labeled his young lover "Ganymede," a reference to the mythological hero whom Jupiter abducted for physical pleasure, and he delighted that neither the ancient gods nor the men who wrote about them felt shame for having sex with other men. The archbishop purportedly observed:

> *Jupiter* left his *Juno*, left all his Goddesses, and all his pretty
> moral Girls, for *Gannymede*, and dispatched an Eagle whom
> he sent from the Skies to bring him up to his Caresses.
> You may read *Virgil* and there you'll find he was one of us.

It was not just the sexual acts that made the archbishop worthy of ridicule; rather it was how his desires set him apart from other men.[22]

Batt's account of Newburgh emulated the takedown of Stone in many ways. Batt did not fear Newburgh's past but his future intentions. He saw the chaplain as unashamed in his desires and predatory in his actions. Batt may even have believed

Jupiter and Ganymede

Source: John August Nahl II [after Wilhelm Böttner],
Zeus and Ganymed (1790–1800). British Museum, Prints and Drawings,
01613852648.

that Newburgh recognized Stone and other infamous buggerers as "one of us."

❖ ❖ ❖

Robert Newburgh had to formulate a response. When Ensign Hamilton gave testimony before Judge Bryan, he could
simply poke holes in the story and argue that Hamilton had
reached an incorrect conclusion. But when Batt offered far more

explicit stories and named several prominent men who could corroborate the rumors, he had to explain his sleeping arrangements in more detail.

Men accused of having sex with other men employed a variety of defenses. Some cited the fact that they were married and had children as proof that they were unlikely to desire other men. But Newburgh could not make this claim. Nor did he offer tales of sexual conquests like bachelors accused of sodomy sometimes did. Instead, he admitted that he had slept with his servant but then tried to explain why this was not sexual. To do so, he explained to the court that his supposed buggery partner was actually his foster brother.[23]

In the fall of 1773, as gossip engulfed the Philadelphia barracks, Robert Newburgh sought to tamp down rumors by explaining his situation to the various officers in the regiment. He had a friendly relationship with Captain Benjamin Payne, so he tried to explain to him that Batt's stories were simply a misunderstanding. In a subsequent trial, Newburgh asked Payne to recall their conversation.

> Q. Does he recollect Mr. Newburgh's mentioning any thing of his Servant's Sleeping with him?
> A. Yes. Mr. Newburgh said, that the Servant was his foster Brother, and had frequently Slept with him; that the Servant had lived with his family for Eight & Twenty Years, and had been by them appointed to attend him.
> Q. from Mr. Newburgh—Did not he mention that it was when he was a Boy, the Servant had Slept with him?
> A. He does not recollect.
> Q. Did He not tell Capt. Payne, that he, as well as his elder Brother, had been subject to an Infirmity, which rendered it absolutely necessary for a Servant to be immediately about his Person?
> A. He did.

The servant was not a mysterious stranger, but a sibling he had grown up with. Because brothers often shared a bed in the eighteenth century, Newburgh thought that pointing out his familial relationship rendered his sleeping arrangements above reproach. He elaborated on this point by insisting that he needed a servant to be on hand at all times because of his chronic illness and noted that his brother had done the same thing.[24]

This was a dubious defense. By bringing up his health, Newburgh emphasized his physical weakness, which did little to answer rumors that he was a buggerer. Early modern medical authorities referred to sodomy as an "effeminate disease" that revealed both physical and moral sickness. Eighteenth-century literature reiterated this point. The characterization of Captain Whiffle in *Roderick Random* portrayed homoerotic desire as the result of a nervous condition. Rather than rendering his relationship with his servant innocent, this admission of illness confirmed Newburgh's reputation as a buggerer.[25]

Batt was dubious of the chaplain's explanation. He had heard the same tale but doubted its veracity. In the fall of 1773, while Newburgh attempted to persuade Payne of his innocence, Batt gathered contrary evidence. He tracked down a man named John Patten who had once rented a room to Newburgh in Ireland. He then transcribed his conversation with Patten and submitted it at a subsequent trial to prove that the claims of brotherly companionship were false.

Q. Did not his Servant and *He* Sleep together in the *same Bed?*

A. Yes, *to be sure*, they slept in the same Bed; But then, he told me, it was a Family failing, and that his Brother, Broghill Newburgh, has a Servant to sleep in the Room with him, and I believed him, because when his own Servant was abroad, he had some other Servant to sleep in the Room.

Q. Pray, was there not a distinction in that Case; Was there not a Mattress brought in for any Servant, but his own?

A. Yes, for he always kept his own Servant remarkably neat.

Q. Have you not known his Servant & him to quarrel, & behave very oddly to each other?

A. Yes, and if he had belonged to me, I would not have born it.

This testimony confirmed Batt's earlier characterization of Newburgh as a persistent buggerer. According to Patten, it was not just a foster brother whom Newburgh had slept with in Ireland; rather, it was a habitual act that did not depend upon a familial relationship.[26]

Patten's testimony also intimated that it was not just an untouched bed that led observers to conclude that there had been repeated acts of buggery. He had witnessed the two men interact neither like master and servant nor like brothers. Instead, Newburgh doted on his companion, presumably providing him with clothes and effects to keep him looking "remarkably neat." The two also behaved "oddly to each other," and quarreled like an old married couple. If the relationship between the chaplain and his servant was platonic, it certainly did not appear this way to anyone who observed it.

As the trials proceeded, the servant was forgotten. Newburgh seems to have realized that citing the relationship with his foster brother was an ineffective defense, so he devised other strategies. As a result, we have no further information about this man. We do not know his name or what became of him after Newburgh left Ireland. It is also unclear if this was a loving relationship or an instance of exploitation. We cannot know whether the foster brother had a unique liaison with Newburgh or whether he was only one of many men whom the young priest invited into his bed. Without a name, Robert Newburgh's sexual partner is lost to history.

❖ ❖ ❖

Christmas was a festive season in late colonial Philadelphia. By 1773, most of the old Quaker restraints had fallen away, and holiday masquerades and mummers were commonplace. With the weather turning cold and ice regularly forming on the Delaware River, most people sought warmth with family and friends. Those of every station gathered for noonday meals, enjoying a day of festivities, and staying for supper. Such conviviality must have made unattached newcomers like Robert Newburgh feel lonely for home. As an Anglican priest, he would have been expected to attend the joint service of Christ Church and St. Peter's, which gathered on December 25, 1773, to hear the Reverend Thomas Coombe preach on "the harmony between the Old and New Testaments respecting the Messiah" before a collection was taken for the poor.[27]

Throughout the festive season, Newburgh continued to rent a room at Brooks's house, nearly a mile from the barracks and its malicious gossip. Yet such distance from the army made him susceptible to errors in judgment. Since arriving in Philadelphia four months earlier, he had obtained bread from a local baker and beef from a butcher, both of whom had contracts to provision the Royal Irish. He had the provisions delivered to his room and billed the army. But this was a breach of protocol. Officers who quartered among civilians were not allowed to take bread and meat at the army's expense. Presumably because he did not know any better, Newburgh flouted these rules "without the knowledge or Consent of the Commandg Officer or any other Person."

In the latter part of December 1773, the regiment's adjutant and acting quartermaster Captain John Mawby noticed the discrepancy. "As soon as it came to my knowledge," he later testified, "I instantly put a stop to it till Mr. Newburgh should comply with the method usual in such Cases." Mawby fretted that the chaplain's extravagance would fall "upon me or the Pay

Master," so he ordered the baker and butcher to stop supplying him. Newburgh was surprised by this development and claimed to be "ignorant of the necessary forms." But if he wanted to keep eating, he had to relocate to the barracks.[28]

Sometime around Christmas, Robert Newburgh traveled to the Northern Liberties and made a formal application for a room in the barracks. As acting quartermaster, Mawby was responsible for assigning men rooms. But on the day that Newburgh arrived, Mawby was in town, so he spoke to the quartermaster sergeant, Joseph Pyrah, who showed him what was available. Newburgh "fixed on convenient apartments and Marked them with his Name." He chose two chambers in the northwest gallery, one to sleep in and one to store his firewood. He then instructed his servant, Private Isaac Hudson, to prepare the rooms for his arrival.[29]

When Captain Mawby returned, he found Hudson eager to set up Newburgh's rooms. The army typically removed windows from unoccupied rooms, so Hudson applied for sashes. But Mawby directed Hudson to a different site in the barracks. He thought "that the room Mr. Newburgh had fixed on would be a very Inconvenient one," so "he Chose a much better one for him" in the "Opposite Gallery." Mawby had no ill will toward Newburgh, he later claimed; rather, he provisioned Newburgh as well as any officer and "furnished him with a Table and Chair from my Appartments, there being none of those Articles then in the Barrack Store."[30]

Newburgh was not pleased with his new accommodations, which he found to be "the most Inconvenient room in the Barracks at Philadelphia." He demanded to know why Mawby had voided his choice of lodgings. Mawby explained that the alternative was better, but Newburgh found this answer unsatisfying. He "missed no Opportunity of accosting me whenever he saw me," Mawby recalled, and repeatedly "complained that he had not the Appartments he was entitled to." The captain soon tired of the chaplain and "found it necessary to shun him."[31]

Newburgh found the change of quarters to be a severe insult. He had originally chosen two rooms, but Mawby assigned him to a single chamber. He thus had no place to store his firewood. The question of how many rooms an officer was entitled to was the subject of an ongoing debate throughout North America. Although sumptuous barracks in Britain and Ireland allowed two rooms per officer, the rudimentary state of colonial quarters meant that captains often received only one chamber and subalterns had to share a room. As a chaplain, Newburgh was ranked the same as a subaltern, which meant that he was entitled only to one room. Mawby was simply following regulations.[32]

Yet Newburgh could not help but notice that every *other* officer enjoyed more space than he did. Each ensign and lieutenant had additional rooms and "Capt. Chapman three or four." The Philadelphia barracks were designed to accommodate nearly two thousand men, but the Royal Irish was only at half strength. There were certainly extra rooms available, but Mawby did not believe that the priest deserved a second room.[33]

Newburgh had to watch the rooms in the northwest gallery sit empty for the next eight months. "There might have been Hay or Straw in some of them," Lieutenant Fowler recalled. Although he was not positive about the room in question, he thought "he saw a Beagle bitch & some pupies in one of the rooms of that Gallery, which he understood was one of those Mr. Newburgh had pitched on." Maybe Newburgh was not being overly sensitive to the slight.[34]

He also did not like Mawby's rationale for moving him from one gallery to the other. Mawby was surprised that Newburgh wanted rooms in the northwest corner as they "lay near a Necessary House and was in the same Gallery where the

Taylors worked." There was something unusual about these preferences. Subsequent testimony indicates that Mawby connected the rumors of Newburgh's buggery to his desire to be closer to an outhouse, a notorious site of male-male trysts. In wanting to be close to the tailors, was Newburgh reaffirming his queer interest in clothing or even looking for new men to seduce?

Mawby also might have thought that Newburgh wanted an extra room so that his servant could be closer to him. Although Private Hudson lodged with his company, Mawby reported seeing "the Servant lock up the room where Mr. Newburgh's Lumber was in the Gallery." This closeness reminded Mawby of Newburgh's sleeping arrangements in Ireland and led to the inference that he had designs on Hudson. Mawby uncomfortably watched the chaplain dote on the private, which confirmed tales from Sligo. When Newburgh was later granted the use of a place in the basement to store his effects, Mawby observed that it was not "usual for Officers to be Indulged with Cellars for their Servants."[35]

Mawby had been persuaded by Batt's stories that Newburgh was guilty of buggery and sought to isolate him. The chaplain's adamant response to this further soured the adjutant's opinion of him. Newburgh did not soon forget his poor treatment; five months after he moved into the barracks, he filed charges against Mawby and demanded that he be court-martialed.

❖   ❖   ❖

Once Robert Newburgh settled into his room, he adjusted to living cheek-by-jowl with the other members of the regiment. Relocating to the officers' quarters made his duties as chaplain easier. Now he only had to walk a few feet to minister to men in need spiritual guidance. He led worship services and read prayers in the barracks. As there were no churches in the Northern Liberties, Newburgh's ministrations may have attracted worshippers from the neighborhood as well.[36]

He also grew closer to the subalterns. Newburgh's room in the barracks was in the same gallery as those occupied by Lieutenant Alexander Fowler and Ensign Nicholas Trist, and the three men began to spend considerable time together. Fowler initially had second thoughts about the chaplain. Shortly after Newburgh moved in, Fowler noticed "a coolness arise" and "none of the Officers came into the Gallery to see him as they used to do." This troubled Fowler, who was incapacitated by his disability, and "He wished that Mr. Newburgh was out of the Gallery."

But Fowler was willing to overlook the charges of buggery. He decided that "he could not Shut the door" in Newburgh's face "as he had no reason for it." Fowler had been hasty in his judgment of Colonel Wilkins, and he did not want to make the same mistake again. The chaplain presented "very Honourable testimonies in his favour," and the lieutenant found these persuasive. After that, Fowler became Newburgh's steadfast friend and let him store lumber in his extra room.[37]

Newburgh also befriended Lieutenant Robert Collins of the Fourth Battalion of the Royal Artillery. Since the Eighteenth Regiment was an infantry unit, the British army assigned artillery officers, bombardiers, gunners, and matrosses to man various field pieces that accompanied the soldiers. For this reason, several members of the Royal Artillery lived in the Philadelphia barracks, including Lieutenant Collins. Collins found nothing objectionable in chaplain's words or appearance but believed him to be "a Man of exemplary Morals, agreeable Behaviour, and to have Supported his Clerical Character with the Uttmost Propriety." Soon, Collins joined Fowler and Trist in Newburgh's circle.[38]

Like Fowler, Collins was married, and his wife lived with him in the barracks. Newburgh befriended both Mrs. Collins and Frances Fowler, and he soon became as intimate with the subalterns' wives as he was with their husbands. Collins reported that his wife and the chaplain "exchanged snuff Boxes," adding that "Mrs. Collins observed at the time that the one Mr. Newburgh had from her, was most proper for a Clergyman on account of a Church being painted on the lid of it." Such familiarity with another man's wife was considered effeminate in the eighteenth century, and it increased the regiment's suspicions of the chaplain.[39]

Newburgh's presence in the barracks also aggravated his relationship with the captains. It was a poor coincidence that he relocated to quarters a week or so after he began his civil case against Batt. Captain Benjamin Chapman stood with his former fellow officer, and after witnessing Newburgh's inappropriate appearance, vowed not to speak to him unless compelled to. The other members of Royal Irish followed his lead. According to Collins, "Mr. Newburgh has been shun'd by all the Officers of the Regiment, (Mr. Fowler & Mr. Trist excepted)."[40]

Despite his treatment by the captains, Newburgh continued to demand that he receive the respect to which his rank entitled him. In early March 1774, he wrote to Mawby and "Complained of Indignity being offered to him" because he received only one pile of lumber per week. As with rooms in the barracks, a man's firewood supply corresponded to his rank, and chaplains and lieutenants only received one pile. However, Mawby often made exceptions. Newburgh pointed this out when he observed "that Mr. Fowler tho onely a Subtn was allowed two pile pr week."

In response to Newburgh's letter, Mawby composed a tart reply. He informed Newburgh that extra firewood was "an Indulgence" granted to Fowler because he was "a married man." This harsh response highlighted Newburgh's marital status, which he perceived to be an insinuation of buggery. The absence of a wife not only meant that he deserved less fuel, but that he deserved less respect. Mawby added that if Newburgh "Could reflect he would find his Character and behaviour deserving of Contempt and reproach." In effect, he blamed the chaplain for his own predicament.[41]

Newburgh responded with a second letter, but Mawby refused to accept it. He reported, "I soon had reason to suppose his intention was to draw me into Altercation & Dispute which I wished to avoid," so he broke off all communication and "return'd his Letter unopened." Even their epistolary relationship had come to an end.[42]

As the winter waned, a fourth captain turned against Newburgh: Benjamin Charnock Payne. Payne had been friendly when the chaplain first arrived in Philadelphia, even recommending a private from his company as a servant. But like Mawby, Payne worried that Newburgh might have lurid designs on Hudson. In early March, he removed Hudson from the chaplain's service, and ordered him "into the ranks, without his, or Mr. Newburgh's knowing the Cause of it."[43]

As the officers of the regiment divided over the chaplain, the enlisted men found themselves caught in the middle. Some sided with the captains and began to joke about Newburgh's appearance and behavior. He was an easy target and soon became the victim of harassment. Hudson reported that Newburgh had to start "putting the wood in his Bed Chamber" because someone in the barracks was stealing his supply. Other enlisted men withheld judgment of the chaplain and the stories of buggery. When Payne ordered Hudson back into the ranks, Newburgh had no problem hiring Private William Osborne as a replacement.[44]

By moving into the barracks, Newburgh strengthened the existing divide between the captains and the subalterns. Much as had happened with Colonel Wilkins two years earlier, Chapman led the effort to expel a hated member of the regiment, and he garnered the support of most other officers for this cause. This time, however, Fowler opposed Chapman's move and assembled supporters of his own. For his part, Newburgh refused to be cowed. Even though he could not disprove the rumors that he was a buggerer, he would fight to stay in the British army.

❖ ❖ ❖

As Robert Newburgh settled into life in Philadelphia, events around him continued to shake the British Empire. On Christmas night 1773, colonists in the Pennsylvania capital celebrated the Boston Tea Party as a fitting defiance of a hated law. When word arrived the next day that the rapidly approaching *Polly* carried tea for Philadelphia, eight thousand colonists gathered outside the Pennsylvania statehouse to demand that nothing be unloaded from the ship. This demonstration of popular will by nearly a third of the city convinced the captain to return to England. The Tea Act remained unenforced in Philadelphia.

Over the next six months, tea parties were held in South Carolina, New York, and Maryland, effectively voiding parliamentary law. In response, Prime Minister Lord North devised a series of coercive acts to punish the colonies for their defiance. On March 31, 1774, King George III granted his assent to the Boston Port Act, closing the port of Boston to all commerce until Massachusetts made restitution for the lost tea. Other intolerable laws soon followed.[45]

The Eighteenth Regiment played no role in these events. The Philadelphia barracks were a world away from the protests at the statehouse. Governor John Penn had no interest in calling out the British army to crush protestors, so Major Hamilton's men sat out the events. No one wanted a repeat of the Twenty-Ninth Regiment's massacre in Boston, or the Eighteenth's seizure of wagons at Carlisle. Instead of worrying about events that were leading to a revolution, the captains and subalterns were obsessed with their chaplain's homosexual acts.

Or perhaps the two matters were not so different. The Sons of Liberty pressed a series of nonimportation and nonexportation agreements that no merchant liked. As an aspiring wine merchant, Thomas Batt must not have thought much about efforts to restrict trade, and he probably blamed the colonists. Meanwhile, Benjamin Chapman sought to ingratiate himself with the royal governor of New York, a placeman with royal connections. Despite his rude education, Chapman may have hoped to advance in America through patronage, and he was no doubt annoyed by the Patriot cause. The same men who stood for king and country also lined up against the Robert Newburgh.

The world of the barracks and the civilian concerns of Philadelphia were not entirely separate in early 1774. The legal actions that followed over the next few months would suggest that the impending revolution and the parson's buggery were not wholly unrelated either.

CHAPTER FOUR

A Man of Infamous Character

ON A LAZY SATURDAY IN MARCH, a dozen officers and soldiers gathered in the tailors' room in the Philadelphia barracks and started joking around with one another. Like other infantry units, the Eighteenth Regiment tasked five privates with repairing uniforms. The work was slow, so the tailors took on piecemeal work, sewing garments for cash. The tailors had a large workroom, and this space attracted men with nothing better to do. On March 12, 1774, several men of the Royal Irish congregated in the tailors' room and started to get rowdy.

Present that day were the five tailors: master tailor Private Samuel Lee and his assistants Privates Thomas Beversley, George Douglass, John Green, and Robert Jeff. Also present were two sons of Captain Mawby: Lieutenant John Mawby Jr. and his little brother, Sebright, who was "about three or four years old." Captain Mawby had ordered a waistcoat and pair of breeches for little Sebright, and he sent his older son to retrieve the clothes. Captain Benjamin Charnock Payne and Ensign Edmund Prideaux accompanied the Mawbys into the tailors' room. As the highest ranking officer, Payne took control of the situation and began to issue orders.

The exact details of what happened next are unclear. Various testimonies indicate that Payne asked the tailors whether

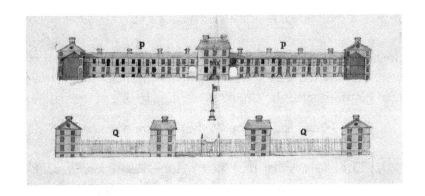

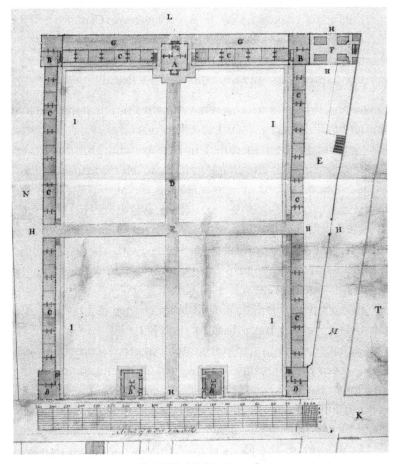

The Philadelphia Barracks

Source: Benjamin Loxley, Plans and Sections of Houses for Officers and Barracks
for Soldiers Near the City of Philadelphia (1757). British Library,
Add MS 57715.

the boy's clothes were ready, and when he discovered that they were, he ordered Sebright to try them on. Then "the Gentleman began to teize the Child." According to one of the tailors:

> after the Child had got the Clothes on Capt. Payne desired him to go down and Cuckold old Daniel the Master of the band of Music; that the Child put his hand upon Capt. Paynes Thigh to make a kick at him and called him *Foutre*, upon which Capt. Payne made answer to the Boy, Aye, and the Parson's a *Bougre*; that the Boy answered to Capt. Payne, that nobody was a Bougre, Lt. Mawby then took the Child by the hand and told him that those were not Gentleman-like Expressions, and then they left the Room together.

Payne and Prideaux followed the Mawbys out, leaving the five tailors bewildered by what had taken place.[1]

Captain Payne had called Robert Newburgh a buggerer. Three months after the chaplain had moved into the barracks, things were only getting worse. He was the butt of the joke and everyone, even a three-year-old child, was in on it. Although his civil suit against Thomas Batt had stalled, Newburgh thought that he had put the stories of sex with a servant behind him. But now, in the early spring, a former friend was laughing at him because he was a buggerer.

Payne's use of language signaled a change in how the captains talked about the priest. In the civil trial, Batt sought to prove that Newburgh had committed buggery by providing evidence about the chaplain's sleeping arrangements and repeating salacious gossip about his desires. Payne, by contrast, did not concern himself with such matters. He did not offer any details about Newburgh's sexual activities, only that he was a buggerer.

At this point, the focus shifted from what Newburgh had done to who he was. In the trials that followed, his acts would be forgotten as the accusers focused entirely on his character. To some extent, this was understandable as he ostensibly did not commit any acts of sodomy in the barracks. Yet it also reveals that Payne and the other accusers believed that there was something inherently wrong with Robert Newburgh; a deeper truth about his soul that surfaced not only in his sexual acts but in his general disposition. At the heart of any man was his character, and the parson's was stained as a buggerer.

❖ ❖ ❖

Captain Payne's choice of term is revealing. He did not call Newburgh a sodomite or a catamite, but a *bougre*. The phrasing was cleverly French, but the connotation was clear. The captain had identified the chaplain as a man who had sex with men.

Bougre derives from the term Bogomil which was the name of a religious sect that arose in the Balkans in the tenth century. *Bogomil* was initially a geographic designation and an variation on the demonym Bulgarian. Bogomil beliefs later spread to France, where they were adopted by the Cathars. In 1289, Pope Innocent III declared the Bogomil tenets heretical and launched the Albigensian Crusade against the French bougres. Thereafter, bougre meant heretic. As part of their heresy, Bogomils were suspected of sexual depravity: specifically anal intercourse and bestiality. When bougre entered the English language three hundred years later, these sexual associations were part of the definition. In time, *bougre* transmogrified into *buggerer*. People might prefer one spelling over the other, but they meant the same thing.[2]

By the eighteenth century, bougre was a generic expletive. An English newspaper reported how a group of bandits robbed a coachman at gunpoint, shouting: "Blast your eyes, you Bougre, stop!" The term could take on a ring of ethnonationalism, such as when a group of French prisoners condemned their English captors as "Bougre Anglois, Bougre de Chien" (English buggerer, dog buggerer).[3]

The word made occasionally appeared in the events that led up to the American Revolution. During the Black Boys Rebellion of 1765, James Smith ordered his men to fire on British soldiers and "Shoot the bougar!" Five years later, in the melee the followed the Boston Massacre, British soldiers hunted down heckling boys, exclaiming: "where were the boogers? where were the cowards?" While bougre in these instances was not necessarily a claim of sexual acts or identity, the men mouthing the word understood that it could imply sodomy.[4]

When Payne called Newburgh a bougre, he used a term that in another context meant jerk or asshole. Bougre was an angry word, one of derision and insult. But the humor of the situation was that everyone knew that Newburgh was accused of having sex with other men, and in this respect, bougre was double entendre. Payne would have known that the term also implied heresy, which was a fitting irony for the regimental chaplain.

Certainly, bougre was an inappropriate word to use in the company of a child. It was an expletive, like *foutre*, and often the words were used together. Foutre means *damn* or *fuck* in the context of "I don't give a damn!" (Je n'en ai rien à foutre!) When Payne heard a small child call him a foutre, he apparently found this amusing and responded with bougre, which almost rhymed. As often happened, the mention of a man who had sex with men evoked laughter; this was choice blue humor. Lieutenant Mawby, however, found such wordplay inappropriate for a child, so he removed his little brother from the room.[5]

The incident included racial anxieties. In his teasing, Payne told Sebright to go "Cuckold old Daniel the Master of the band of Music." The lack of a surname for Daniel as well as his place in a regimental band suggests that he was a person of African descent. British units often employed Black drummers, and Daniel may have served this function for the Royal Irish. Much like calling Newburgh a buggerer, the idea of harassing old Daniel because he was Black meant that Payne was deriving humor from marginalized men's identities.[6]

It would be incorrect to assert that Payne called Newburgh a homosexual. The men in the tailors' workroom were confined by the terminology of their era. Yet, by March 1774, the officers and soldiers had ceased to discuss the chaplain's acts of buggery and focused on his reputation instead. Newburgh's intercourse with his servant, whether confined to his foster brother or not, was too long ago and too far away to be of concern to the men of the Eighteenth Regiment. But they suspected that Newburgh had an unnatural desire and worried that he would try to have sex with a man again. By the eighteenth century, the perpetrator of a criminal act could find himself defined by that act, especially where sex was involved.[7]

❖ ❖ ❖

The incident in the tailors' room also sheds some light on Benjamin Payne. Payne and the other captains were usually overshadowed by Benjamin Chapman, but not this time. Payne was English and a decade older than Chapman and Batt. He had joined the British army in 1757, and he spent much of the Seven Years' War in the Caribbean. He transferred between regiments after the war ended, such that when the Royal Irish arrived in America in 1767, he was a captain in the Twenty-Eighth Regiment. He transferred to the Eighteenth in August 1771, shortly before the regiment was deployed to Philadelphia.[8]

Payne drew numerous lessons from his age and experience. First, he had a violent streak that surprised many in the regiment. According to Ensign Trist, Payne routinely beat soldiers, including noncommissioned officers, for minor infractions. Trist claimed that a sergeant and at least seven privates deserted because of such cruelty. Lieutenant Fowler likened Payne's violence to slavery and later testified that Payne's "System of Discipline" was "more fitted for a West India Plantation than a British Parade."[9]

Payne's aggressive demeanor matched his rigorous nature. Chapman noted that Payne possessed "the most unshaken Zeal for the service, and the most Exact attention to every point of his Duty." He was loyal to king and country, and he rebuked anyone who was not. One private whose religious beliefs strayed from Anglicanism reported that "Captain Payne called him a swadling rascal, a Presbetorian rascal, and a Jesuit." Payne was outraged that Newburgh brought shame on the regiment, and although he was forbidden from striking the chaplain, his linguistic violence was a means of punishing him.[10]

Payne also had his defenders. Sergeant John Brogden said that Payne "was the best Capt. he ever had," and Sergeant George Smith received "many favours from Captain Payne; such as having a Physician sent to attend him, and being supply'd with Wine, spices, &ca." Other soldiers testified that Payne provided money to help an enlisted man support his family, and that he paid to transport a man's wife who was not allowed to travel with the regiment. Of course, Chapman and Batt admired him, insisting that Payne possessed "the strictest Integrity and Honour" and "the most Humane and Benevolent Disposition."[11]

Payne was also more refined than the other officers, and he portrayed himself as a man of learning. In his version of what transpired in March 1774, Payne claimed that he and Ensign Prideaux were discussing a passage from the novel *Tristram Shandy* when they entered the tailors' room. Payne had lent Prideaux a copy of the book a few days earlier and the two men were discussing "the odd Passage relative to the Abbess of *Andoullet* and her Mule." As little Sebright tried on his new breeches, the boy insisted on knowing what they were talking about. "This passage Mr. Prideaux was repeating to the child," when Sebright began repeating expletives. This "made them all Laugh," so Payne "ask'd the Child who was a *Foutre* and a *Bougre*," to which Sebright replied "the Parson." Payne had never called Newburgh a buggerer: a little boy had.[12]

British officers were known for being well read, and they carted boxes of books with them into battle. Most were accounts of war, both ancient and contemporary, but they included less serious titles similar as well. *The Life and Opinions of Tristram Shandy, Gentleman* was written by Laurence Stern, and published serially from 1759 to 1767. It was purportedly the biography of the eponymous character, but *Tristram Shandy* was actually a collection of stories, many of which engaged in sexual humor.

In the story that Payne cited, the abbess of Andouillets and a novitiate named Margarita are trying to goad a pair of mules up a hill. Unable to budge the obstinate animals, the two women grow exasperated. In response, Margarita tells the abbess that there are two words that will prompt any beast to act: bouger and fouter. But neither of them can utter the words because to do so would be a mortal sin. In response, the abbess suggests they divide the filthy business so that neither will be guilty.

And accordingly, the abbess, giving the pitch note, set off thus:

Abbess	} Bou—bou—bou—
Margarita	}—ger,—ger,—ger.
Margarita	} Fou—fou—fou—
Abbess	}—ter,—ter,—ter.

The trick works, and the women succeed in driving the mules up the hill.[13]

Like Chapman, Payne was ambitious. He had staked his fortune on his career in the British army, and he no doubt wondered about this decision once he found himself embroiled in a controversy in Philadelphia. While *Tristram Shandy* was hardly Caesar's *Commentaries*, Payne's reference to it indicates a worldliness that most men in the Royal Irish lacked. Yet this sophistication did not include an acceptance of men who had sex with men; if anything, it encouraged a firm rebuke of buggerers.

❖ ❖ ❖

The Reverend Robert Newburgh also liked new clothes. Even though he had arrived in America with several trunks of

Scene from *Tristram Shandy*

Source: George Cruikshank, "He Caught the Attention of Both Young and Old,"
in Laurence Sterne, *The Life and Opinions of Tristram Shandy, Gentleman*, ed.
Wilbur L. Cross, 4 vols. (New York: Taylor and Co., 1904), 1: 31.

clothes, Newburgh contracted with the regimental tailors to make him a new suit. In March 1774, while making clothes for Sebright Mawby, the tailors also sewed a new jacket and breeches for the chaplain. Once again, Newburgh eschewed the traditional black cassock worn by a clergyman and opted for something more colorful and modern. For a man accused of buggery, this was a foolish choice, especially given that several people in Ireland and America had already taken note of his flamboyant appearance.

In fact, the color of Newburgh's new clothes may have inspired Payne's observation that "the parson's a *Bougre*." In his version of events, Lieutenant Mawby did not remember any discussion of *Tristram Shandy*, but testified that "there was a Coloured Coat lying by one the Taylors, which he believes was Green, and Somebody said that it belonged to the Parson." It was the sight of this green coat that led the officers to begin "teazing and Joking with the Child" and prompted Sebright to make "use of the words *Bougre* and *Foutre*."[14]

It would soon be spring, and perhaps the choice of color marked the upcoming Irish holiday. "A day or two before or after St. Patrick's day," Private John Green visited Newburgh's chamber in the barracks. Green was one of the regimental tailors, and he brought with him a pair of breeches to take measurements on. While the chaplain tried on the new pants, he groused that it was taking the private a long time to complete his work. Green explained that "he was kept extreemly busy by Captain Payne, and could not get them done sooner." Newburgh bristled at the mention of Payne's name and probed Green for more information. He recalled that he

> then ask'd him if Capt. Payne had Spoke of him; And Green told him, that he would not bring his name in question he could tell him of a very Extraordinary thing being said of him, that he promised him, that nothing but

necessity should oblige him to mention his name, & that
he would bear him blameless, and then he Inform'd him
that Capt. Payne had said, the Parson is a Buggerer.

Standing there, in a state of undress, Newburgh coaxed the
story out of Green, offering assurances that he would not tell
anyone that the tailor was gossiping about his superiors.[15]

Newburgh lied. Instead of concealing Green's story, he
acted on it. Newburgh had to address Payne's words or else he
would be tacitly acknowledging he was a buggerer. He filed a
civil suit against Payne, repeating the action he had taken against
Batt in December. This time, however, he wanted the army to
weigh in. Upon hearing Green's story, Newburgh went to Major
Isaac Hamilton and "Complained to him that he (Capt. Payne)
had accused him before a room full of Soldiers of being a *Buggerer*." He wanted the army to punish Payne for malicious words.

But instead of Payne facing a court-martial, Green and his
companions did. Speaking ill of an officer was a serious offense,
so once Payne heard that the tailors were gossiping about what
he had said about Newburgh, he demanded that they be court-
martialed. Predisposed to believe a long-serving captain over a
troublesome chaplain, Hamilton granted the request. Payne violently arrested the four privates and confined them to quarters.

On Easter Tuesday, April 5, an unidentified group of officers formed a regimental court-martial to hear the case against
Privates Beversley, Douglass, Green, and Jeff. The four stood
"accused of having made a false Accusation against Capt. Benjamin Charnock Payne." Indicative of the casualness of a regimental court-martial, no one made a transcript of the trial or
informed the commander in chief of the verdict. Subsequent
legal action indicates that the court moved quickly to convict
the tailors. Although the punishment is unclear, they were
most likely whipped.[16]

Robert Newburgh testified at the trial. Upon being asked if he was acquainted with the tailors, he stated that he never "Knew them before or had any Conversation with them relative" to the incident in the tailors' room. This struck the court as an outright lie. Had Newburgh not asked Green what Payne had said about him? The officers on the court expressed "their astonishment at such a Deliberate Instance of Preverication." Newburgh had lied under oath.

The members of the court and several other officers "Mr. Triste excepted, afterwards waited on Major Hamilton" to "desire an Enquiry might be made into Mr. Newburgh's Conduct." The men were led by Chapman, who believed that the chaplain's actions required a thorough review. Chapman no doubt added his own negative experience with Newburgh to the "Several reports that prevailed Concerning him."[17]

Hamilton deferred to Chapman. Earlier, the major had attempted to avoid involving the army in deciding whether Newburgh was a buggerer, but with a groundswell in the officers' corps, he had to act. Once again, Hamilton allowed his views of Newburgh to be swayed by the captains. "He at first treated Mr. Newburgh with some attention," Fowler observed, "but latterly he has treated him like most of the Other Officers, which has been with every mark of disrespect that they possibly could."[18]

Although a weak leader, Hamilton was also a peacemaker. He had healed the regiment's divisions in Illinois, and now he sought to do so again. Seeking more information, he asked Thomas Batt to detail his accusations against Newburgh in writing. Batt agreed, and on April 7, the former captain swore a statement before William Parr, a Philadelphia justice of the peace. Batt repeated the tale of how officers in Ireland had relayed stories about "Our Chaplain," and how he had avoided sailing to America with Newburgh to avoid his lustful intentions.

Batt also added new details, citing the names of other men who heard about Newburgh's buggery. "In short," Batt's statement concluded, "his general *Character is an infamous one*."[19]

Batt's testimony was explosive. He provided lurid details that fleshed out the jokes that Payne had told in the tailors' room. He stated, under oath, that Newburgh had shared a bed with his servant, and relayed accounts that the two had acted with inappropriate familiarity. Although Batt had not personally witnessed Newburgh's acts, he drew conclusions about him based upon information from reputable men. These confirmed the account that Ensign Henry Hamilton had given before Justice Bryan four months earlier. Moreover, Newburgh's obfuscation and combativeness only confirmed the low opinion that the captains had formed against him.

On April 8, Major Hamilton convened a meeting in his quarters to resolve the matter once and for all. Reverend Newburgh was in attendance, as were the captains and subalterns. Hamilton began the meeting by reviewing Batt's testimony and then asked Newburgh for his response. Newburgh spoke "for about fifteen minutes and laid his papers before the Officers." Since first being accused of being a buggerer a year before, he had collected statements from respectable men in England and Ireland that testified to the quality of his character and his work as a priest. He expected that these letters would invalidate Batt's cruel rumors and lewd observations. Then he gave the officers an ultimatum: "if you believe Gentlemen that I am the wretch Mr. Batt has made me to be, I will immediately deliver my Commission into the Major's hands."

No one said anything. The officers of the regiment were neither willing to accept Newburgh's testimonials and proclaim his innocence, nor did they have sufficient evidence to convict him of buggery and force him out of the army. Instead, "there was a Silence, and no one seemed willing to give his opinion." At length, Lieutenant Fowler spoke. He "thought Mr. Newburgh deserved an answer and that he was not sent for there to remain Silent." He wished to hear what the captains thought about the matter, but in their silence, "he would Speak what he thought; that the letters and testimonials which Mr. Newburgh had produced were full & Satisfactory." Whether he had had sex with his servant was immaterial, and the chaplain deserved to resume his duties unimpeded.[20]

The captains were unmoved. "Capt. Chapman soon after left the Room, saying, *that he had no Opinion to give.*" Several other officers trailed after him. Payne also departed, and Captain Mawby crossed the room to follow him out. At that moment, Newburgh accosted the adjutant. "For god's sake! Capt. Mawby let me have your Answer," he insisted, "are my papers satisfactory or not"? But Mawby was unpersuaded by the letters. He told Newburgh that he "looked upon them of no Consequence & left the room."[21]

As the room emptied, Major Hamilton offered a solution. As a peacemaker, he wanted to end the growing number of lawsuits and return amity to the regiment. He advised Newburgh to drop the suit against Batt, and "offered to give him leave to go home Immediately." Hamilton reasoned that Newburgh could only clear up the rumors in Ireland, but that once he had done this, he could rejoin the unit. In truth, he simply wanted to get rid of the chaplain. Newburgh was marked as a buggerer, and no amount of paperwork could refute this.

Newburgh considered Hamilton's offer. Nearly all the officers refused to speak to him, and even little children laughed at him. Maybe he had made a mistake by joining the army in the first place. But the subalterns quickly disabused him of the idea. Alexander Fowler, Nicholas Trist, and Robert Collins urged him to stay and fight for his reputation. Fowler and Trist had watched Colonel Wilkins leave America to save his name, and they had observed that by leaving, Wilkins had confirmed his corruption in the eyes of the regiment. If Newburgh dropped his suit and left for Ireland, his career would be over, and everyone would know that he was a buggerer.

The subalterns goaded him into action. According to one account, Fowler, Trist, and Collins told Newburgh that "if he did not prosecute Capt. Batt, they would thro' him off, and have nothing to say to him more."[22] A soldier who disobeyed his commanding officer did so at extreme peril, but the chaplain also recognized the truth of the subalterns' advice. So Newburgh proposed a compromise. He was willing to accept Hamilton's offer to return to Ireland, but he had some conditions. He insisted that the regiment issue a certificate of his good behavior, and that Payne and Batt state before the regiment "that they had not Declared or called him a Buggerer." He also wanted the officers "to accompany him to Church as a Mark of respect and to show the inhabitants than any impressions, the officers had recd. with respect to his character were wiped away."[23]

It was a tall order that neither Hamilton nor the captains could stomach. They rejected his conditions, so Robert Newburgh decided to stay in America and scrap for his reputation. What had begun as a childish joke in the tailors' workroom had metastasized into a regimental crisis.

❖ ❖ ❖

At numerous times, various accusers cited Robert Newburgh's *character* to explain why he did not belong in the British army. In his sworn statement before Judge Parr, Batt disparaged the chaplain's character three times, while Mawby vowed never to speak to him "till his Caracter is free from those black Aspersions which at present stain it." Following his questionable testimony during the tailors' court-martial, the officers of the Eighteenth Regiment ("Lieut. Fowler & Ensign Trist Excepted") announced the "impropriety of doing duty with Mr. Robert Newburgh" on account "of his Character's being impeached." Character was so prevalent during the attacks that even the subalterns employed the term to defend the chaplain.

In short, the debate over whether the parson was a buggerer was an argument about his character.[24]

The term *character* derives from a Latin word for a branded or impressed mark. In the fifth century, Augustine of Hippo used *character* to describe the indelible impression that baptism and other sacraments left on a person's soul. In this way, it became a metaphor for personhood. Just as a stamp marked a coin, a piece of wood, or a wax seal, a person's actions and beliefs permanently marked his character.[25]

Character had both a public and a private quality. In the eighteenth century, it was synonymous with reputation; thus, a man who sought respect or prominence carefully cultivated how he presented himself to the world. Yet character was no mere disguise. Philosopher David Hume used the term to describe an inner self that might or might not be revealed by outward actions. Similarly, Jean-Jacques Rousseau wrote that character was a deeply personal trait that was shaped in youth, and for this reason, he advocated for the expansion of education. Character was also part of the growing interest in emotions and sensibility.[26]

A man's character was especially important to the British army as it stretched across the globe. In a vast empire, there was a great degree of uncertainty about the quality of men, so officers routinely sought "a Person of good character who can be well recommended." A lieutenant seeking appointment in America carried the recommendation of a captain who had "known his Father many years," while another subaltern carried a major's letter testifying to his "good Character" even though he was "not personally acquainted with this Gentleman." The more respectable the recommender, the better the testament. When a German aristocrat endorsed "a Man of irreproachable Character" for service in Quebec, a British army recruiter complied without consulting with his commanding officer because he "could not refuse him."[27]

Robert Newburgh clearly understood the importance of character. When he sought entrance to the Eighteenth Regiment, he sent letters of recommendation from high-ranking officials in the church and government to General John Sebright. Likewise, when Thomas Batt first accused Newburgh of buggery, he urged him to confront those who spoke ill of him and "procure Such Certificates of your Character as will enable the regt. to receive you."[28]

But reputation could be misleading. A recommendation might prove false, sometimes because the recommender was untrustworthy. When the Reverend John Stuart opened a school in Montreal, he hired a man who claimed he could teach mathematics. "But as I had taken his Character from himself, and some others, who were inadequate Judges," Stuart discovered that the man was "utterly unqualified for the Undertaking" and sought to dismiss him.[29]

In these situations, patient observance could reveal a man's true character. In the New Testament, the term *dokimē* appears several times and is rendered as *character* by modern translators. But in the King James version of the Bible from which Newburgh preached, *dokimē* was translated as *experience* and *trial*, ideas that were part of character. Once Batt and the captains heard that the new chaplain had had sex with a man, they grew skeptical of his recommendations. Upon observing his actions and words, they came to know the truth. For this reason, when the Royal Irish officers met in Major Hamilton's room in April 1774, they dismissed the letters that Newburgh presented. His actions were far more revealing than his recommendations.[30]

Character was not the same thing as sexuality. Men of low character were associated a host of immoral acts of which sexual transgression might be only one manifestation. However, like sexuality, character was an indication of a man's true self, or what was sometimes referred to as his *nature*. Payne and the other captains believed stories about Newburgh's sleeping arrangements and untoward desires, and they did not see these as isolated actions. They could read his character on his body through his appearance and deportment, and they understood that his lowly character was something specific. Newburgh had the character of buggerer.[31]

Character was a powerful political force in the eighteenth century. In England, lawmakers and wits routinely made judgments on another man's political ability based on personal qualities, including his sexual reputation. Drawing on ancient writings, Georgian theorists posited that a man's character was determinative of his actions rather than the reverse. Foreshadowing the sexual revolution of the 1960s, the personal was political in the eighteenth-century Anglo Atlantic. Once the captains decided that Newburgh was guilty of buggery, they found nonsexual manifestations of his character. The civil suit against Batt, complaints about his room, and lying at the tailors' court-martial all confirmed that the parson was a buggerer.[32]

Once a man was accused of low character, there was little he could do to rebut it. When the focus was on his sexual acts, Newburgh asked for proof and attempted to explain away the circumstantial evidence. But as the line of attack shifted from acts to identity, he took a different tack, producing letters of recommendation to prove his good character. In this, the chaplain inverted the captains' logic; he argued that because he was a man of stellar character, he could not be guilty of having had sex with another man. For this reason, he stopped talking about his servant's familial status and his own ill health. Instead, he emphasized his intelligence, dedication, and morality, arguing that such qualities were inconsistent with the character of a buggerer. But this was a poor strategy. To defend his reputation, Newburgh had to exert a level of belligerence that further betrayed his good character and led him to make missteps like lying under oath. Character, especially that of a buggerer, was indelible.

❖ ❖ ❖

On April 10, 1774, Major Hamilton ordered a court of enquiry to "Examine into the Conduct of said Robert Newburgh." Two days earlier, the officers meeting in Hamilton's room had rejected Newburgh's papers and declared that they would no longer work with the chaplain until a full investigation of his character was made. Hamilton had tried to restore the peace, but he was a weak leader who deferred to the demands of his subordinates. He appointed Major Charles Edmonstone to preside over the proceedings, but the power on the court was held by the captains. Benjamin Chapman, John Mawby, and four other Royal Irish officers joined the court, while Alexander Fowler and Nicholas Trist were conspicuously excluded.[33]

A court of enquiry was essentially a fact-finding commission. Too many aspects of Newburgh's character were subject to rank speculation, thus a hearing was needed to determine their truthfulness. A court of enquiry was less formal than a court-martial; there was no prosecution or defense. Instead, the court and the accused reviewed written testimony and questioned witnesses in no particular order. A court of enquiry could not mete out punishment, but if it concluded that the chaplain was a buggerer, it could recommend that a general court-martial be ordered.[34]

On April 12, the court of enquiry convened at the Philadelphia barracks. The officers began by reviewing the testimonies of Ensign Hamilton and Thomas Batt. The court then called Batt, who testified that throughout Ireland, Newburgh "was violently suspected of being a *Buggerer*, from his Sleeping repeatedly with his Servant-Man."[35]

Robert Newburgh lost no time inserting himself into the proceedings. He asked Batt about events in Ireland before the two had left for America. Specifically, he asked about a promise Batt had made to Cliffe Tottenham to keep the rumors of his buggery secret until he could investigate the matter. Tottenham was a former officer in the Twenty-Eighth Regiment and had since died. Had not Batt broken his word, Newburgh wanted to know, and thus tarnished his own character? Batt responded that he had promised "Mr. Tottenham, who was then *dying*" to keep the rumors to himself, but that once Tottenham died, he felt no need to keep his word "in prejudice to a Corps he had served & esteemed." Newburgh hoped that Batt's response would paint him as cold and heartless, but the captains appreciated Batt's avowed loyalty to the Eighteenth.[36]

Batt was not one to be intimidated, and he countered Newburgh's pathos with pornography. Responding to a question from the court, Batt explained how he had refused to sail with Newburgh because he feared that the chaplain "would be into my beef." Such explicit language left Newburgh aghast. He "beg'd permission of the Court for Leave," claiming that he was "in want of some Papers." However, he was apparently so gutted by Batt's words that he did not return that day. "The Court waited a considerable time for his Return, to no purpose," the transcript reads, and "therefore Adjourned 'till to morrow morning at 9 o'clock.[37]

When the court of enquiry reconvened on April 13, it heard from Captain Payne. Payne confirmed Batt's testimony and added more details. He had also been in Ireland a few years earlier, and when quartered in Arklow, he had been "frequently told by a Clergyman of that Town, and several others, that Mr. Newburgh was Suspected of being Guilty of an unnatural Crime, with his Servant-man." Payne referenced the summer of 1772, when Newburgh was a curate in County Wicklow near Ballinaclash, ten miles from Arklow. It is unclear who the clergyman at Arklow was or what relationship he had had with the young curate.

Newburgh pushed back immediately. He disparaged the source of the rumor, asking Payne about the "little drunken Parson who lived at Arklow." But Payne responded that the

Irish clergyman was not the only source of the rumor. He had heard the same story several times "in different parts of the Kingdom." He claimed that Chapman had also heard that Newburgh "was a Man of *Infamous Character*," and that before he applied to join the Royal Irish, the Forty-Seventh Regiment had rejected him "on account of his being reported as a *Buggerer*." With such candor at trial, probably no one wondered if Payne had called the parson a bougre.[38]

Payne's mention of his fellow captain suggests that Benjamin Chapman was directing the proceedings. Following Payne's comments, an officer on the court asked whether Newburgh had allied himself with Colonel Wilkins. Did the chaplain say, "You, Gentlemen, will all obey Colonel Wilkins e'er long, or Words to that Effect?" Payne replied that he had. The court then entered a statement into the record stating how "every Officer of the Royal Irish" had signed a letter to General Sebright about Wilkins "declaring *that they never would do Duty with him*, 'till he had cleared up his Character." Much as Chapman had once pushed out Wilkins on account of his lowly character, he now looked to do the same to Newburgh.[39]

On the third day, the court of enquiry considered whether Newburgh had lied under oath at the tailors' court-martial on April 5, only a week earlier. Payne returned and testified that before the trial began, he had stated that he did not like how the chaplain was "tampering with the Taylors." Two privates then testified that Newburgh had asked them and the tailors what they thought about Payne. But the real evidence was a portion of the tailors' trial that was read into the record: one portion quoted Private Green stating that Newburgh had asked him what he thought of Payne, but a second portion quoted Newburgh saying that he did not know the tailors. It was a clear case of prevarication.

At last, the court permitted Robert Newburgh to call witnesses. Predictably, he produced the subalterns to speak to his character. He called Lieutenant Fowler and asked whether he ever had "the remotest Grounds from his conversation or behavior" to think him "Guilty of any Immorality whatever." Fowler answered emphatically that he did not. Newburgh then asked about the papers he had presented and whether these did "sufficiently satisfy Mr. Fowler of his Innocence?" They had, the lieutenant responded. Because of his papers and actions, Fowler believed the chaplain to be a man of good character; it was thus unimaginable that he could be a buggerer. Newburgh also questioned Lieutenant Collins who made the same point.[40]

At this point, the events of the court of enquiry become somewhat uncertain. According to the record, Newburgh "acquainted the Court, that he had some papers to lay before them," but that it would take some time for him to copy them, so he asked for a day's recess. The court then adjourned, but it did not return the next day; in fact, it did not meet again for another week. Then, on April 21, the court reconvened for the sole purpose of entering a letter from Thomas Batt into the record. In the letter, Batt claimed that Major Hamilton and the court had "requested of me to inform them, of what I knew, relative to Mr. Newburgh's Character," and so he offered the transcript of a conversation he had had with John Patten, the Irish innkeeper who claimed that Newburgh and his servant had slept together. The details were lurid but not new.[41]

But why had Batt submitted a transcript instead of producing Patten himself? Batt informed the court that he had arranged for Patten to give a deposition before Judge Bryan much like Ensign Hamilton had. However, Newburgh and his lawyer informed Patten that a military court could not compel him to give testimony, perhaps even intimidating him. It was a believable story, but curiously, no one in the court room asked any questions about Batt's letter. Apparently, neither Newburgh nor the subalterns were in the room.

Although eighteenth-century military courts did not follow the strictest rules of evidence, there was something troubling about the court's actions. Accepting the testimony of a person who could not be cross-examined invited hearsay or even outright falsehood. Likewise, not allowing Newburgh to interrogate Patten violated the principle of judicial fairness. But Chapman and the rest of the court had already decided that the parson was a buggerer and should leave the army.

There the record of the court of enquiry ends. It is unclear what, if any, decision the court reached: none is recorded. Hamilton and the captains hoped that Newburgh would depart for Ireland and address the rumors of his buggery there. The major subsequently dispatched the transcript to General Frederick Haldimand. The commander in chief could have ordered a general court-martial for Newburgh, but apparently, he did not think that one was warranted as he took no action.[42]

Watching the regiment turn against the chaplain, the three subalterns composed a statement of "approbation of the Revd. Mr. Newburghs Conduct and Character." Fowler, Trist, and Collins cited the "Recommendations of him from People of the first Distinction in Ireland" as proof of his good character. They had had seen these testimonies confirmed by Newburgh's conduct. They could not believe that he was a buggerer but thought that such stories had "been founded on Malice and totally Unsupported."[43]

The court of enquiry did not heal the divisions of the regiment, nor did it persuade Robert Newburgh to go back to Ireland. Instead, he remained with the Royal Irish, and his reputation as a buggerer continued to aggravate the division between captains and subalterns. Soon, enlisted men would turn against their officers, motivated largely by this man of "infamous character."

CHAPTER FIVE

Assisted Privately by Some Miscreant

ONE NIGHT IN EARLY FEBRUARY 1774, it was Private Nicholas Gaffney's turn to mount guard. The Eighteenth Regiment was quartered at the Philadelphia barracks, and although no one feared an attack from colonists, it was military protocol for a soldier to serve night watch. On that particular night, Gaffney informed his corporal that another private would have to take his place as Captain John Shee had given him permission to stay in his room.

For the next two months, Private Gaffney skipped patrol. Twelve or thirteen times when it was his turn to mount guard, he insisted that he had his captain's liberty to remain in the barracks. But he was not being honest: Shee had not excused Gaffney from guard duty.

In late March, Shee was reviewing the duty roster, and he noted that Gaffney's name was missing. Shee asked several noncommissioned officers about Gaffney's absence, and they informed him that the private had claimed to have received his captain's permission to be absent. Outraged at such insolence, Shee ordered Gaffney to mount duty at once.[1]

Nicholas Gaffney and John Shee had a long history together. Both men were from Ireland, and they had spent a decade together in the British army. But Gaffney had soured on Shee when the Royal Irish was in Illinois, perhaps due to his demotion from corporal to private. He shadowed Shee and began to suspect him of selling poor-quality goods to the soldiers for a profit. When the regiment returned to Philadelphia, Gaffney made his opinions about Shee known.

Upon being reprimanded for shirking his duty, Gaffney dressed for patrol and headed to the parade at the center of the barracks yard. However, instead of taking his post, Gaffney marched to Major Isaac Hamilton and handed him a list of six charges against Shee. These rehashed claims of corruption in Illinois: selling alcohol and coffee for personal gain, promoting a fight between soldiers, and allowing a private to be "Murdered by the Savages." Gaffney then returned to his room, insistent that the commanding officer had excused him from duty.[2]

Gaffney perplexed the officers and annoyed the enlisted men. He defied the standing order that all lights be extinguished at 9:00 p.m. because, according to Corporal Thomas Smith, he had permission to stay up late to work on his case against Shee. And Gaffney continued to refuse to serve night watch. At length, the regiment's adjutant, Captain John Mawby, arrested Gaffney for "Insolence, Contempt and Disobedience of Orders."[3]

Major Hamilton ordered a regimental court-martial, but Private Gaffney was irrepressible by this point. At trial, he offered his charges against Shee as a defense. The trial record has not survived, but subsequent testimony indicates that it was a disaster. The court dismissed Gaffney's charges against Shee as "vexatious, scandalous, &ca.," but this only made him unrulier. Even after his was put in chains, Gaffney proceeded with "a great many disagreeable Questions and words, Laughing and telling them that he paid no regard to what they did."[4]

Gaffney's court-martial became so discordant that the officers brought a halt to the proceedings. They then told Hamilton that they could not adjudicate the case due to "the constant Interruption, Insolence and Contempt of the Court by the

Complainant." They recommended that Hamilton ask the commander in chief to order a second trial to bring Gaffney to heel. There was no resolution for Shee or Gaffney.[5]

Gaffney's court-martial coincided with Robert Newburgh's court of enquiry. They occurred within a few days of each other, and both took place in the Philadelphia barracks. Several officers were involved in both trials. Major Charles Edmonstone went from presiding over the one trial to the other, while Captain Mawby served on both courts. Newburgh's friends, Lieutenant Alexander Fowler and Ensign Nicholas Trist, sat on Gaffney's court-martial, while his nemesis, Captain Benjamin Payne, took down the proceedings.[6]

There were other connections as well. Both Gaffney and Newburgh were defiant of military authority in ways that outraged the officers. There was no suggestion that Gaffney was a buggerer, but the two men shared a reputation of low character. Neither followed orders nor exhibited the proper deference of his station. Gaffney's claim of privileges enraged the captains as much as Newburgh's flamboyance. Ultimately, both the private and the chaplain embroiled the regiment in legal proceedings that nearly everyone thought pointless.

In the spring of 1774, the Eighteenth Regiment not only concerned itself with a buggering chaplain; it also sought to punish an insolent private. The intersection of the two cases put homosexuality and rebellion into conversation with one another. A man who had sex with a man was no better than a one who disobeyed his superiors, and both revealed that the divinely ordained hierarchy was crumbling in North America.

❖ ❖ ❖

On May 16 or 17, 1774, a contingent of the Royal Irish Regiment packed up and departed Philadelphia. They ferried across the Delaware River and began a four-day march across New Jersey to Perth Amboy. The group included Reverend Newburgh as well as Captains Chapman, Payne, Mawby, and

Shee, and the subalterns: Lieutenant Fowler and Ensign Trist. A handful of enlisted men came along as well, including Privates Green and Gaffney as well as the other tailors who had been court-martialed a month earlier. The group stopped several times along the way and quartered at local taverns. On the first night, Green and Gaffney struck up a friendship at the Sign of the Red Lion, sharing a bottle of rum at night and breakfast the next morning. Days later, Gaffney, who was still in chains, got into a scuffle with Sergeant William Williams at the Black Horse Inn.[7]

The officers and soldiers headed to Perth Amboy to sort out several legal disputes that were roiling the regiment. Ten days earlier, Major Hamilton had written to General Frederick Haldimand asking for help with "the Mutinous & Disobedient Spirit in the Soldiers under my Command." Specifically, he

Sign of the Red Lion

Source: Historic American Buildings Survey and Nicholas Sooy. *Sooy Place, Red Lion, Burlington County, NJ*. New Jersey Burlington County Red Lion, 1933. Library of Congress, Prints and Photographs Division, HABS NJ,3-REDLI.V,1-.

wanted another court to discipline Gaffney. Hamilton fretted that the privates had become infected "with a Notion of their being independant of their Officers," which he claimed they had learned "from the relaxed and partial Discipline of Collo. Wilkins." Because the former commanding officer had been unable to discipline the troops, soldiers like Gaffney now brought discord to the Eighteenth Regiment.[8]

Haldimand issued a warrant to try Gaffney, and the pertinent parties marched closer to New York City so that the deputy judge advocate, Captain Stephen Payne Adye, could assist with the proceedings. Apparently, Haldimand and Adye decided that since so many members of the Royal Irish would be in attendance, they would decide not one case but three. In addition to retrying Gaffney's case, the court-martial would also hear the case of Green, who wanted to appeal his conviction for gossiping that Payne had said "the Parson is a Buggerer." Also to be decided was a new case filed by Newburgh against Captain Mawby. The chaplain was angry at the contemptuous way that Mawby had treated him when he had moved into the Philadelphia barracks five months earlier, so he demanded that the captain be punished. Although none of the three cases dealt with sex between men, Newburgh's character as a buggerer haunted all three.[9]

Each of the three cases took the form of a general court-martial. A general court-martial was more formal than the regimental variety. As the name indicates, a general court-martial could only be ordered by a senior officer such as the commander in chief, and the officers who sat on the court were selected from other regiments to ensure impartiality. A general court-martial was longer, and it generated a formal transcript that was dispatched to the War Office in London. British officers were entitled to a general court-martial, and if convicted, they could face a fine in the form of an unpaid leave of absence or, in extreme cases, the loss of commission. A general court-martial could also be ordered to hear an appeal from an enlisted man who had been convicted by a regimental court-martial, or to decide on a case that proved too contentious for a single unit to handle.

Upon reaching Perth Amboy, the officers and enlisted men of the Eighteenth headed to the city's barracks on the edge of town. Perth Amboy was considerably smaller than Philadelphia with approximately five hundred inhabitants. The city's barracks were smaller as well, with an officers' quarters and rooms with bunks for enlisted men. Nevertheless, some members of the Royal Irish made their own accommodations. Robert Newburgh rented a room on the second floor of "a large house near the water side," which he shared with Fowler and Trist.[10]

As the members of the Royal Irish settled into Perth Amboy, Captain Adye assembled a court to hear the three cases. Following army protocol, Adye impaneled thirteen officers from the Twenty-Third Regiment, the Forty-Seventh Regiment, and the Royal Artillery who were stationed in New York and New Jersey. Lieutenant Colonel William Nesbitt was the highest-ranking officer among the group, so he was named president of the court. Among the officers from the Forty-Seventh Regiment was Ensign William McDermott who, seven months earlier, had faced a general court-martial for sexually assaulting little Kitty Shaw. Having been cleared of the charges, McDermott now sat in judgment in a series of cases that involved another man's purported sexual acts.[11]

❖ ❖ ❖

The first trial began on May 24. Private John Green "having appealed from the Sentence of a Regimental Court Martial" asked the court to reconsider the decision that officers of the Eighteenth had rendered two months earlier. Unlike an appeal in a civilian court, Green's case was relitigated. He "was brought prisoner before the Court and accused of having made a false Accusation against Capt. Benjamin Charnock Payne." But

Green hoped that the new judges might render a more favorable verdict.[12]

It was unusual for an enlisted man to obtain an appeal, and it is not clear why Green received one. Several members of the regiment thought that the tailors had been unfairly punished when it was Payne who had called Newburgh a buggerer. Green may have been encouraged to pursue an appeal by Fowler, as Green later testified that he told the lieutenant about the "ill treatment of Capt. Payne's." The subalterns were eager for an opportunity to knock the captains down a peg, which would have appealed to Newburgh as well.[13]

Green's court-martial did not have a prosecutor and defense counsel; rather, the court called various witnesses and asked them questions. Payne and Green asked their own questions, although the trial did not have the adversarial quality of subsequent legal actions.

The court first heard from Payne, who testified that Green and the other tailors had sullied his character. He accused them of harboring animosity toward him because "he has Sometimes given them Strokes with his Rattan." Payne was well known for striking soldiers, and although he insisted this was innocuous, he believed that this action "Inspired those Men with passion and revenge" to falsely accuse him of spreading rumors about Newburgh.[14]

This was the same strategy that Payne had employed two months earlier. He said nothing about buggery but instead, emphasized his strong leadership and Green's insubordination. This strategy had worked at Green's previous trial, and he had reason to believe that it would work again. But he was mistaken. The court's questioning of Payne revealed that it was less interested in rank than it was in the truth.

Q: from the Court) Did he ever in the Presence of the Prisoner call Mr. Newburgh a Bougerer?

A: Never that he recollects, he may Indiscriminately have used the Expression *Damn the Bougre* in speaking of him as he has of many other Persons, it being an Expression he often makes use of when he is angry or displeased with any one.

With this line of questioning, it became apparent that it was not Green who was on trial, but Payne. This created an opportunity for the tailor. Green had been convicted of falsely accusing Payne of speaking ill of Newburgh, but if he could prove that the captain had called the parson a buggerer, then his conviction would have to be overturned.[15]

The court also heard from Reverend Newburgh, who repeated the story of how he had come to learn of what Payne had said about him. Newburgh was sympathetic toward Green and explained that he had pressured him to divulge details. But he had good reason for doing so. He had thought "Capt. Payne was his Friend," but when Payne "withdrew that friendship," he "supposed that he had some reasons for it, and might naturally be talking of him."[16]

Two other officers testified, then the court moved on to the tailors. Beginning with master tailor, Samuel Lee, all five stitchers were called before the court and asked what Payne had said about Newburgh in March. Green, "being put upon his Defence," testified that Payne had asked Sebright Mawby "is not the Parson a *Bougre*?" Privates Thomas Beversley, George Douglass, and Robert Jeff repeated this same story with minor variations.[17]

The tailors' testimonies inverted the normal order of military hierarchy. In their effort to get at the truth, the court asked the privates about the captain's actions, a line of inquiry that was rarely allowed outside of a military trial. In response, the tailors showed no compunction about criticizing an officer. Robert Jeff was particularly critical of Payne's deportment.

Q: Upon the Gentlemen's leaving the Room, was there any conversation passed among the Taylors?

A: There was.

Q: What was that Conversation?

A: That it was very odd words for one Gentleman to speak to another.

It was not Green's character that interested the court, but Payne's.[18]

As the tailors relayed their account of events in the workroom, the court began to question not only Payne's words, but his behavior. Beversley, Douglass, and Jeff stated emphatically that they had never told Newburgh what Payne had said. This sat poorly with the officers on the court because after they finished interviewing the tailors, the officers asked Payne why he had charged all four men if only Green's words were in question. Payne attempted to blame Newburgh, claiming that the chaplain had told Major Hamilton "that there were several Taylors" who had spoken against him. He added that the regimental court-martial had punished "the other three not so great as Green."[19]

A willingness to accept the words of a private over a captain infuriated Payne. He interrupted the court's questioning of the tailors to call Captain Mawby as a rebuttal witness and asked him to impeach the soldiers' characters.

Q: from Capt. Payne) What is the Character of Thos. Beversly?

A: In General he is given to Drunkenness, and he has during the fitting up of this years Clothing been confin'd by the Deponent five or six times, and at some of them for being drunk at 6 or 7 oClock in the morning and neglecting his work and his character in General as a Soldier he looks upon as a bad one, he once Deserted from the Regiment and afterwards

took the advantage of the Kings General Pardon to
return to it.

In effect, the captains attacked Beversley's testimony by disparaging him as a soldier. Payne and Mawby insisted that
because of his repeated drunkenness, poor work ethic, and desertion, the court could not trust him to tell the truth.[20]

The use of the word *character* in the captains' exchange is
revealing since they used the same word to attack Newburgh.
Payne and Mawby did not insinuate that Beversley was guilty
of sexual impropriety. Like reports of buggery, however, drunkenness, indolence, and desertion were windows into a man's
true nature.

Green's court-martial stretched into a second day. By now, it
was clear to everyone that Payne had been careless in his words.
Even Payne figured this out as he insisted on clarifying his previous day's remarks as the second day of the trial began. The
court then heard from four other privates who each supported
Green's claim that Payne had called Newburgh a buggerer.

The second day's testimony also revealed that enlisted men
were remarkably taciturn in discussing matters of sex. Under
questioning from the court and Green, Private Thomas Wallace refused to offer any details about the meaning of what
Payne had said.

Q: Does he particularly remember the words that passed?
A: Those words, he particularly recollects, the Jest that
passed before he does not remember.
Q: from the Prisoner) Did not all the men in the Shop
believe that the words Capt. Payne made use of, were
alluding to the Chaplain of the Regiment?
A: He thought it might lean that way as there had been a
dispute between Mr. Newburgh and Capt. Batt, but
what it was he does not know.

It is curious that Wallace was so confident that Payne had called the chaplain a buggerer but claimed to be ignorant as to what this meant. The soldiers had certainly heard the rumors about Newburgh and, of course, they knew what a buggerer was. Yet neither Wallace nor any other private wanted to get involved in a dispute between officers. Such reticence is understandable, but it also means that we have little information on what enlisted men thought about homosexuality.[21]

As the case against Payne mounted, Captain Chapman attempted to rescue his friend. Near the end of the trial's second day, Payne called Chapman and asked him about Wallace's character. Like Mawby, Chapman described the private as a deserter and therefore untrustworthy. But even Chapman could not save Payne. The court tired of the attacks on the soldiers, so Chapman had to address the words in question. "Capt. Payne did not say himself that the Parson was a Bougerer," Chapman testified, "but ask'd the Child, was the Parson a Bougerer." It was a minor distinction that did little to sway the court.[22]

Green's general court-martial ended abruptly. Both Green and Payne claimed that they had additional witnesses who were still enroute to Perth Amboy, but the officers had heard enough. "The Court having duly considered the Evidence for and against the Prisoner," Colonel Nesbitt and the twelve officers found Green "not Guilty of the Crime laid to his Charge, and doth therefore acquit him." They opined that "the whole may have arisen from a Misapprehension of words." With that, the court adjourned for the day.[23]

John Green had accomplished something unusual. Through his appeal, he had corrected an injustice, and in the process, embarrassed a long-serving captain. To be sure, Green's case was tightly circumscribed; it focused only on a single incident, and Green made no effort to suggest that Payne's words were indicative of his character. Yet the officers no doubt felt uneasy at how easily a private had triumphed over a captain.

The decision in Green's case left Robert Newburgh in an awkward position. The man who had joked about him being a buggerer had been reprimanded, and he certainly delighted in this. However, the court's ruling had effectively established that Payne, Green, and nearly everyone else in the regiment had been talking about him. The court offered no opinion on Newburgh's character or the truthfulness of Payne's statement. Although Green had been cleared, the parson remained a buggerer in the regiment's eyes.

❖ ❖ ❖

The day after Green's trial ended, the general court-martial of Captain John Mawby began. It appears that the same court of thirteen officers sat for this case as well. Mawby's court-martial was Robert Newburgh's third attempt to refute the rumors that he was a buggerer. His civil suits against Batt and Payne were still pending, yet he felt the need to go after a third captain. Newburgh had not forgotten the disrespect with which Mawby had treated him when he moved into the Philadelphia barracks five months earlier. Instead of forgiving him, he sought to hold Mawby accountable before a military tribunal.

Newburgh believed that he had been treated poorly because he was perceived to be a buggerer. For this reason, he pursued the same tactics against Mawby that he had deployed in his civil suits. If the court would reprimand the captain for inappropriate words and actions, then implicitly, the army would declare the chaplain not to be a buggerer. Newburgh thus accused Mawby of three wrongs: having "declared his Character and behaviour Deserving of Contempt and Indignity," having withheld "from him the Convieniencies usually granted to all other officers," and having "treated him in a Contemptuous manner."[24]

But Mawby had never called Newburgh a buggerer. Unlike Batt and Payne, he had chosen his words more carefully. This meant that Newburgh had to attack Mawby's character without providing context. As before, the court found such high dudgeon peculiar and took the case down a different path than was intended. Worse, Mawby's court-martial opened the door for the captains to introduce evidence against the chaplain. If it could be proven that Newburgh deserved rebuke because of his poor character, then the case against Mawby would have to be dismissed.

On May 26, Mawby's trial began. Newburgh appeared before the court and took up his first charge against Mawby. He produced the letter that Mawby had sent in March which chastised him for demanding extra firewood. Newburgh thought that the letter spoke for itself, so he moved on to the second charge. He told the court that he had been "put into a room the most Inconvenient in the whole barrack," and he explained how Mawby had allotted him less firewood than he gave to the subalterns.[25]

The court was skeptical of Newburgh's charges. The officers wanted to know what specifically was wrong with the room that Mawby had selected, and they demanded that he "be more particular with regard to the woods and firing which was refused to him." In response, Newburgh called the quartermaster sergeant, but Joseph Pyrah offered little to support his claims. Instead, Pyrah recalled how the chaplain had selected one set of rooms, but that Mawby thought these "would be very Inconvenient," so he assigned him to another one. Pyrah also testified that Newburgh had "received his wood and Candles as any other Subtn of the regiment."[26]

Pyrah then spoke to the events that had prompted Newburgh to relocate to the Philadelphia barracks. When he had rented a room in the city, Newburgh had taken beef and bread at the army's expense in violation of military protocol, so Mawby cut off his food supply. Newburgh attempted to seize on this testimony and called Private Isaac Hudson to testify that Mawby had stopped his rations the previous December. However, after only four questions, the adjutant stopped the interrogation of the private. As the trial transcript notes,

> Captain Mawby having declared to the Court that he in order to Save the trouble of Examining any further Evidences, Acknowledged that the Issuing of Mr. Newburghs provisions were stopp'd by his order, Mr. Newburgh declined calling any more Witnesses in Support of this Charged, and proceeded to the 3d and last Charge.

Newburgh may have thought this concession a victory, but the court believed the opposite to be true. Mawby's actions were harsh but correct. It was his job as adjutant and acting quartermaster to ensure that all members of the regiment abided by the rules regardless of their character.

Newburgh then moved on to his third charge, that Mawby had treated him with contempt. Like the first charge, this accusation related to Mawby's refusal to accept a letter from him in March. He called Private William Osborne, but Osborne testified that he did "never Carry a letter from Mr. Newburgh to Capt. Mawby." Newburgh was dumbfounded by this response, so the court ended the proceedings for the day.[27]

The case against Mawby fell apart almost as soon as it began. Sharp words in a letter were hardly proof of indignity, nor was the refusal to accept a letter a form of contempt. The court also had little interest in opining which rooms were inconvenient and whether a man's firewood supply was adequate. Newburgh had failed to demonstrate that Mawby's actions deserved a court-martial, and he convinced no one that he should not be labeled a buggerer.

Mawby's trial stretched into a second day. Having heard the chaplain's side of the story, the court now allowed the captain to "put upon his defence." Mawby introduced a document into evidence and briefly questioned a lieutenant, both of which refuted Newburgh's claim of being treated with contempt.

Mawby then called Captain Chapman. Chapman had a low opinion of Newburgh and had no compunction about admitting this to the court. Mawby asked about the letter he had sent to Newburgh, and Chapman responded that "he thought Capt. Mawby Justified in the Expression" that the priest deserved his contempt. Mawby then asked Chapman *why* he believed Newburgh should be treated with such disdain.

Q. Have not the Officers of the 18th regiment Lieut. Fowler and Ensn. Trist Excepted, determined not to keep Mr. Newburgh Company, till Such time as he had Cleared himself of the Crime generally reported of him in Ireland?

A. The Officers of the 18th regiment present at Philadelphia Lieut. Fowler and Ensign Trist excepted, did observe that Mr. Newburg's Conduct was highly reprehensible In many respects, and for that reason they entered into that resolution.

With Chapman's testimony, Mawby turned the case against Newburgh. The adjutant may have treated the chaplain with contempt, but this because Newburgh was a buggerer.[28]

Chapman was not finished. When Mawby asked him why the officers had turned against the clergyman, Chapman repeated the litany of gossip that had surrounded Newburgh since before he entered the army. He had been denied a commission in the Forty-Seventh Regiment "on Acct. of his behaviour," and Ensign Hamilton had testified that Newburgh "had been guilty of a Great and unnatural Crime." Chapman reported that he had learned these stories from Batt, although he had also observed

Newburgh's indecency firsthand. Chapman then recounted the story of how he had been walking with Colonel Fanning the previous November when "the revd. Mr. Newburgh Galloped Close by him at full Speed, in a very unbecoming dress."[29]

Chapman's testimony revealed few new details, but it was devastating to the case against Mawby. Newburgh attempted to address the captains' rebuke "by producing Testimonials from the principal Gentlemen of the Country he Came from," but as before, these epistolary character witnesses proved ineffectual. More important, he had no answer to the rumors Chapman entered into evidence other than to say that they were not true. This did little to impress the court.[30]

It is unclear how Mawby's trial concluded. The only surviving record of the trial cuts off without listing a verdict. At the end of the second day, the court adjourned, but when the officers returned, they had moved on to another case. Most likely, the court felt that the evidence was unworthy of continuing the trial. In retrospect, the trial only made matters worse for the chaplain. Chapman offered further evidence that the parson was a buggerer, while some of Robert Newburgh's own testimony would later be used against him three months later.

❖ ❖ ❖

As the Perth Amboy tribunal discharged its second case, it was apparent to some that buggery had infected the regiment. The courts-martial of Green and Mawby had not been about men who had sex with men, yet a buggerer was central to both. Reverend Newburgh's reputation had led to the dispute between Private Green and Captain Payne, and it was used to defend Captain Mawby's interactions with the chaplain. It was as if every disagreement and division in the regiment was colored by the stain of homosexuality.

In the eighteenth century, buggery was not a private act between two men but a public expression of instability. A man who could not control his lusts threatened institutions like the army, while a man who had sex with his servants inverted the social hierarchy. For this reason, the identification of a buggerer could be predictive of future troubles. Much as rumors of sex with other men offered a window into a man's character, the presence of a man who desired sex with other men revealed a deeper societal corruption. A country that suffered a sodomite invited anarchy and revolution.

Buggery had long held political implications. When the Glorious Revolution elevated William of Orange to the throne of England, critics used the specter of homoeroticism to attack the king. William III was accused of being a buggerer and his reign was denounced as unholy because he had introduced the foreign vice into the country. As one 1693 pamphlet opined, the king's "Reformation" had "Turn'd all things Arsy Versy in the Nation."[31]

The politics of buggery intensified over the course of the eighteenth century. By the time King George III began his reign, sexual peccadillos had become major public features of British political life. In 1776, the popular London actor and playwright Samuel Foote was accused of sexually assaulting his coachman and faced a highly publicized trial. When the king and queen came to Foote's defense, a pamphlet titled *Sodom and Onan* appeared that bemoaned how did "Sodomy contaminate the Land." Foote was a "Coward, and Catamite," the pamphlet claimed, and it questioned the morality of anyone who had dared to support Foote, including George III.

> As heaven's Viceregents Kings on Earth are plac'd,
> But G——e the seal majestic hath disgrac'd;
> Inveigled by Scotch Insinuation
> To pardon Sodomites and damn the Nation.

King George was not accused of buggery, but his leniency toward Foote undermined the social order and threatened to turn an Arsy-Versy nation into a topsy-turvy one.[32]

The animosity toward Robert Newburgh followed a similar logic. The rumor that he had had sex with his servant in Ireland revealed that he was unacceptable for the British army, so the captains sought his dismissal. But Newburgh stayed with the Royal Irish, and his character corrupted the regiment. He launched lawsuits against Batt, Payne, and Mawby, and these besmirched the names of good men. Worse, his presence gave opportunities for subalterns to challenge captains, and enlisted men to question their officers. The British army was a strictly hierarchical institution, and a buggerer could upend the whole thing.

Newburgh and the subalterns did not see matters this way. They believed that it was not the chaplain's buggery that corrupted the army, but the captains' cruelty. Payne's physical abuse, Mawby's contemptuous speech, and Chapman's obsession with appearance were the true problems in the regiment. The prosecution of the tailors was further evidence of this, and they applauded the vindication of Green. Newburgh, Fowler, and Trist believed that good order could not exist without justice and that military hierarchy could not be used to rationalize persecution.

This division was only hinted at throughout the first two trials, but as the general court-martial moved on to Private Gaffney, the disparate views of the captains and the subalterns came into greater relief. Although the case had nothing to do with either Robert Newburgh's reputation or treatment, his character as a buggerer played a decisive role.

❖ ❖ ❖

At 8:00 a.m. on May 28, 1774, the general court-martial at Perth Amboy reconvened to hear its third and final case. Compared with the previous two, it was long and convoluted. Private Nicholas Gaffney stood accused of "Exhibiting a variety of Slanderous and Infamous Charges" against Major Isaac Hamilton and Captain John Shee. Specifically, Gaffney had filed six counts against Shee related to his command at Cahokia, and three against Hamilton for his actions since the regiment had returned to Philadelphia. Because the charges were untrue, the two officers asked the court to punish the private for his "Mutinous & Disobedient behaviour."[33]

As with Private Green, the court gave Gaffney the opportunity to make his case against Hamilton and Shee. If he could prove that his accusations were true, then he would be cleared of all charges. Unlike Green, however, Gaffney's accusations were numerous and involved events from many years earlier when the regiment had been in Illinois. It was a difficult case for a skilled private to make, and Gaffney was not a skilled private.

The court began by examining Gaffney's previous court-martial, and it interviewed Captain Mawby about the proceedings. Mawby recounted how Gaffney had misbehaved during his trial, and "frequently told the Court that he did not look to them for Justice." In response, Gaffney tried to make Captain Payne the villain. Deploying Green's strategy, he asked Mawby about incidents during the court-martial when Payne's well-known temper had exploded. "Did not Capt. Payne say," Gaffney asked, "that he deserved to go where four Men went the day before, which was to execution for Murder"? But Mawby denied these charges. Payne also appeared before the court and refuted Gaffney's claims.[34]

The court then heard from several soldiers, each of whom gave evidence against Gaffney. Sergeant William Williams reported that the private had "said with an Oath, he never would return to the Barracks" and that "he would rather knock Capt. Shee's brains out." Vows to desert the army and kill a captain surprised Williams, who warned Gaffney not to make such threats in his presence, but in response, Gaffney "Called him a Malignant Cowardly Scoundrel & Puppy." This and similar testimony confirmed that Gaffney was a troublesome private and

A Soldier of the Eighteenth Regiment

Source: British War Office, *18th Regiment or Royal Irish, Sebright's* in *The Uniform of the Several Regiments of Foot of His Majestys Service* (London, 1771). The Society of the Cincinnati, Washington, D.C., MSS L2019F56 [Bound].

that his charges against Shee and Hamilton were based more in anger than in truth.[35]

On the second day of trial, Gaffney "desired to make his Defence" and began calling witnesses. He had been unable to disprove the charges of his insolence, so he attempted to argue the veracity of his claims against Shee and Hamilton. But

Gaffney lacked the rhetorical skill that the occasion necessitated. He was not an educated man but a shoemaker who had spent the last dozen years in the British army. He dredged up already disproven charges against the captain and major, which only irritated the officers on the court.

Gaffney began with Captain Shee. He claimed that Shee had provisioned his company with subpar victuals and profited from the men's misery. Gaffney called three privates and a sergeant, each of whom recounted the terrible provisions at Cahokia, including "a Quantity of Bears meat and Venison." However, no one could verify Gaffney's claim that Shee was to blame for this. Gaffney then claimed that Shee had overcharged his men for "Savage Rum" as well as coffee, tea, and sugar. Sergeant Martin Bell and others confirmed the high prices and low quality of provisions in Illinois, but none testified that Shee had made a profit from the situation.[36]

Gaffney also criticized Shee's leadership in Illinois. He insisted the captain had ordered him "on unlawful Fatigues" and told him to husk corn, tend to the hogs, and unload hay as part of his daily chores. While such work was not uncommon, Gaffney insisted that "no man was by orders of Colonel Wilkins to be so employed without his own Consent." Yet Gaffney could not back up his claims. He questioned several soldiers, all of whom placed the blame on him instead of Shee. Private Robert Sparrow reported that Gaffney "never was willing to do that or any other part of his duty when he could avoid it." Corporal John Dutson also testified that when an order was given for men to grind swords, Gaffney had shirked this duty because he "had a Clap."[37]

By the time Gaffney's court-martial entered its fourth day, it was clear to everyone that he was not mounting an effective defense. Having been unable to prove Shee's poor leadership and corruption, Gaffney moved on to other charges, which he also was unable to substantiate. He accused Shee of exempting a private from duty to work on his farm. Shee admitted that he had, and the court moved on. Gaffney also held Shee responsible for the death of Private John Knight, who had been killed by Native Americans, but none of the witnesses faulted Shee for Knight's tragic end. Lastly, Gaffney charged that Shee had promoted combat among two privates, but no one had observed this event.

Then Gaffney moved on to his charges against Major Hamilton, all of which had to do with work ordered when the regiment returned to Philadelphia in late 1772. Hamilton had charged the private for a new firelock and hat band, which Gaffney thought "it Illegal to Stop his pay for." But this was standard protocol, and the court moved him along. He also claimed that Hamilton had ordered repairs to the soldiers' uniforms but had not compensated him for it. However, given the informal nature of such work, this was difficult to prove. Gaffney's weak evidence against Hamilton did little to sway the court in his favor.[38]

Suddenly, on the fourth day of his court-martial, Gaffney took his defense in a new direction. For three days, he proceeded methodically, attempting to prove his innocence by litigating his case against Shee and Hamilton point by point. He relied heavily on witnesses who were like him: enlisted men who had served in Illinois. Yet these testimonies were largely ineffective. Then, all at once, his tactics changed.

The first hint of Gaffney's new approach was the appearance of Lieutenant Alexander Fowler. Although Fowler had served in Illinois, Gaffney directed him to recent events in Philadelphia.

Q: from the Prisoner) Was he not a Member of the Court Martial before which he exhibited his Charges against Capt. Shee?
A: He was.

Q: Does he think that he behaved in a mutinous or Contemptuous manner before them?

A: He did not he thinks behave with Contempt to the
Court, but he behaved with Insolence to Capt. Shee.

Q: Was he not threatned to be struck before that Court by
Capt. Mawby?

A: He thinks he was.

Q: Did not Capt. Payne threaten to send him to Senegal?

A: He does not remember; there might be some such
expression made use of.

In questioning Fowler, Gaffney shifted from cataloguing the
abuses of Hamilton and Shee to documenting the cruelty of the
captains. He insisted that it was Mawby and Payne who had
acted inappropriately at the regimental court-martial, not him.[39]

When the court reconvened the next day, Gaffney called
other men who did not match the profile of earlier witnesses,
including Ensign Nicholas Trist. Trist had not served in Cahokia nor had he had much interaction with the Gaffney, but
he offered a more sanguine opinion of the private's reputation
anyway.

Q: from the Prisoner.) What is Gaffney's Character since he
has known him?

A: He knows but little of him as he does not belong to the
same Company, but he never heard of any thing to the
Contrary of his having always behaved as a good Soldier.

Gaffney's use of the word *character* is revealing. The term had
only appeared a few times before in the trial, and when it had,
it was officers who had used it. Now, suddenly, Gaffney showed
great comfort looking deep into a man's soul.[40]

Gaffney's new defense also exhibited more eloquent language. Between questioning Fowler and Trist, he addressed the
court directly. In contrast to his defiant tone of the first few

days of trial, now Gaffney was deferential. "It cannot be supposed that I," he began, "in the humble Object station of a private Soldier would dare to bring a Charge such as has been presented to you, had I not the firm Basis of truth to rest my assertions on." He was but a "poor and Illiterate man opposed to wealth and power." He then revisited the earlier testimonies of several enlisted men and carefully explained to the court why they proved he had never threatened Shee's life.

As part of his direct appeal to the court, Gaffney referred back to the regimental court-martial in which he had been accused of disrespecting his officers. "It is not impossible I, might have smiled before this Court of Enquiry," he observed, "but Sure such a harmless Circomstance could not offend those Gentlemen." It is curious that Gaffney mistakenly referred to his previous case not as a *regimental court-martial* but as a *court of enquiry* as he never did this in any other instance. Gaffney's words did not sound like him.[41]

When Gaffney concluded his case, the court allowed Shee and Hamilton to respond to the charges against them. Hamilton went first, explaining that stopping Gaffney's pay for a broken musket and uniform were neither unusual nor excessive; he then recalled Mawby and Payne to support this point. For his part, Shee did not respond to the charges point by point because he did not believe Gaffney had offered sufficient evidence during "that *unnatural Prosecution* of himself." Instead, he described how he had done his best to provision men in Illinois, even though "I lost a very considerable Sum by doing so." As for forcing men to work or being responsible for the murder of a soldier, Shee found these charges "so absurd, & extravagantly rediculous" that he "should have passed them over in Silent Contempt." Nevertheless, he called a few soldiers and officers to indemnify himself, including Payne and Chapman.[42]

Then Shee delivered a second address to the court. The change in Gaffney's defense was too stark not to notice; the appearance of the subalterns, references to previous trials, and adroit language revealed that Gaffney was not speaking for himself but was being manipulated by another man. As Shee told the court:

> I have however so much Charity for the Man as to imagine he would not have carried Matters to those violent lengths, had he not been assisted privately by some Miscreant, Enemy to the peace & harmony of the Regt. Thus much is certain that the Revd. Mr. Newburgh has since his Arrival here offered to supply Gaffney with what Money he might want, & charitably added he wanted no Return for it. Not satisfied with this he has had (I am well informed) him frequently at his Lodgings in private Conference, & no doubt assisted him with his advice.

It was all Robert Newburgh's fault. According to Shee, Gaffney would not have pursued his case had it not been for the chaplain's interference. Newburgh hated the Eighteenth and would stop at nothing to destroy it, including setting a private against his captain. Although Shee had stayed out of the controversies involving the parson, now a fifth captain turned against him.[43]

With Shee's revelation, the treachery of Newburgh and Gaffney intersected. The low character of the buggerer with his disregard for the natural order undermined the military hierarchy and upended the social order. Buggery was a form of communal corruption, and it had infected the Eighteenth Regiment. Newburgh's unnatural lusts had led him to litigiousness, disrespect, falsehood, and now, had inspired unfounded claims against Shee and Hamilton.

Newburgh would later admit that he had assisted Gaffney. His motivations were unclear when Gaffney's case concluded, and they would not be revealed until a subsequent court-martial. Although the captains suspected all sorts of nefarious intentions on Newburgh's part, both prurient and political,

Fowler and Trist did not agree. They thought that Gaffney had been forced into an untenable situation by ruthless captains, not unlike Green. Had Shee and the others treated Gaffney with respect, this otherwise good soldier would not have been tried. For the subalterns, whether the parson was a buggerer was immaterial to Gaffney's case.

❖ ❖ ❖

At 9:00 a.m. on June 3, 1774, the general court-martial at Perth Amboy reconvened for the last time. The tribunal of thirteen officers granted that Gaffney's wages had been inappropriately stopped but that every other charge the private had lodged against Hamilton and Shee was "Slanderous and Infamous," frivolous, or groundless. As a result, the court found Gaffney guilty "of mutinous and disobedient behaviour" and sentenced him to receive "one Thousand lashes on his bare back with a Cat of nine tails."[44]

With that, the court-martial ended, and the men of the Eighteenth Regiment began their four-day march back to Philadelphia. The extended stay in New Jersey had done little to heal the divisions among the Royal Irish. Although the three cases had been resolved, the friction between captains and subalterns were exacerbated, and relations between officers and enlisted men remained tense. Nor did the three trials improve anyone's view of Newburgh's character. He remained suspect for his flamboyant clothing and defiant attitude, while his assistance of Gaffney convinced some that he was willing to pull down the British king, army, and empire.

But Robert Newburgh's pursuit of justice had just begun.

CHAPTER SIX

A Patriotick American

IN THE SPRING OF 1774, events in America were moving quickly toward crisis. In early May, Lieutenant General Thomas Gage resumed command of His Majesty's forces in North America. The second son of an aristocratic family, Gage had ascended the ranks of the British army, rising through the officers' corps until he was named commander in chief of the North American Establishment. Along the way, he married an American woman and fathered eleven children. Gage was an exceptional bureaucrat, but he had no idea how to stop a revolution.

For the past nine months, Gage had been in London, sharing his thoughts on how to suppress American insubordination. He met with the king and prime minister, and he impressed them with his knowledge of colonial affairs. Events had grown steadily worse in America since 1763, and repeated conciliation had not worked; Gage advised taking a harder line.

Gage was in London during the Boston Tea Party and thus was on hand to offer a solution. He identified Boston as the locus of a rebellion and suggested that the empire isolate the city in order to bring the colonies to heel. The result was the Boston Port Act, which closed the main harbor in New England until the colonists paid for the lost tea. This was the first of the Coercive Acts passed by Parliament in the spring of 1774; accompanying legislation allowed British officials to be tried in more sympathetic courts and reorganized the government of Massachusetts. The Coercive Acts were the most strident action yet against the Americans, and the colonial response was expected to be hostile. It followed that Gage should be named governor of Massachusetts, making the commander in chief the chief executive of America's most rebellious colony.[1]

Gage was also in London when Robert Newburgh joined the Eighteenth Regiment. In Gage's absence, Major General Frederick Haldimand had managed the British army in North America, handling affairs including military trials. When the general courts-martial of Privates Green and Gaffney concluded, Haldimand received a transcript of the proceedings, and he personally approved Green's reprieve as well as Gaffney's flogging. Upon Gage's return, it was expected that Haldimand would relinquish such matters. But the new Massachusetts governor had no time for a buggerer. Gage wanted to focus on quashing rebellion, so he ordered that Haldimand continue to handle the army's day-to-day matters such as courts-martial.[2]

Much to Gage's dismay, Newburgh had no intention of letting the matter drop. Even before the three trials in Perth Amboy ended, he demanded that the army intervene. By June 1, 1774, Newburgh had launched suits against three captains to prove that he was not a buggerer. But he remained an object of scorn in the regiment and unable to perform his duties as chaplain. He knew his rights, and he demanded a general court-martial to restore his good name.

Talk of rights was suspect in the summer of 1774. Gage had been sent to suppress declarations of liberty, and Newburgh's demands struck many officers as insubordinate if not rebellious. Jokes about buggery seemed humorous in the tailors' room, but when it was revealed that the chaplain had helped a private criticize his superiors, no one was laughing. It was also disconcerting how the subalterns rallied to his defense. They were apparently not bothered by his reputation as a buggerer, and this raised questions about their loyalty.

As Gage began his task of bringing Boston to heel, he ignored Newburgh's case. But it was not so easy to separate homosexuality and revolution; both revealed a society turned upside down. The captains in the Royal Irish Regiment were beginning to see this connection, and they could no longer distinguish between the breakdown of the regiment and the collapse of the empire. Yet these were deeply British sentiments in a land that did not necessarily share them. A rupture was coming, and the subalterns were being drawn to a more liberal view of sexual character. As Robert Newburgh pursued his case, he exposed the ways in which buggery and political divisions overlapped and how they pointed a way forward in the nation to come.

❖ ❖ ❖

On May 27, 1774, a dozen or so members of the Eighteenth Regiment were quartered in Perth Amboy, New Jersey. That day, the Reverend Robert Newburgh concluded his case against Captain John Mawby, and it was clear that the chaplain had not prevailed against the adjutant and acting quartermaster. Sometime after the court adjourned on that Friday, Private Robert Jeff delivered a letter to deputy judge advocate, Stephen Adye, stating:

> You will be pleased tow acquaint the President of the Courte Martiall that I Dow hear-by axcuse the Revd. Mr. Robert Newburgh Chaplin of the 18th Regiment of Buggery and that I think it improper in me as a private Solder to pay him aney Complimt or call upon him to discharge his Duty untill he is either Condemd or acquitted.

For the first time, Robert Newburgh stood formally accused of having had sex with a man.[3]

Private Jeff was one of the four tailors who had been court-martialed for gossiping about Captain Benjamin Charnock Payne, and he had traveled to Perth Amboy with other members of the regiment to testify in Green's trial. Jeff had been born in Yorkshire, England, and as his accusation indicates, had only a rudimentary education. He may have become friends with Newburgh in the tailors' room or during the trials. Jeff was also married with children, including a newborn, making him conspicuously heterosexual.[4]

According to subsequent testimony, Newburgh "persuaded Jeff to give in a Charge against him." The plan was clever but convoluted. The chaplain reasoned that once charges were filed, Jeff would be asked where he had heard about Newburgh's buggery, and Jeff would reply that he had learned it from Payne. The captain would then be questioned under oath, and Newburgh could prove once and for all that "Capt. Payne had Called him a Buggerrer." After that, he could pursue damages against Payne in the Pennsylvania courts.[5]

Newburgh promptly admitted to General Haldimand that he "did desire and consent to Robert Jeff A Soldier in our Regiment to give in the Charge against me." He even coached Jeff on how to write his charge. As his wife had recently given birth, "Jeff was to say that as his wife might want Churching &ca, he, as a private Soldier, thought it improper to apply to him till his Character was Cleared up," claimed Gaffney. Apparently, it took some work to convince Jeff to make the accusation, and he almost immediately regretted it. The captains no doubt observed that Newburgh had tempted yet another enlisted man to invite chaos and disorder to the regiment. Of course, with Jeff married, they did not believe that his refusal to spend time with the chaplain was the result of an unwanted advance.[6]

A day after Jeff produced his accusation, Major Isaac Hamilton filed charges of his own. Hamilton had no interest in buggery; rather his concern was Newburgh's disruptive behavior.

> I Do Accuse the Reverend Mr. Robert Newburgh Chap-
> lain to his Majestys 18th Regimt of Foot, of Wilful perjury,
> Prevarication, & falshood, and of having, by his Vicious
> and ungentleman like behavior, derogated from the Sa-
> cred character with which he is invested.

Hamilton did not offer any specifics, but the charges were
linked to Newburgh's actions in the tailors' court-martial and
the civil suits against Batt and Payne. Meddling in Gaffney's
case was soon added to the mix. Hamilton handed his charges
to Lieutenant Colonel William Nesbitt, who was presiding at
the time over the general court-martial in Perth Amboy. Hamilton hoped that the court would take up the case against Newburgh as soon as it was through with Gaffney.[7]

Newburgh agreed. He wrote to General Haldimand on
May 29, explaining that he had wanted to court-martial Payne
but was told "to prosecute him at Civil Law." Now that he had
been charged with "Crimes notoriously cognisable by the Civil
Law," however, Newburgh worried that a colonial court might
try him for sodomy. "I have Reason to fear," he wrote to Haldimand, "I shall not without your Excellency's Interposition
obtain proper means of Vindicating my Character." He would
agree to drop his civil suit against Payne in exchange for a
court-martial.[8]

Colonel Nesbitt, however, had no interest in buggery. Writing to Haldimand on the second day of Gaffney's trial, Nesbitt
washed his hands of Newburgh's case, which to him seemed
"a vexatious, & tedious affair." Although "some of their Evidence have already been examined (by our mistake) upon the
Subject," he hoped that the general would refuse to order a
court-martial, and refer the chaplain "to either a Bishops, or
Civil Court."[9]

Nesbitt's decision was confirmed by Haldimand. Sending
word through the major of the brigade, he ordered that "when

the Tryal of Gaffney is Clos'd, You will please to Dismiss all the Parties Concern'd at the Genl. Court Martial to their Respective Quarters." Although Haldimand thought that charges "of so Serious a Nature" were worthy of attention, he deferred any action until "he has General Gage's Opinion." Now that Gage had resumed command, it was his problem. For good measure, Haldimand transmitted "an account of the whole affair" to Gage. Haldimand had no opinion on buggery or the disruptive chaplain other than that "He earnestly wishes this Disagreeable Business had never occurred."[10]

With the general court-martial unwilling to hear Newburgh's case, Major Hamilton took alternate measures. On June 1, he arrested the chaplain and ordered him to "be confined to the Barracks." Hamilton acknowledged that Newburgh stood "accused of having committed a most unnatural Crime" and also cited his "Vicious & ungentlemanlike Behaviour," effectively combining Private Jeff's charges with his own. Until a general court-martial could be convened, Hamilton ordered that no one "shall apply to the said Mr. Newburgh, as Chaplain, to Discharge the Dutys of his Function" including the holy rites of baptism, marriage, and burial. In his place, the regiment would appoint a substitute to be compensated out of his salary. Not surprisingly, Newburgh was outraged, and he informed Hamilton, "I apprehend you were ill advised to give such an order." But he had no choice but to comply. Newburgh soon departed Perth Amboy under an armed guard much like the one that had escorted Green and Gaffney to New Jersey two weeks earlier.[11]

By June 4, Robert Newburgh was back in Philadelphia, imprisoned in the barracks. As adjutant, Captain Mawby had the responsibility for incarcerating prisoners, and he no doubt took some pleasure in locking up the man who had court-martialed him only a week before. Because Newburgh was an officer, Mawby could only confine him to his chamber, although this effectively trapped the chaplain in a room he deemed, "the most Inconvenient in the whole Barrack." At this point, a third accusation was leveled against Newburgh. Because of his hostile response to Hamilton during his arrest, he was also charged with "insolence to his Commanding Officer."[12]

As the officers and enlisted men of the Royal Irish returned to the Northern Liberties, they prepared for their second summer in the largest city in British North America. By June, the temperatures in Philadelphia push into the 80s, and this quieted complaints about who deserved more firewood. Robert Newburgh would have been accustomed to considerably milder Junes in Dublin. He probably threw open the window to catch a breeze, but confined to his room, he had to watch events in the city from afar.

❖ ❖ ❖

As temperatures rose in Philadelphia, tempers cooled in the Eighteenth Regiment. The trip to Perth Amboy settled several regimental disputes and gave some of the soldiers a break from the day-to-day tedium of army life. The chief troublemakers also disappeared. Newburgh was silenced by his incarceration, while the muster roll for June 24 listed Captain Benjamin Chapman as "On Duty at New York." At the same time, Major Hamilton's health improved, and the commanding officer led the regiment effectively for a change. For the first time in many months, things returned to normal in the Philadelphia barracks.[13]

Meanwhile, tensions heated up among the nearby civilian population. In response to the Boston Port Act, a group of Philadelphians met at the City Tavern on May 20 to form a committee of correspondence. The committee wrote a "friendly and affectionate answer" to the New England city, which was immediately carried north by Boston silversmith and Son of Liberty Paul Revere. Unlike Bostonians, however, Philadelphians tended toward moderation and had little interest in a boycott of British goods. In fact, one committee leader even supplied information to the British government about machinations in Pennsylvania. Instead of a protest, Philadelphia marked the day that the first Coercive Act went into effect with solemnity. On June 1, "many of the inhabitants" of the city chose "to express their sympathy and concern for their distressed brethren, by suspending business on *this day*." The port was closed, "the houses of worship were crowded," and muffled bells tolled throughout the city.[14]

Many of Royal Irish had been in Perth Amboy during Philadelphia's initial response to the Boston Port Act, but nearly everyone had returned by the time a growing number of colonists began to question the city's restrained position. Many mechanics found prayer and patience to be a tepid response, and on June 9, twelve hundred working men gathered in the statehouse yard to openly criticize the committee of correspondence. In response, a number of radicals were added to the committee. Eleven days later, a mass meeting of eight thousand Philadelphians turned out to demand that Pennsylvania no longer simply observe the tyrannical treatment of Boston but join with Massachusetts and the other colonies in proposing a solution.

Soon after, momentum in Philadelphia shifted to the radicals. In mid-July, an extralegal gathering that termed itself the Provincial Congress of Pennsylvania gathered at Carpenters' Hall. The group resolved that the convening of a continental congress was "an absolute necessity" as it would provide a forum "to consult together upon the present unhappy State of the Colonies, and to form and adopt a plan for the purposes of obtaining redress of American grievances." An intercolonial gathering could proclaim "American rights upon the most solid and constitutional principles," while also avowing its sincere hope to reestablish the "Union & harmony between Great-

Britain and the Colonies." The provincial gathering then appointed seven delegates to join the First Continental Congress in September.[15]

The officers and enlisted men of the Eighteenth Regiment watched nervously from the Philadelphia barracks as the city demanded a more forceful rebuke of British policy. Since returning to barracks in late 1772, the Royal Irish had been well treated, without the parsimony or violence of Boston. The provincial legislature faithfully appropriated £1,200 annually for "Firewood, Candles, Small-beer, &c.," and there were few conflicts between soldiers and civilians in the city.[16]

However, as Philadelphia abandoned moderation, some inhabitants cast a wary eye on the redcoats in their midst. In early July, the *Pennsylvania Packet* advertised a pamphlet that denounced standing armies as agents of tyranny. Written by Massachusetts Patriot Josiah Quincy, it recounted how Caesar and Cromwell had used soldiers to oppress their own people. "But as to America, the armies which infest her shores, are in every view FOREIGNERS, disconnected with her in interest, kindred and other social alliances; who have nothing to lose, but every thing to gain by butchering and oppressing her inhabitants." Although Quincy's tone was Bostonian, Philadelphians found his reasoning persuasive. In addition to appointing delegates, the provincial congress called for "a repeal of all statutes for quartering troops in the Colonies, or subjecting them to any expence on account of such troops."[17]

Philadelphia's change in spirit had real consequences for the Eighteenth Regiment. Major Hamilton discovered this new hostility toward British soldiers inside a Philadelphia courtroom. In the spring of 1774, a man turned himself in to Hamilton and claimed that he was a deserter from the Forty-Seventh Regiment. Hamilton dispatched the man to New York to be court-martialed, but this aroused the ire of a Philadelphia

merchant. Since deserting, the runaway soldier had been working on a ship and the merchant resented losing a laborer, so
he sued Hamilton.

In early July, a Philadelphia civil court heard the merchant's
case against Hamilton. The major argued that he had acted legally under Britain's Quartering Act, which gave a British officer the right to arrest any soldier who absconded from his
unit. Captain Payne testified on the major's behalf, and Hamilton even produced the man's own written confession that he
was a deserter. But it was to no avail. The jury returned a verdict against Hamilton and left him owing £13 in damages.

Hamilton relayed the court's decision to General Gage. The
fact that a jury had chosen to ignore British law astonished
him, and it came to "the great Surprize of the King's Attorney,
and the whole Court." He placed the blame for the misguided
decision on the judge overseeing the case, who instructed the
jury that despite "positive Proofs that the fellow was a Deserter,
they ought now not to pay the least Attention to any of the
English Acts of Parliament." Hamilton named the disloyal judge
as "Mr. Ross." This may have been the Honorable John Ross,
the same man who was handling Robert Newburgh's civil case
against Thomas Batt.[18]

Hamilton also connected the political upheaval in Philadelphia to the divisions in the Eighteenth. In late July, Ensign
Nicholas Trist asked Hamilton for permission "to retire on half
pay" from the British army. Apparently, like his friend Fowler,
Trist had begun to suffer from physical ailments. He had become "Afflicted with Violent pains in my Breast and Rheumatic
pains in my Shoulders," and despite repeated efforts to find a
cure, he was "very unfit for Active Service." But Hamilton was
skeptical of Trist's motives. Writing to Gage, he said of Trist:

> He is now endeavouring to quit the Service on Account
> of His Marriage with the Daughter of a Woman who keeps

Hon. John Ross (1714-1776), Royal Attorney-General.

The Honorable John Ross

Source: Harmon Pumpelly Read, *Rossiana: Papers and Documents Relating to the History and Genealogy of the Ancient and Noble House of Ross of Ross-Shire, Scotland, and Its Descent from the Ancient Earl of Ross* (Albany: Read, 1908), 166.

a Lodging House in this City, and I suppose intends be-coming a *Patriotick* American as he had Address to declare to a Gentleman of the City that his Brother Officers Dis-like to him was occasioned by expressing his Sentiments in favor of America.

On June 10, Nicholas Trist married Elizabeth House, the daughter of an Anglican family in Philadelphia. Little is known of House's father, but her mother, Mary, ran an upscale boarding-house at Fifth and Market. As Hamilton's letter indicates, the

House house enjoyed a reputation as a locus of revolutionary fervor; indeed, several delegates to the upcoming Continental Congress would lodge there in September.[19]

Hamilton also drew Gage's attention to Trist's conflict with the other officers in the regiment. He did not explain that the captains and the subalterns were divided over their opinion of Reverend Newburgh, although he referred to this implicitly. The division had grown deeper with Gaffney's trial, and now colonial politics also seemed to be pulling the regiment apart. On one side were the loyal captains and, on the other, suspect subalterns who allied with a buggerer.

Hamilton advised Gage to grant Trist's request. A few months earlier, the major had attempted to heal division in the regiment by asking Newburgh to return to Ireland, and now he sought to do the same by evicting a second troublemaker. There was no question about Trist's sexual character, although his sudden physical ailment echoed the chaplain's chronic illness. However, Gage denied Trist's request. With rebellion imminent, the British army could not spare any officer, even one of questionable strength and allegiance.[20]

Although eight companies of the Eighteenth Regiment were stationed in Philadelphia, parts of two others were still scattered across the west. Captain Hugh Lord commanded troops in Illinois, and in the summer of 1774, he reported that the barracks at Kaskaskia had "suffered exceedingly by the violence of the season" such that he worried about the health of his men. Another handful of Royal Irish soldiers quartered in Pittsburgh, where they were commanded by Corporal James Tucker. Tucker's troops also lacked adequate clothes and housing, and the corporal reported that agents for Virginia governor Lord Dunmore had stolen his river boats. Both Lord and Tucker pleaded for help, but none came.[21]

Instead, Gage focused on the brewing conflict in the east. In July 1774, he contemplated removing part of the Eighteenth to Massachusetts to help suppress the extralegal congresses breaking out in that colony. Haldimand concurred, opining that "le 18" was of no use "a Philadelphie." Before he could remove the regiment, however, delegates for the Continental Congress began to descend upon the city, and Haldimand thought better of it.[22]

❖ ❖ ❖

In the summer of 1774, the American Revolution was at hand. Although it would take another two years for the colonists to declare independence, the gathering of the First Continental Congress was an important step. Revolutionary ideas had been circulating in the colonies for more than a decade, creating a language for Americans to criticize Britain's treatment of them. In particular, the colonists argued that they were entitled to liberty, freedom, and rights. This discourse of revolution implicitly included homosexuality.

The American Revolution was the result of both long-term cultural trends and short-term political conflict. On one hand, America had always stood apart from the mother country. The oldest colonies—Virginia and Massachusetts—had never looked like England: the first was filled with feudalesque tobacco plantations and the second with regicidal religious radicals. When the colonies matured, they grew less dependent on Britain. As America gained an international economy, mass consumer culture, racial diversity, religious pluralism, and broad participatory politics, the basis for a modern nation emerged. By 1776, many believed that there was no good reason why the colonies should be tethered to England.[23]

On the other hand, independence occurred because of specific events. Triumph in the Seven Years' War nearly bankrupted Britain, and Parliament calculated that the colonists should bear some of the burden of their defense. The result was the Stamp Act, which taxed nearly every scrap of paper in America: newspapers, court documents, and even playing cards. Britain also sought tighter control over the colonies, passing the Sugar Act to regulate Atlantic trade, while the king stationed fifteen regiments of regular soldiers in North America to secure recent gains.[24]

The Americans balked at the new taxes and strictures. The Stamp Act prompted a continental congress, boycotts, and riots. Although the colonists hated the financial burden, they also believed that their rights had been violated; taxation without representation was unconstitutional. Britain's subsequent attempts to corral the colonies resulted in further assertions of rights such as religious liberty, an independent judiciary, and freedom of the press. When the Americans finally broke from Britain in 1776, their Declaration of Independence was not just a list of grievances, but a statement of universal principles.[25]

Sexuality followed a similar trajectory. On the one hand, ideas about sex deviated sharply in the first years of colonization. The colonists were remarkably fruitful, populating a land that they erroneously believed to be empty. In Plymouth, the first three generations of women bore 7.8 to 9.6 children on average, about twice as many as their English sisters. Ministers praised motherhood, and the age at first marriage averaged two years younger in New England than old England. The reliance on enslaved labor in the southern colonies likewise prioritized fecundity. Because of this "reproductive matrix," sexual behavior set the colonies apart from the mother country long before independence.[26]

Like Britons, Americans recognized that some men were queer. In her 1755 diary, New Jersey socialite Esther Edwards Burr recorded the day that she learned that her cousin Billy Vance was engaged. "Did you ever here the like?" Burr wrote. "Pray what can he do with a Wife?—he is more of a Woman than of a Man." Curiously, cousin Billy only appears one other time in Burr's diary, when he insisted that Esther dress her brother "in womens Cloths" in order to rehearse a play. Burr consented but insisted that it be "done quite privately."[27]

America also deviated from Britain on views of homosexuality. Although the colonies adopted the English legal prohibitions on sodomy, only a handful of colonists were ever put to death for buggering each other. Conditions of colonial life partly explain this reluctance. The patriarchal structure of society and high demand for labor meant that American courts tended not to ask too many questions. The colonists preferred to "correct" young men who had wandered astray with whippings, and they looked the other way when older, more established men engaged in male-male relations.[28]

As a result, Americans were more tolerant of same-sex intimacy than Britons. The lack of eligible women seems to have prompted an acceptance of male partnerships. In the Chesapeake, former indentured servants took up housekeeping together, and one even left a deathbed missive to his "Loving Mate." The diversity of cultures also encouraged nonconformity. In Pennsylvania, the Quaker founders minimized the number of capital offenses, preferring to mete out life imprisonment or floggings for buggery. The death penalty was added only in 1718, when Britain required that the province comply with English law.[29]

Non-whites also offered alternatives to procreative sexuality. Various Indigenous groups included "two-spirit people" who were born male but assumed a third gender. Labeled *berdache* by the French, they adopted feminine attire and undertook sacred responsibilities such as the transmission of tribal traditions. Similarly, Africans who were enslaved and brought to America came from cultures with same-sex practices. Homosexuality persisted on the plantation, and occasionally, two people of the same sex ran away together. Such deviant acts were viewed harshly by the colonizers, but they were nevertheless part of the broader colonial landscape.[30]

American views toward male-male sexuality were also shaped by the impending break with Britain. By the middle of the eighteenth century, English accounts of "Sodomitical Clubs" and literary depictions of effeminate men had found their way into American newspapers. Some colonists even emulated the harsh treatment of buggerers. In 1751, the *Boston Evening Post* printed a cartoon of one man sodomizing another, which was intended as a political satire on the homoeroticism of Freemasonry. However, once Parliamentary taxes and colonial protests came to the fore, Americans diverged from their British brethren once again. In the 1770s, sex scandals dominated English political life with the high-profile cases of Isaac Bickerstaff, Robert Jones, and Samuel Foote, but nothing of comparable import appeared in the colonies.[31]

For Americans, the real scandal was not sodomites but tyrants. In the summer and fall of 1774, references to the biblical story of Sodom and Gomorrah appeared several times in the colonial press, yet in every instance, the story was used to condemn Britons rather than buggerers. A letter printed in at least three colonies lamented how the "present parliament have begun the destruction of Great-Britain." England had been corrupted by luxury and immorality, the author contended, such that "the sins of the nation are like those of Sodom, and religion despised.—*Awful times!*" An article published in the *Hartford Courant* compared the Boston Port Act to God's destruction of the cities on the plain. Whereas the Lord had heard the cry of Sodom and judged its inhabitants, the British government was deaf to the pleas of Americans and ignored their calls for justice. It was unconscionable, the Connecticut writer insisted, that God had listened to "the Sodomites, naturally inclined to Lust, Revenge, in a word, every Vice," but Americans were "unheard in their own Defence." Although the author insisted that the colonists were "remarkable" for "the practice of every moral Virtue and Christian Grace," metaphorically at least, he equated Americans and Sodomites.[32]

The coming break with Britain created an ambivalence on the part of Americans toward buggerers. The Stamp Act and other parliamentary laws did not suddenly inspire toleration of homosexuality; rather they diverted attention away from harsh diatribes against sodomy and an interest in sex scandals that gripped Britain at the same moment.

These divergent views matched the division between captains and the subalterns on the matter of Robert Newburgh. The captains' opinions of the chaplain were consistent with the prevailing British understandings of same-sex desire. Chapman, Payne, and the other captains believed Newburgh's buggery to be a sign of corruption that inverted the social order and threatened to pull down the empire. Conversely, the subalterns were less concerned with what Newburgh had done, focusing instead on the tyranny of the captains. Like the colonists, Fowler, Trist, and Collins did not accept sodomy, but they could ignore it.

Perhaps colonial ambivalence inspired liberality. The Revolution coincided with the decline of large families. Starting around 1760, all groups of Americans women, regardless of race or region, began having fewer children. This demographic shift was revolutionary: the moment when American women demanded to be free of constant childbirth. A new ethos was emerging, one that offered more opportunities for nonprocreative sexuality. Maybe this included space for same-sex affection as well.[33]

As protests grew into war, the idea of personal rights gained traction throughout the land. In declaring independence, Thomas Jefferson set forth the revolutionary proposition that "all men are created equal" and declared that everyone had "inalienable" rights. Nor was this sentiment confined to white men in wigs. Following the Stamp Act protests, Black Charles-tonians marched the streets shouting "Liberty!" while, in Mas-sachusetts, enslaved men petitioned Governor Gage for their emancipation because they had "a natural right to be free." Abigail Adams urged her husband to "Remember the Ladies" while drafting the Declaration of Independence, and in 1780, Judith Sargent Murray composed one of the first feminist treatises in the Anglo Atlantic. These demands produced results; the northern states moved to abolish slavery, albeit gradually, and at least one state granted women the right to vote.[34]

Newburgh's trials suggest that the American Revolution may have had a similar effect on the people who would come to be known as homosexuals. The same language of revolution, equality, and rights was available to buggerers and those inclined to reconsider the outright condemnation of such men. Although there was no campaign for gay rights during the creation of the United States, in many ways, Robert Newburgh came the closest of anyone to making the case. He possessed rights, and he demanded the liberty to exercise them, in spite of the widely held view that he had had sex with a man.

❖ ❖ ❖

Throughout the summer of 1774, Robert Newburgh remained confined to the Philadelphia barracks. This, however, did not prevent him from demanding redress. He wrote first to General Haldimand, complaining about his arrest. He deplored being relieved of his duty as "A Minister of Gods Word," adding that having to pay for a substitute would be "A Reproach stamp'd on my Character which must be fatal to me." Yet not all of his appeal to Haldimand was couched in the language of humble pathos; he also asserted that he was entitled to fair and equal treatment. He explained that he had been "deprived like a Culprit of my Liberty and Freedom." Only a general court-martial would afford him "a proper Means to vindicate my Character from the shocking Aspersions."[35]

Although a court-martial had not been Newburgh's first choice, it was his best chance of putting to rest the assault on his character. A military trial assembled with the blessing of the commander in chief would *have* to accept his testimonials and silence the rumors; it would establish as a matter of fact that he had not had sex with another man. At the same time, a court-martial posed great risks. If the court ruled against him, he would be formally declared a buggerer. He could even be cashiered and deprived of his commission, which would force him out of the army and end his career. A general court-martial could not sentence a chaplain to the type of corporal punishment that Private Gaffney received, but it could do violence to his character.

When no immediate response came from Haldimand, Newburgh wrote to General Gage. Again, he demanded a court-martial to clear his name. This time, he amplified his rhetoric:

> I am confined like A Culprit, deprived of my Rights as A British Subject, Excluded from the Discharge of my Duty as A Clergyman, tho honord with A Commission from the best of Kings, glorious in the Support of his Subjects Priviledges.

This was the first time that Newburgh invoked the term *rights* in his correspondence. He also identified George III as the *protector* of his rights rather than the source of them. Yet he was no revolutionary. Despite sharing language with the Boston rebels, he leaned on the entitlements of his status. "I had the Honour to be recommended to the King by the Devonshire family," he informed Gage, such that "Were I at home Their Influence might assist me." This was a cleverly worded inflation of the status of Sir Henry Cavendish, who had endorsed Newburgh's entrance into the army two years earlier. Cavendish was only an Irish MP, but he was also a distant relative of the former prime minister, the Duke of Devonshire.[36]

Major Hamilton also weighed in on Newburgh's situation. In early June, he wrote to Gage summarizing the events that had recently rocked the Royal Irish, including Gaffney's court-martial. "But, Sir, our Uneasiness does not arise from the Private Men only"; rather, the regiment was now saddled with a man "whose Character reached us before himself." Citing stories from Batt and others, he recounted how Newburgh had "officiated in many Parts of Ireland, and wherever he went he was Stigmatized as a Buggerer." Hamilton suspected that Newburgh "look'd upon the Service as not only a sure but a proper retreat" from his low reputation, and he detailed the chaplain's actions since joining the regiment. Newburgh exhibited "Spleen and Mortification" when the captains shunned him, and he befriended "the greatest Villains in the Regiment," entering into cabals with Fowler and Trist "to undermine Subordination." He even manipulated "a most worthless Soldier" to accuse him of buggery in order to force a court-martial.

Hamilton drew a straight line from Newburgh's reputation as a buggerer to his disregard for military order. By itself, sodomy was a charge unworthy of the British army. "I should not have taken any Notice of the Unnatural Crime," Hamilton insisted, except that he worried that the "Honour and Virtue" of the Eighteenth Regiment might suffer "If the Accused is not punished." He saw buggery not as a crime to be prosecuted, but as a window into Newburgh's soul. Because "His Character in other respects is exceedingly Disgraceful," the major supported a court-martial to try the chaplain for his crimes. Hamilton could overlook Newburgh's sexual activities but not the disorder he brought to the regiment.[37]

Three weeks after his arrest, Newburgh remained imprisoned in the Philadelphia barracks. Again, he wrote to Gage, requesting "a speedy Court Martial" because "my Health is greatly impaird by my Close Confinement." But Gage was preoccupied by events in Massachusetts, devoting his attention to

quartering troops in Boston and establishing a colonial government more loyal to the king. Eventually, however, he conceded
that Hamilton was correct; a trial was the only remedy. But
Gage did not possess the proper paperwork to order a general
court-martial. He had delegated such things to Haldimand, so
he had to request "the Forms of the Warrants for the President
and Judge Advocate" in New York. This delayed matters for another three weeks, such that the general did not order a court-
martial until July 13.[38]

Gage continued to prioritize the events in Massachusetts
over Newburgh's case throughout the summer of 1774. It was
only the day before the court-martial began that he revealed
his opinions in a letter to Haldimand.

> The Court Martial I fear will be troublesome and long, and
> perhaps a great deal of Dirt and bad Language given which
> will raise Suspicion without Proof. There was no avoid-
> ing it, for all Sides demanded a Tryal with much Warmth.
> That Regiment will never be good for any thing till they
> get a good Commander, and your drawing them from Phil-
> adelphia will be of no hurt to them.

Like Hamilton, Gage had no interest in trying a man for
buggery.[39]

Sodomy trials in the North American Establishment were
rare on the eve of the Revolution. During Gage's twelve-year
tenure as commander in chief, Newburgh's case was the only
time that the British army in North America court-martialed
an accused buggerer. Gage viewed sodomy as a sin not to be
named, believing that talking about it would do as much dam-
age as the act itself. That it had led to a trial was a testament
to the divisions in the regiment and weak leadership. He was
already planning on drawing the Royal Irish closer to Boston,
in part so that they could be placed under a more competent
commander.[40]

With that, Gage turned to more pressing matters. In the same letter in which he discussed Newburgh's case, he wrote of diplomacy with Native Americans, the movement of soldiers to New York, and intelligence from a British agent spying on colonists in Massachusetts. Gage believed that subverting rebellion was far more important than buggery, and on this point, most British officers would have agreed. But the captains and subalterns of the Eighteenth had lost the ability to differentiate homosexuality from revolution.

The delay in paperwork meant that Robert Newburgh continued to languish in the barracks. Gage's request did not reach New York until July 20, and it took three more weeks for the trial to begin. Meanwhile, the chaplain remained confined. In another letter to Gage, he claimed that he had been prevented from meeting with his lawyer and was not given "an Oppertunity of attending on divine Worship." He missed Trist's wedding, Hamilton's day in court, and the building colonial movement against British rule.[41]

As he waited, Newburgh caught wind of a recent development in the barracks infirmary. Two months earlier, he had assisted Private Gaffney at his court-martial. Although Newburgh had composed questions, located witnesses, and drafted the closing argument, his efforts had been unsuccessful, and Gaffney sentenced to a thousand lashes. The private returned to Philadelphia and faced his punishment, although he only received six hundred lashes because it was feared that any more would kill him. In a sorry state, Gaffney was admitted to the barracks' infirmary.

Consistent with his position as chaplain, Newburgh attempted to provide spiritual guidance to Gaffney. According to Sergeant John Brogden who ran the infirmary, he went to see Gaffney shortly after his flogging, but the private refused to see him. In response, Newburgh offered "to get a Clergyman for Gaffaney" and he solicited help from the Anglican priests in town. But neither the Reverend Jacob Duché of Christ Church nor the Reverend William Stringer of St. Paul's were available.[42]

At the end of July, Newburgh returned, and this time Gaffney agreed to see him. Newburgh had a letter "from a Friend at New York" that testified that Major Hamilton's poor character "was well founded, throughout the Continent," but Gaffney was indifferent. According to Sergeant Brogden, the chaplain then told the private that "he had one Question to ask him." When Gaffney had refused his visit two months earlier, had he said that "he would not have Mr. Newburgh nor no such fellow, as he was"? The use of the term *fellow* in this context appears to be a euphemism for buggerer. Gaffney denied that he had ever denigrated the chaplain in this way. To this, "Mr. Newburgh answered, No, Gaffaney, I do not Imagine you would make use of Such a word, as I have been Such a friend to you."[43]

But the private was in league with the captains by this point. Angered by Newburgh's interference in Gaffney's court-martial, Chapman and Batt concocted a plan to use the private against the chaplain. In the trial that followed, Nicholas Gaffney would be the army's star witness against Robert Newburgh.

As August approached, Newburgh spent his solitude preparing for trial. He monitored the selection of the thirteen officers who would sit in judgment of him. When he heard a rumor that officers from the Eighteenth might be included, he complained. In response, Haldimand chose a "nombre d'Officier" from New York because "le Chapalain Objecte." Newburgh also made sure he had all his papers in order. On August 2, he wrote to Major Hamilton, demanding to know on "what Instance" he thought him guilty of perjury and prevarication so he could "Summon such Evidence as may be requisite." Hamilton ignored this request.[44]

Newburgh also filed countercharges against Hamilton, Chapman, Payne, and Mawby. Most of these repeated accusations from previous trials, but he added some new charges as well. He blamed Hamilton for treating him poorly during his incarceration, Chapman for ungentlemanlike behavior, and Payne for accusing him "of an unnatural Crime, before the private Men of the Regiment." Over time, his relations with the captains grew even more bitter, and he charged Payne with "Offering Violence to my Person, and kicking my Servant." Although there is no evidence that Payne struck Newburgh, Private William Osborne later testified that Payne exploded when he brought him a letter from Newburgh. Payne threw Osborne out of his room, "kicked him; and when he had got down the first step he kicked at him again." Payne then told Osborne that if he should ever bring him another letter from the chaplain that "he would break every bone in his hide."[45]

Newburgh's accusations grew more strident as his trial approached. The day before his court-martial, he sent Gage a list of additional charges that he hoped "may be taken Cognizance of, as soon as my Trial is over." Gage, however, declined to act on any of these complaints. "From what I have seen," Gage wrote to Haldimand, "I have no doubt that the Court-Martial will have trouble enough."[46]

❖ ❖ ❖

In the first week of August 1774, Reverend Newburgh, the captains, subalterns, and more than a dozen enlisted men headed to New York City for the trial. Much like moving the courts-martial to Perth Amboy, the journey to New York was intended to ensure a fair hearing; it placed the case in the hands of officers who knew little of the divisions in the Eighteenth Regiment. It also allowed Haldimand and the deputy judge advocate to closely monitor the case. Given the magnitude of the trial, little was left to chance.

New York City during the Revolution

Source: Franz Xaver Habermann, *Debarquement des troupes Engloises a Nouvelle Yorck*
Die anländung der Englischen trouppen zu Neu Yorck (Augsburg, 1778?).
Library of Congress, Prints and Photographs Division, 2004670214.

The move to New York did improve Robert Newburgh's living conditions. During the trial, he was allowed to live in "the House of one Bowden," probably the Reverend John Bowden, who had been named assistant minister at Trinity Church on Wall Street one month earlier. Like Newburgh, John Bowden was an Irish clergyman who had come to America to make his fortune. He was a bachelor at the time, and this made the two men good company for one another.[47]

New York had a smaller population than Philadelphia, but it was rougher and more divided. Religious and racial rifts were sharper, with battles between Anglicans and Presbyterians, and occasional executions of African Americans when a slave conspiracy was uncovered. The British army also had a permanent presence in New York that it lacked in Philadelphia. For more than twenty years, New York had been the center of the North American Establishment, with a constant presence of at least a regiment of regulars who quartered in barracks on the most public of places in the city: the Battery and the common.[48]

Newburgh's court-martial took place in New York's Upper Barracks, the place where other cases involving military justice were adjudicated, and corporal punishments were meted out. The Upper Barracks was a massive structure, standing two stories tall, measuring 420 feet in length, and capable of housing at least eight hundred soldiers. It stood on the Fields, the city's common, located at the northern terminus of Broadway. The Upper Barracks was also the site of violent confrontations between colonists and soldiers as the American protests grew into revolution.[49]

New York had been rocked by more contentious protests than Philadelphia. In November 1765, at the height of the Stamp Act riots, a crowd of over a thousand rushed Fort George, threatening the governor and troops inside. Five years later, soldiers and civilians faced off in the streets of New York in what became known as the Battle of Golden Hill. New Yorkers responded more aggressively to the Coercive Acts than the Philadelphians did. By the time Newburgh's trial began, the colonists had elected five representatives for the upcoming congress.[50]

In early August 1774, John Adams passed through New York City. The Boston lawyer and future founding father was headed to Philadelphia as a Massachusetts delegate to the First Continental Congress. Adams had grown restless under Gage's governorship, especially once he was dismissed from the provincial council for being insufficiently loyal. On August 20, 1774, Adams recorded touring New York and strolling past "Two setts of Barracks." Although Adams did not know it, Robert Newburgh's court-martial was going on inside the structures. Had civilians been allowed into the court, perhaps Adams would have been impressed to hear a presumed buggerer speak of rights in a way that emulated his own declaration of liberties.[51]

Adams was about to embark on the creation of a new nation that protected individual rights. Would there be a place for homosexuals in the America that followed?

CHAPTER SEVEN

The Advocate of an Injured Man

ON MONDAY, AUGUST 8, 1774, the general court-martial of the Reverend Robert Newburgh finally began. After more than a year of vicious rumors and regimental infighting, a military tribunal would decide the chaplain's fate. By this point, the accusation of buggery had become entwined with other charges, such that it was no longer possible to separate sex from lying under oath and disobedience. Marking the start of "La Conseil de Guerre," General Frederick Haldimand observed that he did not expect the trial to finish in a week. Given the complexity of the case, this was an understatement; it lasted three.[1]

Presiding over the trial was the commanding officer of the Forty-Seventh Regiment, Lieutenant Colonel William Nesbitt. Nesbitt was familiar with the Eighteenth's legal disputes, having served as president of the regiment's courts-martial in Perth Amboy two months earlier. Joining Nesbitt on the court were ten majors, captains, and lieutenants from the Forty-Seventh, and one officer each from the Eighth Regiment and the Royal Artillery. Deputy judge advocate Captain Stephen Payne Adye was also on hand to advise on matters of military law.

The trial began with swearing in the members of the court and a reading of the charges. Newburgh stood accused of "Vicious and Immorral Behaviour," which broke down into six

A Court-Martial

Source: James Gillray, *A Court Martial, or a Scene at the Horse Guards* (London: Darchery, 1782). British Museum, Prints and Drawings, 01613852650.

separate charges: perjury, prevarication, falsehood, "Scandalous and Indecent acts," conduct "Derogatory from the Sacred Character, with which he is Invested," and having treated his commanding officer "in a Disrespectful manner."

Captain Benjamin Chapman assumed the role of prosecutor and argued the army's case. Chapman informed the court that Major Hamilton was unable to attend due to "his ill State of Health," so he had delegated the duty to him. No doubt, he was pleased to have the sick, old man out of his way. Chapman declared that prosecuting Newburgh "was one of the most ungrateful & Irksome Tasks he ever undertook," yet he did so for "good of the Service and the Honour and respect of an Honourable Corps."[2]

Robert Newburgh served as his own defense attorney. He was assisted by a "very eminent Advocate employ'd by him":

most likely, John Ross, the attorney who was handling his civil case against Thomas Batt. However, civilians were not allowed to participate in military trials, so Newburgh was effectively on his own. Several officers took turns transcribing the case as the handwriting on the transcript changes numerous times over the course of the trial.[3]

Chapman began by explaining that the Eighteenth Regiment had previously attempted to resolve the case on its own. However, a simple solution had been precluded when Newburgh was "Formally accused by a private Soldier of having Committed a Most unnatural Crime." Now a court-martial was required. Chapman hoped that the tribunal would finally resolve the case and "if possible get rid of a man, whom they had every reason to Suppose, had by his Subtle Machinations and Insinuating address been the Grand promoter of all their trouble." By Chapman's account, Newburgh was the source all the problems among the Royal Irish.[4]

Yet as soon as Chapman introduced the topic of an unnatural crime, he announced that he would not attempt to prove that the parson was a buggerer. "Robt. Jeff, the soldier who accused Mr. Newburgh of sodomy, before a General Court martial, had since deserted." Efforts had been made to locate Jeff, but to no avail. More important, Chapman insisted, sexual acts were immaterial to the army's case. There was "only circumstantial and Hearsay evidence" regarding buggery, so he would "draw a Veil over this matter" and move on to the other charges. The army would not prosecute Robert Newburgh for sodomy.[5]

The disappearance of Private Jeff is curious. Two months earlier, Newburgh had convinced Jeff to accuse him of buggery in order to trigger a court-martial. But this action had angered the captains. According to a fellow private, shortly after filing charges, Jeff was "debarred from working as a taylor, and his wife and family turned out of the barracks." It appears that Captain Benjamin Charnock Payne was responsible for this cruelty, and that he also beat the private. Jeff deserted the Eighteenth Regiment on July 8, and a month later, an advertisement appeared in the *Pennsylvania Packet* offering a reward for his capture.[6]

It is plausible that Payne and the other captains induced Jeff to desert. Not prosecuting Newburgh for buggery was clearly in the army's interest. As several trials had already made clear, it was impossible to prove what had or had not happened in Ireland. Without Jeff, Chapman could dispense with buggery and avoid the morass that had hindered Newburgh's other legal opponents. It was far easier to prove the chaplain's disobedience than whether he had had sex with a man.

Although Chapman dispensed with buggery, he nevertheless prosecuted Newburgh as a buggerer. It had never been about acts for the captain. Since seeing the chaplain gallop by dressed like a jockey, he had decided that Newburgh's character made him unfit for the British army. Like Thomas Batt, Benjamin Chapman worried that past actions were predictive of future desires, and he assumed that the officers on the court felt the same way. He could thus emulate Hamilton and Gage by insisting that sexual acts were beneath the dignity of the military tribunal while simultaneously using sexual innuendo to smear Robert Newburgh as a buggerer.

❖ ❖ ❖

As if to demonstrate that his case was motivated by more than prurient curiosity, Captain Chapman began by enumerating some of the drier instances of Reverend Newburgh's misbehavior. In the first three days of the trial, he presented evidence to prove that the chaplain was guilty of perjury, prevarication, and falsehood. They all pointed to Newburgh's poor character and his unfitness for military duty.

Chapman first called Captain John Mawby and questioned him about Newburgh's testimony at Mawby's court-martial the previous May. At that trial, Newburgh had claimed that Mawby had seen his testimonials and "had said that they were Satisfactory to him in Every respect." Now, Mawby denied that he ever made such a statement. Mawby also testified that Newburgh had complained that he had been assigned to "a room the most Inconvenient in the whole Barrack" and that he received an inadequate supply of firewood, but neither claim was true. It was not the strongest start. Although he called two enlisted men in support of Mawby's claims, what Chapman described as perjury was a matter of opinion.[7]

Yet it was not the quality of the room or the quantity of firewood that Chapman was interested in; rather, it was what Newburgh's words revealed about his disrespect for military hierarchy. Mawby attested that he was "almost Certain" that Newburgh had claimed "that he was Intitled to a Captains allowance." Chapman corroborated Mawby's account by offering his own testimony to the court. Any additional firewood, he insisted, *"was regarded as a piece of Indulgence from Capt. Mawby, not as his right."* This revelation set the stage for his prosecutorial strategy. Time and again, Chapman would insist that otherwise innocent comments and differences of opinion were actually windows into Newburgh's low character.[8]

The evidence for prevarication was also underwhelming. For this charge, Chapman returned to the tailors' regimental court-martial in April, when Newburgh had claimed he did not know Privates Beversley, Douglass, and Jeff. Chapman interrogated Lieutenant William Blackwood, who had served as scribe at the tailors' trial. Blackwood stated that he and the other members of the court-martial found Newburgh's denial alarming. Again, Chapman argued that lying under oath revealed a man's true character. According to Blackwood, although Newburgh was given multiple opportunities to clarify his statement, he "said that he looked upon it that no one had a right to enquire into his Conduct but his peers, meaning the

Clergy." In other words, Newburgh had set himself above his proper place in the British army.[9]

Several times in the first three days, the term *right* made an appearance. Each time, it was someone asking if the chaplain had claimed privileges. Newburgh had used the word himself several times, and the officers and enlisted men of the regiment took note. An assertion of rights was out of place in the British army, an institution based on sublimating personal desires for the good of the unit. It was too close to the protests and riots of the American colonists who threatened the unity of the British Empire.

On the third charge, falsehood, Chapman was on firmer ground. Turning to Newburgh's court of enquiry, he asserted that Newburgh had complained that the officers who judged him "Irregularly made Several addittions to thier proceedings without his knowledge or Consent." Here, obliquely, buggery made an appearance. At the April trial, Batt had submitted a transcript that detailed how Newburgh had slept with his servant. Subsequently, Newburgh had insisted that these prurient details had been placed into the record without his knowledge, thus depriving him of an opportunity to refute them. However, Lieutenant Blackwood testified that Newburgh had known about Patten's testimony, and Ensign John Peter DeLancey concurred.[10]

Robert Newburgh was anything but passive during the first three days. As Chapman presented evidence on perjury and prevarication, Newburgh repeatedly interrupted him, questioning witnesses and disputing evidence. On the charge of falsehood, he resorted to ad hominem attacks. Taking over interrogation of Ensign DeLancey, he asked:

> Q. (from Mr. Newburgh) Were there not very Indecent, Gross, and Horrid Expressions made use of before that Court, and suffered to be entered into the Minutes,

inconsistant with the respect that is due to a Clergyman
and a Gentleman, in the Course of Mr. Batts hearsay
evidence?

A. There was an expression made use of by Mr. Batt in the
Course of Examination, relative to Mr. Newburgh,
which he thought a very Indecent one, but he thought it
however Necessary to be Inserted in the proceedings, as
they were then examining into Mr. Newburghs Conduct.

It was one of the few times that Newburgh deployed the same
argument that the captains often made against him: he deserved respect for his rank, not his actions. He even lashed
out at Chapman, insisting that he had had a hand in keeping
Patten's testimony secret. But DeLancey denied it, adding,
"Capt. Chapman treated him with great Humanity." Such an
aggressive response suggests that Newburgh had deduced that
the prosecution was determined to argue subtly, but insistently,
that he was a buggerer.[11]

Of the charges that Chapman had presented thus far, this
instance of falsehood was by far the most persuasive. Fortunately for Newburgh, the captain moved on to a second occur-
rence. He turned to Newburgh's civil suit against Batt. Captain Payne testified that Newburgh had claimed the subalterns
"would thro' him off, and have nothing to Say to him more" if
he did not prosecute him. The purpose of this charge seems to
have been to highlight divisions in the regiment and to introduce the civil suit against Batt.[12]

Chapman then presented a third instance of falsehood:
that Newburgh had wrongfully claimed that Batt had offered
him money to drop the civil suit. Chapman questioned Private
John Robinson, a grenadier in the Forty-Seventh Regiment, on
this point.

Q. (from Capt. Chapman) Has he ever Conversed with
Mr. Newburgh?

A. Yes, he has.

Q. Did Mr. Newburgh ever tell him that Capt. Batt offered him a sum of money, if he would withdraw his prosecution or words to that effect?

A. He did.

Q. Does he recollect the Sum mentioned by Mr. Newburgh?

A. Three Hundred pounds, to the best of his knowledge and recollection.

Robinson further attested that Newburgh's claim was common knowledge among soldiers in Philadelphia. He had even asked Newburgh himself about it, and the chaplain confirmed the story. Two lieutenants from the Forty-Seventh corroborated Robinson's story.[13]

Chapman then questioned Thomas Batt. All he had to do to prove that Newburgh was lying was for Batt to deny that he had ever offered the chaplain any money to drop the civil suit.

Q. (from Capt. Chapman) Has he at any time made an offer to Mr. Newburgh of a Sum of money to Induce him to withdraw his prosecution?

A. He never thought of Such a thing.

Although Newburgh briefly questioned Batt, it was clear that Chapman had persuaded the court of at least one instance of falsehood.[14]

For three days, Chapman offered evidence that Newburgh was guilty of various counts of perjury, prevarication, and falsehood. It was an impressively disciplined effort by a man who had no legal training. Chapman had always been ambitious. Like Robert Newburgh, Benjamin Chapman was a Protestant Irishman who saw the British army as an opportunity for advancement. He understood the low esteem in which buggerers were held, and he was determined to evict one from the Royal Irish Regiment.

❖ ❖ ❖

On Wednesday, August 10, 1774, Captain Chapman moved on to the fourth charge: "Mr. Newburgh's behaviour had been not only Vicious and Immorral," but he "had committed other Scandalous and Indecent acts." Chapman then called Private Nicholas Gaffney, a man whom he described as "an unhappy Soldier, who had been tried for accusing his Captain, and had suffered in Consequence." Chapman intended to prove that Gaffney's false accusation was "Encouraged nearly to his own ruin by the artifices of Mr. Newburgh."

After three days, Chapman had come to the heart of the army's case: Newburgh's manipulation of Gaffney. Two months earlier, a general court-martial in Perth Amboy had found Gaffney guilty of disparaging Captain John Shee and sentenced him to a thousand lashes. But the captains believed that Gaffney's spirited defense, if not his entire case against Shee, had been driven by Newburgh. For challenging military hierarchy, Chapman argued that the chaplain should be drummed out of the corps.

Chapman began asking Gaffney about how he came to know Newburgh. The private replied that he first met the chaplain the previous spring in Philadelphia. He then took the court back to April 1774, shortly after Gaffney's disastrous regimental court-martial had concluded. Newburgh approached him one night when Gaffney was on sentry duty, and he said that had something to discuss. Newburgh preferred to talk in private, so he invited Gaffney to "Come to his room that evening or the next." Gaffney was reluctant to be alone with a suspected buggerer, but once he learned that Newburgh intended to "assist him all that lay in his power" including procuring a lawyer, he warmed to the chaplain.

Gaffney told the court that it was Newburgh who had convinced him to pursue a case against Hamilton and Shee. "He would have withdrawn the Charges, or Petitioned to have withdrawn them, had it not been" for Newburgh's advice. He claimed that he had always liked and respected Shee, but that since "Mr. Newburgh was a Gentleman and a man of Sence, he thought that he would not give him bad advice or Encourage him." Oddly, Gaffney's newly sanguine opinion of Shee caught no one's attention. At his court-martial, Gaffney had been Shee's greatest critic, but now he was an innocent victim led astray by a man of low character.[15]

Gaffney continued. He claimed that Newburgh's promise of legal help had turned out to be hollow. Newburgh's Philadelphia lawyer was unable to travel to Perth Amboy for the court-martial, so the chaplain found an alternative: the lawyer's brother, who was also a merchant. Although this put a man who had never practiced law in charge of Gaffney's defense, Newburgh insisted that the merchant "understood the law himself and that he would give him all the assistance he Could, and Mr. Newburgh would pay his demand." However, this second counsel was also unable to attend, so Newburgh took over the case himself. As the captains suspected, it was Newburgh who had recommended examining the subalterns and wrote questions for them.[16]

The lawyer-merchant brothers that Gaffney referred to were Joseph and Bowes Reed. Joseph was an accomplished attorney in Philadelphia with an extensive client list, while Bowes was a licensed attorney in New Jersey who had never practiced law. Newburgh's association with the Reed brothers is peculiar, as this is the only time that the two are mentioned in the record. John Ross may have been unable to travel to New Jersey, or perhaps there was an affinity among the men. Like Newburgh, the Reeds were Protestant Irishmen and well versed in Anglo Atlantic politics. In the summer of 1774, Joseph Reed provided intelligence to British officials on colonial attitudes.

However, in November, he joined the Philadelphia committee of correspondence, and when the Revolution began, both brothers fought for American independence.[17]

If Gaffney's reference to the Reeds was a coded attack on Newburgh's loyalty, Chapman ignored it. Instead, he redirected Gaffney with a more salacious line of questions. Specifically, he sought to lay out how the priest had convinced this unhappy soldier to prosecute his superiors. Chapman began by asking about the two men's interactions at the Philadelphia barracks.

> **Q.** (from Capt. Chapman) Did Mr. Newburgh tell him that he thought him very ungratefull, for not taking notice of him, when he used to go to and from the Necessary house, or to that effect?
>
> **A.** Yes, Mr. Newburgh told him that he had after Seen him going to and from the Necessary house, whilst he was Standing in the Gallery, and that he had waved his hat to him, which he (Mr. Newburgh) told him he meant as wishing him Success in his Prosecution, and that he (Gaffney) had never returned the Compliment, and he thought from Mr. Newburgh's discourse that he Imagined that Mr. Newburgh looked upon it that the Deponent was offended at him.

There was something untoward in Newburgh's actions. According to Gaffney, Newburgh monitored his movements, including the path to the outhouse. Captain Mawby had previously fretted over Newburgh's desire to be so close to a site notorious for homosexual trysts. The chaplain also signaled to Gaffney in a colorful way, but the private did not return the greeting.[18]

This was just the beginning of the innuendos about the parson's intentions. Responding to questions from Chapman, Gaffney explained that Newburgh had plied him with gifts and alcohol. At Gaffney's general court-martial, Captain Shee had claimed that Newburgh gave Gaffney cash, but now the private dismissed the charge. "Mr. Newburgh never gave him any money," Gaffney clarified, but "said he had a Snuff box, which he had a particular esteem for, and which he would give him as a Small token of his friendship." A snuff box was an unusual gift for two men to exchange as it had a feminine connotation; indeed, the snuff box that Newburgh gave Gaffney had once belonged to the wife of Lieutenant Collins.[19]

The intimacy between Newburgh and Gaffney had a leveling quality. "Did Mr. Newburgh and he ever drink together?" Chapman asked. "Yes, frequently at Amboy," Gaffney replied. "He, as well as the other soldiers," had gathered in the chaplain's room, "and the bowl was handed round from one to another, and Compliments passed among them." The court found this revelation interesting and interrupted Chapman's interrogation. The officers wanted to know how often Gaffney had drunk with Newburgh and how much time they had spent together. Gaffney answered that "he himself was with him Seven or Eight times," for up to three hours at a time. The court then asked what words had passed between them.

Q. Did Mr. Newburgh ever make any Encomium on his (the Deponents) Sense and resolution?

A. Yes, he thought Mr. Newburgh flattered him very much, as he Commended him much for his Sense, Spirit and resolution, and wished to god that he was like him; that he would not have the Countenance to stand and plead his Cause, as he (the Deponent) did, that he told Mr. Newburgh, that it Could not be expected that he had much sence as he was not a Liberal bred man, and that he was onely the Son of a Mechanic, and He thought his Capacity but weak, to which Mr. Newburgh replied that he had a Natural Genius, which was better then education.

It was odd enough for an officer to invite an enlisted man to his quarters, and odder still for him to share alcohol with him. But it was Newburgh's words that were the real problem. He had dismissed the importance of rank and insinuated that every man was worthy of respect. Worse, he flattered the private and further persuaded him to continue his ill-fated case against Shee and Hamilton.[20]

From drinking parties, Chapman moved effortlessly to a discussion of sexual depravity. Had Newburgh ever talked about convincing Private Jeff to accuse him of a crime, he asked, and if so, what was the charge? Gaffney affirmed this, although "He Cant positively say what the Charge was, but he Imagines it was about buggery." Then Chapman asked what Newburgh had said about the court-martial of William McDermott, the ensign who had been tried for sexually abusing a little girl. Gaffney responded that "Mr. Newburgh then swore, by God, that if a Child played with his or any other mans private parts, till he was provoked, that he thought it no Crime for himself or any other man to act with them."[21]

Gaffney's testimony revealed that it was all a case of seduction. Newburgh had promised him legal help, but this was merely a pretext to get closer to the private. He invited Gaffney into his private chambers, where he plied him with gifts, alcohol, and flattery. Then he started talking about illicit sexual acts. To be sure, Chapman never asked Gaffney whether Newburgh had propositioned him, and Gaffney claimed that he had not returned all of his entreaties. But Chapmen was not particularly interested in distinguishing an erotic seduction from a nonsexual one.

❖ ❖ ❖

The fear of seduction was powerful in the eighteenth-century Anglo Atlantic. To be seduced was to be led astray: to be persuaded, often by a person with nefarious intentions, to abandon an allegiance or to do something wrong. Seduction

could lead a man to renounce his nation or a woman to surrender her virginity. As the Revolution approached, anxieties
about betrayal and sexual impropriety intersected in ways that
involved homosexuality.

Seduction was seen as a destabilizing force, and so efforts
were made to punish those who persuaded vulnerable individuals to make poor choices. In medieval England, labor laws
forbad a master from persuading a worker to abandon his or
her employer. Similar laws crossed the Atlantic and prevented
masters from stealing each other's servants and slaves. At
times, seduction took on a political dimension. Following a tobacco cutting riot in 1682, the governor of Virginia issued a
general amnesty to the rioters because they had been "seduced
from their allegiance, by the specious (though false) pretences"
of the riot's leaders.[22]

Seduction was a long-standing concern for the British army.
Commanders feared that soldiers were easily persuadable and
that, especially in a hostile environment, Britain's enemies
would convince enlisted men to desert. This was especially true
in North America as complaints over taxation and standing
armies intensified. "Desertion is very frequent in all the regiments," General Gage reported in 1766. He collected stories
of a South Carolina planter who promised soldiers better wages
to come work for him, and how a private in Boston "was Seduced" by a man "who gave him half a Guinea to desert." With
the Boston Port Act, colonists increased their efforts to depop-
ulate the British army. In the summer of 1774, while Gage
began executing deserters, he asked the Massachusetts attorney general to file suit against Bostonians for "seducing" privates away from the army.[23]

Seduction also had a sexual connotation, especially for
women. The unmarried were warned to be leery of dashing
young men, lest they surrender their virtue. By the eighteenth
century, the idea of female seduction was so powerful that it

served as the basis for the great British novels of the era: Samuel Richardson's *Pamela* and *Clarissa*. These circulated widely and spawned American imitations like *Charlotte Temple* by Susanna Rowson and *The Coquette* by Hannah Foster. Seduction novels nearly always ended in the death of their titular characters, which was presented as a just punishment for women who did not guard their virtue.[24]

In the 1760s and 1770s, the dual connotations of seduction became conflated. With the passage of laws like the Stamp Act, Americans feared that a cabal of dark-hearted ministers had poisoned the good king against colonial rights. Conversely, Britons believed that a few Yankee troublemakers had enticed an overwhelmingly loyal majority. When Gage subjected Boston to military rule, critics like John Adams likened Americans to Clarissa, seduced to give up their rights. Adams also feared that British soldiers were persuading young women to betray their virtue and country; indeed, the villain in *Charlotte Temple* is a dashing British lieutenant.[25]

Gaffney's testimony reveals that there was a homosexual dimension to the seduction narrative in Revolutionary America. Through his questioning, Captain Chapman painted a picture that followed the tropes of seduction tales. Nicholas Gaffney was innocent, simple, and trusting, while Robert Newburgh was elite, educated, and manipulative. Everyone at court knew the stories about Newburgh's sexual relationship with his servant, and Chapman played on this fact to suggest that the chaplain had similar designs on Gaffney.[26]

Like other seductions of the era, Newburgh's attempts had political implications. His temptation of Gaffney was similar to the colonists' efforts to persuade British soldiers to desert. Newburgh was not merely weakening the regiment but sought to destabilize the British army at a moment of imperial crisis. Such lusts were not merely repulsive, but mutinous.

There was a flaw in Chapman's argument, however. As any eighteenth-century novel reader knew, a young woman who gave up her virtue had only herself to blame. For this reason, potential victims were instructed to be vigilant. British soldiers also understood this. During the trial, Thomas Batt approached a private and warned him that Newburgh had "Craft enough to Seduce men and bring them to his own ends" through flattery and gifts. Unlike Gaffney, however, this private found the idea that the chaplain could tempt him laughable, as "he did not believe Mr. Newburgh had rhetorick enough to make him tell anything Contrary to his Conscience" and that "with regard to Bribing him that an Imperial Crown would not do it." Gaffney should have known better.[27]

The most troubling part of Chapman's argument was that it raised an uncomfortable question that neither he nor Gaffney were prepared to answer. If Newburgh had propositioned him for sex, did Gaffney give in? Throughout the Anglo Atlantic, soldiers were known to prostitute themselves for money, primarily to officers and wealthy men. If Gaffney had engaged in buggery with Newburgh, then the private would be as guilty as the chaplain. For this reason, Gaffney repeatedly expressed discomfort with Newburgh's advances, and Chapman maintained that buggery was not part of the army's case.[28]

❖ ❖ ❖

Robert Newburgh waited until the second day of Private Gaffney's testimony before he asked a question. He was timid at first, which was completely out of character. He was stunned by the viciousness of Gaffney's claims, as his questions lacked the vigor of early interrogations: "Did he ever urge him on to the prosecution against Major Hamilton and Capt. Shee?" "Yes, he thought he did, very much," Gaffney replied. He tried to counter this point by insisting that he had advised the private "not to prosecute Major Hamilton." But Gaffney contested this claim and testified that Newburgh encouraged him to lay "Charges against Major Hamilton as he was a quiet man, and no more than an old woman." Gaffney easily brushed off Newburgh's first questions and accused him of misgendering the commanding officer in the process.[29]

With that, Newburgh was quiet for a while. The court probed Gaffney about what role the chaplain had played in arranging Gaffney's charges. When had he decided to file charges against Hamilton and Shee? During the court of enquiry, Gaffney replied, tying his case back to the initial inquiry into the chaplain's buggery.

Finally, Newburgh pushed back. He questioned Gaffney's timeline of events, and then asked an obvious question: Why had the private decided to testify against him?

> **Q.** Has he not been Induced by expecting a remission of the remainder of his punishment, to become an Evidence against Mr. Newburgh?
>
> **A.** He never had any proposals of this sort, but he was Conscious of his having done wrong, and wished to Expose villainy, and as a proof of his never having recd. any Encouragement, produced a Letter to the Court, which he had received in answer to a petition he had sent to Capt. Batt.

Gaffney was only doing his duty to "Expose villainy." But he was lying.[30]

It is difficult to know the depth of the relationship between Robert Newburgh and Nicholas Gaffney. They were both Irish Protestants and about the same age, but otherwise they had little in common. Neither had taken much notice of the other before Gaffney's court-martial, yet during their time in Perth Amboy, they had socialized frequently. Newburgh may have seen this as a sign that the men of the regiment no longer perceived him to be a buggerer. He remained faithful to Gaffney throughout the summer, even visiting him twice in the Philadelphia infirmary. But by this point, Gaffney had become a pawn of the captains in their crusade to expel Newburgh from the army.

The details of why Gaffney turned against Newburgh were revealed in letters subsequently presented at court. While Gaffney lay in the infirmary in July 1774, he reached out to Thomas Batt, seeking his help. Having received six hundred lashes, he spoke with the language of a man about to die. "I Examin my Self a thousand times, and cannot form any other Judgment," Gaffney wrote, "that I, had So often offended the almighty that he left me at last to my Self, and the Devil got power over me and Spirited me up to my Destruction." His only hope was for God's mercy, and toward that end, he asked Batt to help him make amends with Hamilton and Shee.[31]

Batt was moved by Gaffney's letter. The two had gone to the same school and had "lived Long together in the Same Town" in Ireland. Batt's uncle had even recruited Gaffney for the Eighteenth Regiment. He promptly replied to Gaffney's letter and contacted Captain Shee. Shee was sympathetic to Gaffney's plight because he believed that the private "never would have gone such lengths" had not "Mr. Newburgh supported you, and offer'd you money." Batt then told Gaffney that "the most probable method to obtain forgiveness" was to testify "that you were seduced into your behaviour to Captn. Shee, by some artfull, wicked person, or Persons, who only made A tool of you, to execute their own wicked Purposes."[32]

Gaffney dutifully complied with Batt's request. He wrote an account of his interactions with Newburgh including his legal advice, gifts, flattery, loose language, and low opinion of the officers, all of which Chapman used at Newburgh's court-martial. Although Shee, Hamilton, and Batt informed Gaffney that his testimony would not absolve him of his crime, it also appears that Gaffney hoped to gain something from his time as a witness. He asked Batt to help him seek a pardon from General Gage, as "I, am not Capable of doing" it alone. In effect, it was Thomas Batt who had seduced Gaffney, not Robert Newburgh.[33]

Like many young men who enlisted in the British army, Nicholas Gaffney discovered that a soldier's life was tedious and unrewarding. As he watched men from his childhood be promoted ahead of him, he grew jealous and bitter. Yet while many in his situation either made the best of it or deserted, he lashed out at his superiors: first, Shee, and then, Newburgh. It is unclear what Gaffney thought about homosexuality, but he did not believe buggery to be a greater crime than corruption. Indeed, Gaffney probably would have said nothing at all had Batt and the captains not sought his testimony. It is unclear what became of Gaffney after the trial. He disappears from the record after 1774, although he never gained a pardon from Gage for testifying against Newburgh.[34]

❖ ❖ ❖

On Friday, August 12, the general court-martial entered its fifth day, and Private Gaffney returned for further examination. The members of the court took over the questioning and began to explore the details of his meetings with Reverend Newburgh. Where had they met? At Newburgh's house, Gaffney replied, referring to the room that Newburgh had rented in Perth Amboy. "Can he describe the room?" the court inquired. When Gaffney replied that it was "a very Large room, on the left hand, as you go in at the Street door," the officers clarified that what they really wanted to know: "Is it a bed-room?" Gaffney denied that it was, although the question indicates that the court was gauging the intimacy between Newburgh and Gaffney, curious if there had been a sexual relationship between the two men.

Through his questioning of Gaffney, Newburgh attempted to clarify that nothing untoward had happened in his room, either sexually or otherwise. But Gaffney was uncooperative. Although other enlisted men had joined them, Gaffney testified that he had been "alone with Mr. Newburgh at his lodgings." This only whetted the court's appetite for further details about the two men's familiarities.

Q. Was he ever more than once in a day at Mr. Newburgh's lodgings?

A. To the best of his knowledge he has been there in the day time, & has gone there at Ten oClock at Night of the Same day, when Mr. Newburgh has been in bed.

Q. Had he ever any Conversation with Mr. Newburgh twice in one day?

A. Yes.

Q. Did Mr. Newburgh Send for him at that late hour of the night?

A. He Sometimes went to Mr. Newburgh's lodgings after the adjournmt of the Court but Could not Stay, as he had to prepare for the business of the next day, and Mr. Newburgh bid him return again in the evening, but he Sometimes had not finished his business before that Late hour.

Gaffney painted a lurid picture that combined sexual disorder with a disregard for military hierarchy. It was inappropriate for an officer to invite an enlisted man to his room late at night, regardless of whether Newburgh had sexual designs on Gaffney or merely wanted to help him make slanderous charges against his superiors.

Uncomfortable with the tenor of Gaffney's charge, Robert Newburgh attempted to establish that he had not been responsible for this unconventional meeting. "Was he admitted into Mr. Newburgh's bed room?" he asked. "Yes," Gaffney replied, adding that "The people of the house who were up bid him go up Stairs." Gaffney added that he had done so and found him asleep. The chaplain had quickly roused and "upon seeing him, put on his morning Gown, and he went into the Closet to him." Not only had the two men been alone together in a bedroom late at night, but Newburgh had been in a state of undress.

Such answers clearly agitated Newburgh as his next questions flashed with anger. "Did he think himself Sufficiently authorized by an acquaintance of four days to take such a Liberty with a person in so Superiour a Station to himself?" he demanded to know. "Yes," Gaffney replied coolly, explaining that "from Mr. Newburgh's Swearing in his Company and talking upon any foolish Subject that was Introduced, he did not Imagine that he looked upon himself as in a Superior Station." In response, Newburgh demanded to know when he had spoken on "idle and trifling Subjects," to which Gaffney replied that the chaplain "Swore that the almighty wrote a Legible hand in the Faces" of two enlisted men, "meaning that they were rogues." Gaffney apparently viewed such a comment as a sort of blasphemy, which discredited Newburgh's position as a spiritual leader in his eyes. Gaffney further testified that during their various meetings, "Mr. Newburgh told him that he would write Some Questions for him, as a Clergyman's hand might be of Service to him." As such legal advice had not prevented Gaffney from being flogged, it is clear that he meant this sarcastically.

The longer that Gaffney testified, the more acerbic his words became. Having already implied that Newburgh had nefarious designs on him, he was now candidly disrespectful of the chaplain and spoke about him with a nasty tone that he never used to refer to Hamilton or Shee. But this only compounded the case against Newburgh. Because he was perceived to be a buggerer, he did not merit the respect of a convicted private.

Newburgh was deeply wounded by the private's charge that he was unfit to be a chaplain. This seemed to bother him more than the insinuations of buggery, so he sought to prove that he had acted as a clergyman should. When Gaffney had been hospitalized after his whipping, he had offered him comfort. "Did not Mr. Newburgh frequently and Constantly Send him his dinner from his own Table and extend his Charity in many Instances towards him?" he asked. Gaffney dismissed this claim, insisting that any kindness had come from Newburgh's servant alone. If he had not provided food, then had he not provided spiritual comfort? When Gaffney had refused to see him, he found an alternative. "Did not Mr. Newburgh Send Mr. Duché, a Clergyman of the first eminence, to attend him and pray by him?" Again, the private rejected this assertion, claiming that he had sent for the assistant rector at Christ Church. In Gaffney's eyes, Newburgh was no man of God.[35]

❖ ❖ ❖

Given the bile which Nicholas Gaffney directed against him, it is a wonder that Robert Newburgh had assisted him in the first place. Unlike Batt, he had not grown up with him, and unlike Green, he had not employed his services as a tailor. Chapman understood that the two men had little in common and used this to further paint Newburgh as a buggerer and co-conspirator. Yet the distress that Newburgh exhibited when Gaffney attacked his vocation indicates that it was Christian compassion that had drawn him to the private.

Chaplains occupied an unusual place in the British army, and they were often at odds with field officers. Amid a regiment of men who pursued death without emotion, chaplains offered compassion and preached forgiveness. They were the army's conscience and could challenge authority in a manner that no soldier or officer would dare. When British soldiers in Canada stole livestock from civilians, an army chaplain led the charge against the troops and helped arrest ten men. Chaplains could

The Macaroni Parson

Source: The Macaroni Parson (1772). British Museum, Prints and Drawings, 01613852651.

also condemn harsh sentences meted out against soldiers such as excessive whippings. In both instances, the chaplains' actions were censured by their commanding officers.[36]

We do not know much about Newburgh's faith. He left no sermons, and the individuals who testified at his trials had little to say about his religious dogma or practice. The one salient aspect of his ministry that can be discerned is his commitment to charity. Concern for the less fortunate was a central tenet of the Church of Ireland, and the Enlightenment intensified the call to care for all of God's children regardless of rank. Reverend Newburgh's pastoral compassion surfaced most clearly in his efforts to aid Private Gaffney.[37]

Subsequent testimony revealed how exactly this transpired. Following Gaffney's first court-martial the previous spring, several individuals in Philadelphia approached Newburgh and asked him to help the private. In May 1774, as a contingent of the Royal Irish prepared to travel to Perth Amboy for Gaffney's second trial, the appeal for legal aid intensified. The details of what happened were discussed in Newburgh's interrogation of Ensign Nicholas Trist.

> Q. Does he know how Mr. Newburgh came to Interfere in the affair of Gaffaney?
> A. Yes, by the Intreaty of Several Gentleman and Ladies, who frequently desired Mr. Newburgh to give him all the assistance that Lay in his power, not only as being a Christian, & a Gentleman, but they thought it his duty to Interfere, and they had frequently heard it reported that the man was in Danger of his life, at the same time offering to pay Such expenses as Mr. Newburgh should be at, in feeing of Council and such other things, which money then was to be Raised by a Voluntary Subscription; that he frequently heard Mr. Newburgh receive this advice; but as he did not think it his business to interfere, he never gave Mr. Newburgh his advice, whether to take it or not.

The court found this evidence revealing and asked Trist which civilians had involved themselves in Gaffney's case. In response, the ensign named "a Mr. Laugher, Mr. Levy, Mr. & Mrs. Murray and Several others whom he does not recollect."

Of these, the most adamant was Mrs. Murray, who "declared she could and would in one Day or two raise upwards of one hundred pounds for the assistance of that man."[38]

The individuals that Trist named were involved in the western trade such as William Murray and Levi Andrew Levy. Murray, his wife, and two children spent time with the Eighteenth Regiment in Illinois, and apparently, they returned to Philadelphia with the soldiers and remained close afterward. The Murrays and others knew that Gaffney would face a thousand lashes if he were found guilty, and they no doubt found this unusually cruel, as civilian punishments rarely exceeded thirty-nine stripes.[39]

It is noteworthy that the principal advocate for Gaffney was a woman. Although we know little about Mrs. Murray—including her first name—she clearly possessed significant cultural and financial capital. As a woman in the 1770s, she would have understood her role as providing sympathy to a man in need of charity. While her compassion was understandable to the army officers, her power over Newburgh would not have been. The idea that a man could be manipulated by another man's wife further contributed to the perception that the parson was a buggerer.

Ensign Trist was adamant that "Mr. Newburgh motives of assisting Gaffaney arose from the Desire of those Gentleman and Ladies and from charity." He therefore saw nothing untoward in the chaplain's relationship with the private. His deportment was "consistent with the character of a Clergey and a Gentlemen" and he never "observed any improper famailarity between Mr. Newburgh and the Private Soldiers." Although Trist counseled Newburgh that helping Gaffney was a mistake, the chaplain's actions were entirely appropriate.[40]

Ultimately, this was how Newburgh explained his curiously intimate relationship with Gaffney to the court. In testimony elsewhere in the trial, he insisted that Gaffney had called "upon him as the advocate of an Injured man as he thought it his duty as a Clergyman, to assist him." Although no one could substantiate Gaffney's exact words, a private in the regiment reported that "he has heard Mr. Newburgh Say that he looked upon it as his duty to assist him, and was not ashamed to acknowledge it."[41]

While Newburgh's vocation was his best defense, it also confirmed the insinuation that he had unchristian desires. Religious leaders across time have defied cultural norms of gender and sexuality, from celibate Catholic priests to the spiritual gifts of two-spirit people. Within the Christian tradition, the association of homosexuality and the ministry dates back to at least the Middle Ages, and Protestant propagandists exploited this reputation as part of the Reformation in the sixteenth century. Indeed, Protestant clergymen were encouraged to marry in order to prevent sins of the flesh.[42]

Clergymen were commonly accused of buggery in the eighteenth-century Anglo Atlantic. In England, the Reverend Dr. Robert Thistlethwayte was widely suspected of sexual relations with Oxford students. Although a 1739 investigation into the minister's actions proved inconclusive, the negative publicity forced Thistlethwayte to resign his ecclesiastical and collegiate offices and flee to France. The case implicated Thistlethwayte's clerical companions including the Reverend John Swinton, who also faced charges of sodomy.[43]

These associations were particularly pronounced among chaplains. In the masculine ethos of the British army, there was something queer about an officer who consoled wounded soldiers and nurtured the regiment's morals. This idea surfaced in pamphlets of the day. *Mars Stript of Armour* lampoons chaplains' immorality and their flamboyant clothing: "By the various Colours of his Cloathes, you'd sooner imagine him a Son

of Joseph than of Levi." An Irish pamphlet went further, indict-
ing a chaplain "who idled away all his time in playing *Scotch-
hop* and *Shuttle-cock*, with school boys."[44]

Robert Newburgh certainly knew the reputation of clergymen and chaplains. Perhaps this was why he entered the ministry in the first place. The churches of England and Ireland
included a disproportionate number of celibate priests long
after restrictions on marriage had been lifted, and homosexual
men have continued to serve in the Anglican ministry despite
official prohibition. Or perhaps Newburgh saw the chaplaincy
as either unrelated to his lusts or as a means of suppressing
his desires. In many ways, he was not unlike present-day gay
clergy who struggle with the same issues.[45]

Yet Newburgh did not allow such perceptions to interfere
with his duty as chaplain to the Eighteenth Regiment. When
called upon by concerned civilians—including a powerful
woman—he did what he could to assist a pathetic private. He
attempted to hire a lawyer, and when he could not find one, he
helped as best he could. His efforts had been in vain, but he had
not profited from the experience. Perhaps Newburgh harbored
sexual desires for Gaffney or thought he could manipulate an
ignorant man to continue his fight against the captains.
Whatever the motive, it was his position as chaplain that first
brought him to Private Gaffney.

❖ ❖ ❖

By the end of the first week of the general court-martial,
Captain Chapman had made an effective case against Reverend
Newburgh. He had offered several examples of his illegal actions before military courts and elsewhere. Although he had
promised that he would not prosecute Newburgh for sodomy,
he nevertheless attacked his character in a way that relied
heavily on the chaplain's reputation as a buggerer.

Entwined in this seduction was a disrespect for military
hierarchy: Newburgh had not acted as an officer should among

privates. It was fitting for a chaplain to show compassion but not if this emboldened soldiers to challenge their superiors. The way that Gaffney answered Newburgh's questions suggests that he had still not learned his place, and the court took note of this. Robert Newburgh may not have buggered Nicholas Gaffney, but he had nevertheless encouraged a British soldier to rebel against His Majesty's army at a moment when revolution was imminent.

CHAPTER EIGHT

What Is Now Termed a Maccaroni

ON FRIDAY, AUGUST 12, 1774, the general court-martial of Robert Newburgh entered its fifth day. Late summer in New York is sultry and hot, and while the officers and enlisted men sweltered in the Upper Barracks, the case against the chaplain of the Eighteenth Regiment of Foot continued. Captain Benjamin Chapman was artfully painting a picture of a man who had broken the law and undermined military hierarchy, both of which he linked to Newburgh's character as a buggerer.[1]

As Chapman interrogated witnesses, it became clear that he was not the only person who understood that Newburgh was not like other men. Upon being asked how the chaplain and he had initially communicated, Private Nicholas Gaffney responded that a matross in the Royal Artillery named James Ross had transported letters between them. Then Gaffney added a new detail to the story: "he received the message by Ross from Mr. Newburgh and he Stiled Mr. Newburgh *She*; in order that if any body overheard him, it might be thought that the message Came from a woman."[2]

Much like stories of Newburgh's clothes and deportment, this instance of misgendering revealed that there was something unmanly about him. A man's gender performance was a window into his character, so being referred to as *she* confirmed earlier suspicions of the priest's sexual acts and desires. Although Chapman did not inquire into Gaffney's comment, he later returned to this blurring of sex and gender to argue that Newburgh should be expelled from the British army.

There was also something sinister in the application of the feminine pronoun. According to Gaffney, Ross "Stiled Mr. Newburgh *She*" in an act of subterfuge as the chaplain plotted to manipulate a private in his campaign against the captains. An honest man had no need for artifice, but Newburgh blurred gender lines in his attempt to invert military hierarchy. As Chapman concluded his case, he laid blame for the impending revolution squarely on the fact that Newburgh was a buggerer.

❖ ❖ ❖

After questioning Private Gaffney for three days, Captain Chapman moved on to other witnesses. Gaffney's testimony was compelling, and it provided sufficient evidence to convict Newburgh of scandalous and indecent acts. But Gaffney's stories were inconsistent, and the court remained skeptical that a private who had received six hundred lashes for lying about his captain could be entirely truthful about the chaplain. As a result, Chapman called nine enlisted men to testify in support of Gaffney's account, but not all the soldiers were as compliant as Gaffney.

On August 12, Chapman examined Private William West of the Forty-Seventh Regiment. West had befriended Nicholas Gaffney when "he went on furlough to Philadelphia" and the two had been close ever since. He had accompanied Gaffney to Newburgh's house several times, where he drank alcohol and overheard the discussion of lurid topics. West witnessed Newburgh speaking about Ensign McDermott's trial in a way that suggested "he might have some desire to act with the Child, or have his lust kindled." While drinking and engaging in inappropriate conversation, "Gaffney then took pen and Ink, and

Mr. Newburgh Dictated some Questions, by Gaffneys desire, and Gaffney wrote them down."[3]

West, however, did not believe that Gaffney had been seduced. Under questioning from Reverend Newburgh, the private testified that his friend did not "at any time tell him during his Stay at Amboy, that Mr. Newburgh urged him to pursue his designs in Charging Major Hamilton." In West's opinion, the chaplain had acted selflessly. He had agreed to help Gaffney because they were both Freemasons, and "He had reason to think that he meant to give him a Charitable assistance." West had not observed Newburgh do "any thing unbecoming a Gentleman of his rank" or utter any indecent expressions, "except what he has mentioned formerly with respect to Mr. McDermott." Conversely, West thought that his fellow private was very ungrateful. Gaffney had spoken "very Indifferently of Mr. Newburgh" and had plotted to attack his character before his own court-martial ended. While Newburgh worked on the private's defense, Gaffney pulled West aside, "Smiled, and said Let us go and Charge the Parson."[4]

West's testimony revealed that Gaffney was not the innocent victim Chapman portrayed him to be. The eight enlisted men who followed offered similar versions of events. Sergeant William Williams had also drunk a bowl of toddy with Newburgh and Gaffney, and he had seen the chaplain help the private with his questions. But he had "no other reason" to suspect that Newburgh was at fault other "than Gaffaneys telling him, when he was very ill, that it was owing to bad advisers." The soldiers found Newburgh's deep concern for Gaffney unusual, even bothersome. Former Sergeant Thomas Bowden overheard an enlisted man say *"he was tired of going of Messages backwards and forwards"* between the two. But no one believed that Newburgh had persuaded Gaffney to prosecute his superiors. Corporal William Musgrave testified that Gaffney only regretted being "encouraged by Mr. Newburgh" after he was flogged.[5]

The enlisted men also failed to connect Newburgh's purported lust for Gaffney to his desire to upend military order. Following West's testimony, Chapman asked the other witnesses whether Newburgh had offered lurid and immoral interpretations of McDermott's court-martial. To a man, they declined to answer. Private John Nichols twice evaded the topic.

> **Q.** Does he recollect William West telling him, that
> Mr. Newburgh made use of Nearly these words; that if a
> man permitted a Child to play with his private parts
> untill his Lust was raised, he saw no harm in acting with
> it, or words to that effect?
> **A.** He Cant remember that he did.
> **Q.** Did West seem to him to think that Mr. Newburgh had
> expressed himself oddly on the affair?
> **A.** He might but he does not remember that he did.

The court asked a variation on the same question two more times, but in response to both, Nichols claimed not to know Newburgh's opinion about having sex with a child.[6]

Such reticence is not surprising. No soldier wanted to be accused of besmirching an officer and wind up like Gaffney. They also knew that the sexual desires of officers were not appropriate for polite company or the official record. Of course, this makes Gaffney's insinuations about Newburgh's seduction of him all the more unusual. It also suggests that the captains encouraged him to say things that privates rarely did. As the previous trials had revealed, soldiers knew the rumors about Robert Newburgh, and they disapproved of men who had sex with other men. However, it appears that the moral panic over the parson's buggery was a fixation of the captains alone.

❖ ❖ ❖

The court-martial broke for the Sabbath, and resumed on Monday, August 15. Captain Chapman then moved on to the fifth charge: ungentlemanlike behavior. He offered three examples of how the chaplain had failed to maintain the proper decorum for a man of his rank. Chapman's evidence for ungentlemanlike behavior was far weaker than what he presented for the other four charges. He relied heavily on sexual innuendo to allege that Robert Newburgh had inspired disobedience in the ranks. As a result, it was the most homophobic part of the army's case.

For the first instance of ungentlemanlike behavior, Chapman returned to the tailors' regimental court-martial. Although he had already offered the case as evidence that Newburgh had lied under oath, this time he used it to establish that the chaplain had induced enlisted men to "reveal the Private Conversation of their Officers at unguarded Hours." Instead of questioning a tailor, Chapman read the transcript from a previous trial. Specifically, he quoted Private John Green, who had previously testified:

> that on Sunday he Carried home a pair of Breeches to Mr. Newburgh, which he had made for him, and while he was trying them on, Mr. Newburgh among many other Questions asked him, if he had ever heard any of the Gentlemen talk of him, on which he (Green) replied he never had, except one or two words he had heard Capt. Payne Say of him in the Taylors Shop, on which he pressed him much to tell him what they were, and he would save him from any harm, on which he (the prisoner) told him, he heard Capt. Payne Say, the Parson was a Bougre.

This passage revealed no new information. It was well known that someone had called the parson a buggerer and that Newburgh had investigated who this was. The only reason for entering this passage into evidence was to paint a salacious scene: two men meeting in private with the presumed buggerer in a state of undress.[7]

Chapman's second example was also a case of sexual innuendo masquerading as disobedience. He charged Newburgh
with "Suppressing a Letter, which was Intrusted to him" and
called Thomas Batt to testify about it. This took the court back
to Ireland in 1773 when Batt had first accused Newburgh of
being a buggerer. Chapman claimed that General Sebright had
addressed Batt's accusations in his correspondence, but that
Newburgh had "Secreted the Letter in order to make himself
appear the more Innocent before the publick." In other words,
Chapman insinuated that the chaplain had tried to keep his
sexual acts in the closet. This was a weak charge. In cross-
examination, Newburgh asked Batt pointedly: "As it is a long
time since he asked Mr. Newburgh for this Letter; has he not
had time since to write to Sir John and receive an answer?"
Batt's answer was evasive, and the court was unpersuaded.[8]

The third example of ungentlemanlike behavior was the
most astonishing: Newburgh's clothing and deportment. Spe-
cifically, Chapman charged him with "Indecent behaviour and
Dress, such as was in his opinion unbecoming a Clergyman."
Chapman then related a story that he had previously told at
Captain Mawby's court-martial. He described how he had been
walking with Colonel Fanning in Bristol, Pennsylvania, the pre-
vious November when Newburgh galloped by looking "more
Like a fashionable Groom or Jockey than one of that Sacred
Function." Chapman then described Newburgh's appearance:

> that part of his Dress on that occassion, as nearly as he
> Can recollect was a Close Light Coloured Surtout, with a
> Scarlet or Crimson falling Collar, with a round Buck Hatt,
> perfectly in the Stile of a Groom; that at other times he has
> seen him in the Barracks and streets at Philadelphia in a
> Dress that had not the Least resemblance to that usualy
> worn by Clergyman, one Dress that he has seen him in, as

nearly as he Can recollect, is a Light Coloured frock made
of Bath coating, Close Buck or Lambskin Breeches, white
Silk Stockings and a Smart Fashionable Cocked Hatt, in
short what is now termed a Maccaroni Dishabille.

Newburgh's appearance had convinced Chapman that the parson was a buggerer, and now he offered the story into evidence
to prove that the chaplain was unfit for duty.[9]

Chapman provided a very detailed description. He claimed
that Newburgh wore a frock, or a long coat that buttoned down
to the waist with a skirt that flowed to the knees, topped off
with a large red collar. Atop his head, he bore a "Buck Hatt,"
meaning a buckskin or leather hat. When in Philadelphia, Newburgh also wore a frock, which Chapman emphasized was
"Light Coloured" to distinguish it from the more sober garb
of a priest. Underneath his coat, the chaplain sported leather
knickers and white silk stockings. In the city, he wore a tri-
corner hat with feathers or other accoutrements.[10]

Such attire stood at considerable distance from what most
eighteenth-century clergymen wore. At divine services, Anglican ministers typically donned a white surplice over a black
cassock, and they occasionally added preaching bands, tippets,
scarves, and hoods. Outside of worship, most clergymen wore
drab colors, and many Anglican clerics wore cassocks every day.
Although it was not unusual for a minister to own a separate
set of clothes for riding, Newburgh's flamboyant clothing was
certainly unusual for a clergyman in the 1770s.[11]

Chapman further observed that Newburgh's colorful dress
was not limited to his time on horseback. Rather, his "appearance and Deportment" were alarming on multiple "occasions"
such that Chapman imagined that the chaplain "Intended to
Disguise himself." Nor was Newburgh ashamed of his appearance. "During an Entertainment," he had sat in the front row
at a Philadelphia theater much to Chapman's "utter surprize."

A Macaroni

Source: M. Darly, *The Upper Clapton Macaroni* (London 1772).

Chapman also referenced a letter that Newburgh had introduced into evidence from Colonel Eyre Massey. "This style of
Behaviour as one of his Letter writers Humourously observes
might indeed become a Captain of Grenadiers," Chapman told
the court, connecting the colorful attire back to Ireland. Such
an appearance was inappropriate for "the Gravity and Dignity
of a Clergyman, whose character," he added with a telling gender slip, "Should be like that of Caesars Wife, not only free from
Vice but even from the appearance of it."[12]

Chapman then revealed how what he had observed in America matched the stories that Batt and others had told him about Newburgh's sexual activities in Ireland. He told the court that Newburgh had been warned to tone down his clothes and actions, especially since his "reputation was by no means free from blemish." Chapman recalled how he had presented the story of Newburgh on horseback at Mawby's court-martial the previous May. At that trial, he had pointed to the hat that Newburgh was then wearing as evidence of his unfitness for the priesthood. Chapman then detailed how Newburgh had responded:

> that when Impropriety of his wearing a very Fashionable Cockt Hatt was mentioned to him before a General Court martial, he replied in a very Determined Tone of Voice, that he would next day wear another *still* more fashionable, and that no Officer had a right to take Cognizance of his dress or appearance, as for those he was only answerable to his Superiors in the Church, in which Great mistake he was set right by the president of that Court.

Not only had Newburgh dressed in a way that confirmed he was a buggerer, but he had been openly disobedient to Colonel Nesbitt, the very same man who now presided over this court-martial.

Newburgh responded to Chapman's testimony by cross-examining him. He implicitly conceded that he had been flamboyantly dressed when he attended the theater in Philadelphia but asked why this had not come up earlier. He also defended his horse-riding attire, asking "Whether it has been usual in any Country he has been in for a Clergyman to ride in his Gown & Cassock?" He later claimed that he had borrowed the coat in question, but he did not offer any more details at this point in the trial. At length, Newburgh addressed Chapman's association of flamboyant clothing with sexual deviance. He reminded Chapman that at the court of enquiry in April, he had asked a witness if "he had observed any thing Immorral in his behaviour." In response, Chapman, who sat on the court, had declared that such a "Question was unnecessary, for had we heard of any Such thing, we should have put you under an Arrest." In Newburgh's account, his clothing and deportment were immaterial because no one could prove that he had had sex with a man.[13]

Outraged by Newburgh's response, Chapman called the one man who had a lower opinion of the chaplain than he did: Thomas Batt. Chapman asked if he had seen "Mr. Newburgh's appearing in a Dress unbecoming a Clergyman?" to which Batt replied that "He has hardly seen him in any other Coat than a Light Coloured one." Batt added that he knew of a Philadelphia merchant who was "astonished" to discover that Newburgh was a clergyman "as he should not have known him to be one by his Dress or appearance." Batt went on to claim that he had often seen him wearing the type of hat that jockeys donned at Curragh Racecourse, thus repeating Chapman's claim that he looked like a jockey. Asked if he had heard officers express "Surprize at Mr. Newburgh's manner and Style of Dress," Batt replied, "Frequently."[14]

Chapman attempted to add further instances of ungentlemanlike behavior. He claimed that Ensign Edmund Prideaux had seen Newburgh's "frequent indecency at divine Service." This seems to have been another reference to clothing, but Prideaux was not in court and thus was unavailable to substantiate the charge. Chapman also claimed that two women in Philadelphia had signed affidavits that "Newburgh & another person had behaved with uncommon rudeness." However, the affidavits had not arrived, so he dispensed with the point.[15]

Chapman also abandoned the sixth charge: Newburgh's "disrespectfull behaviour to his Commanding Officer." Major Hamilton had not traveled from Philadelphia, so Chapman could only provide the correspondence between the major and chaplain. These were hardly revelatory, so Chapman "concluded the Prosecution."[16]

❖ ❖ ❖

In describing Robert Newburgh's clothing and deportment, Chapman referred to him as "a Maccaroni Dishabille." This term appears only once in all the letters and transcripts of Newburgh's case, but it is the most revealing. *Dishabille* means partly or improperly dressed, and *macaroni* was a term of derision for a man deemed inappropriately masculine. In effect, Chapman used a gender critique to attack Newburgh as a buggerer.

Macaroni entered the English language in the middle of the eighteenth century as a type of food, but it soon became a label for people. A 1773 article explained that macaroni was an Italian word for "a compound Dish made of Vermicelli and other Pastes" that had become popular among "the younger and gayer Part of our Nobility and Gentry." Subsequently, "the Word Macaroni then changed its Meaning to that of a Person who exceeded the ordinary Bounds of Fashion." Macaroni was not a compliment but "a Term of Reproach to all Ranks of People, indifferently, who fall into this Absurdity."[17]

Macaronies could be easily identified by their clothes and deportment, which were ridiculously ostentatious. The archetypical macaroni was a young man who wore spotted or stripped clothes, jockey-style printed cotton waistcoats, ridiculous wigs, and a small tricornered hat; he often carried a small sword, watch fob, and snuff box. In many ways, he prefigured the dandy of the nineteenth century. Matthew and Mary Darly printed dozens of macaroni images in the 1770s that lampooned men of nearly every profession, including soldiers, politicians, and priests. When Chapman called Newburgh a macaroni, the chaplain demanded to know where he had learned what a clergyman on horseback should wear. "He has Seen a Caricature of Such a Figure," Chapman responded, indicating that he knew the macaroni prints by the Darlys or others.[18]

A macaroni's gender was always in doubt. In *The Macaroni: A Comedy*, first performed in York in 1773, playwright Robert Hitchcock parodied an effete young man who proclaims that he and his fellow macaronies "do amuse ourselves sometimes with the Ladies—imitate their manners—but carefully avoid all serious connection with them." The play's title character is named *Epicene*, a term that means a person with features of both sexes or neither sex. In the play, Epicene is humiliated and forced to declare, "I confess that a Macaroni is the most insignificant—insipid—useless—contemptible being—in the whole creation."[19]

A macaroni's effeminacy was a window into his character, which most authors agreed was despicable. In *The Macaroni Jester*, also published in 1773, John Cooke dehumanized "fribbling" hairdressers, boring orators, and London gadabouts as "Monkieronies." Such men wasted their time strolling in the park, attending the theater, and drinking to excess. Luxury enervated them, depriving them of their masculinity. For this reason, Cooke advised macaronies to "Recover the Station you've lost" by "dressing, and thinking, and acting like Men."[20]

Was the macaroni homosexual? Not necessarily. Although macaronies were typically depicted as having no sexual desire for women, few authors thought that this was because they preferred men. Nevertheless, the idea of a man who wanted to dress and act like a woman led some to connect gender and sexuality. One caricaturist labeled a macaroni "Ganymede"—Jupiter's mythical boy lover—and showed him facing the hangman for his crimes. In October 1772, Connecticut's *New London Gazette* reprinted an English article that Captain Robert Jones had been "condemned to die for Sodomy." "He was an Associate of those insignificant Creatures called MACARONIES, whom

A Macaroni Faces the Hangman

Source: M. Darly, *Ganymede & Jack-Catch* (London 1771). British Museum, Prints and Drawings, 01613073529.

all MEN dispise," naming Jones as buggerer and macaroni at once.[21]

The idea that gender reveals a man's sexual desire was not a new concept in the 1770s. Many cultures have asked whether a man who looks like and acts like a woman has womanly desires, and sexual acts are often part of this inquiry. In eighteenth-century London, mollies attracted attention as men who dressed like women and who also had sex like women. But gender has never been a strict binary. Georgian Britain entertained the notion that mollies were a third sex, and macaronies likewise seem to have been epicene if not nonbinary. Yet whereas today trans is distinct from gay, such notions were not strictly segregated two hundred years ago. Because the macaroni was genderqueer, many assumed that he was also a buggerer.[22]

While the term *homosexual* did not exist in the eighteenth century, the presence of macaronies suggests that there was a rudimentary sexual identity in place. The macaroni stood apart from the rest of society, marked by his distinct appearance and ambiguous gender. His flamboyant attire and affectations could be used to prove that he desired sex with other men. Certainly, this was how Benjamin Chapman viewed Robert Newburgh. Having heard rumors that the chaplain had buggered his servant, the captain looked for other evidence of his character and found it in his resemblance to the popular caricatures of the day. *Macaroni* was not synonymous with *buggerer*, but Chapman's use of the word indicates that he saw Newburgh as a man defined by his desire, appearance, and behavior—not unlike a homosexual.

Tales of macaronies circulated throughout the Anglo Atlantic on the eve of the Revolution, and for many people in Britain and America, the macaroni was an object of humor. In 1773, the *Virginia Gazette* reprinted a fictional dialogue between four macaronies extolling the virtues of "drinking Asses Milk." Listening to them, a boy wondered "whether they are Men or Women," to which a woman replied: "they're neither, they are a Kind of Half and Half Breed." Everyone seemed to be in on the joke. When a Member of Parliament described ancient Epicureans as "the Macaronies, of that Time," "A Laugh through the House" was recorded.[23]

However, some saw macaronies as evidence that society had been corrupted by luxury. They were too French, too Catholic, and foretold the downfall of the British Empire. A Philadel-phian unfavorably compared "the orators or heroes of ancient *Rome*, in all the dignity of manhood" who distinguished them-selves on the battlefield to "our modern *Macaronies*." Another American newspaper lamented how "the Breed of Britain is di-minished and dwindled into Pigmies and Macaronies" and con-demned England's unmanliness. "Virtue is always connected with Plainness and Simplicity. Effeminacy always with luxuri-ous Refinement."[24]

Although humorous and deleterious views of the macaro-nies appeared on both sides of the Atlantic, those who worried the most about the collapse of the British Empire tended to see them as a harbinger of doom. Elite men who had been seduced by foreign fashions became half-men and could no longer lead the empire, especially in war.[25] In the minds of men like Chap-man, Newburgh's appearance signaled an inner corruption that matched his flouting of military order through his defense of Private Gaffney. Men like Newburgh *were* the reason why a co-lonial rebellion was imminent.

Conversely, those who saw the impending revolution as a positive thing worried less about macaronies. The term is ab-sent from the writings of Benjamin Franklin and John Adams, while George Washington only mentioned it as the name of a ship and Thomas Jefferson used it to refer to a pasta dish. Where the term described people, it had a less threatening con-notation. For example, in the popular "Yankey Doodle Song," Americans celebrated a young man who "stuck a feather in his hat / And called in macaroni." The humor of the song comes from the irony of the situation: Yankee Doodle affixes the sim-plest decoration to his hat and yet claims that he is as fashion-able as a macaroni. To be sure, Adams and Franklin worried that foreignness and effeminacy threatened masculine virtue, but they blamed British officials for these vices rather than flamboyant men. Americans' lack of interest in macaronies mirrored their ambivalence toward buggery; instead of a homophobic tirade, they launched a rebellion.[26]

The politics of macaronies were hinted at in Chapman's story of Newburgh on horseback. The person who had first pointed out the chaplain's similarity to a jockey was Colonel Edmund Fanning. Fanning had been born in New York, attended Yale College, and earned his title as a militia colonel in North Carolina. He had attached himself to Governor William Tryon and moved north when Tryon was promoted from the governorship of North Carolina to that of New York. Chapman apparently saw Fanning as representative of colonial thought and concluded that other Americans would be equally horrified if they saw the Eighteenth Regiment's parson dressed like a macaroni. Newburgh was a disgrace to the British army, Chapman testified, "Situated as he was in a Country, where Strict propriety and Decorum are the distinguishing Characteristick of almost every Clergyman." The sight of a flamboyant buggerer would only give the colonists more reason to revolt.[27]

But it was not men like Robert Newburgh who pushed Americans to renounce the British king, but men like Edmund Fanning. When Fanning was in North Carolina, he earned the enmity of the people for extortion and corruption. Members of the Regulator movement rebelled against the colonial government and took out their anger on Fanning, whipping him and razing his house to the ground. Escaping to New York with Tryon, Fanning remained at odds with the colonists and raised a Loyalist corps after hostilities began. In effect, Chapman had it backwards; Americans cared less about macaronies and buggerers than they did about corrupt placemen.[28]

❖ ❖ ❖

As soon as Captain Chapman concluded the army's case, Reverend Newburgh began his defense. The challenge was immense. Chapman leveled six charges against the chaplain, and he moved methodically through each accusation, providing detailed evidence for five of them. Although Newburgh cross-examined Chapman's witnesses, much of the army's case remained solid. He had lied under oath, manipulated a soldier, and bore a questionable character.

It was up to Newburgh to refute Chapman's charges and to provide a counternarrative of the events that had led to his court-martial. He had no training in law yet managed to make an effective case nevertheless. He ignored the weaker parts of the army's case and focused on those charges that seemed the most damning, especially the allegation he had offered legal assistance to Private Gaffney out of malice toward the captains. Newburgh did not follow Chapman's methodical approach; rather than arguing one point at a time, he argued them all at once, often asking a single witness questions about multiple events and dates. For this reason, the defense was far more circular and repetitive than the prosecution.

Newburgh's greatest challenge was how to respond to Chapman's insinuation that he was a buggerer. He had to refute charges that he had dressed like a macaroni and had acted with inappropriate familiarity among the enlisted men. Yet as he had learned in previous trials, it was nearly impossible to prove that he was not a buggerer. He could not produce witnesses from Ireland where the alleged act had occurred, although even if he had, it would not have disproven the suspect intentions in his choice of rooms or his assistance of Gaffney. So Newburgh argued for the strength of his character. He presented several witnesses who spoke of his stellar reputation in order to prove that he had not committed immoral acts. Yet this approach was only partially successful. Many people already assumed that he was a buggerer, and Chapman's details about a macaroni appearance only solidified this perception.

On August 16, Newburgh called Private James Ross, a matross in the Royal Artillery. Ross had previously testified that he had relayed messages between Gaffney and Newburgh the previous spring. Returning to court, Ross testified that Gaffney had already "laid his Complaints against Major Hamilton & Capt. Shee" before the chaplain contacted the private. Newburgh also asked Ross about the secrecy surrounding his communications with Gaffney. In particular, he wanted to refute Gaffney's claim that Ross had misgendered him.

> **Q.** Did he call Mr. Newburgh She, by way of concealing who he was, when he spoke of him to Gaffeny?
>
> **A.** No he did not call Mr. Newburgh *She* upon that occation, but he did make use of *She*, relative to one Mr. Ewen a Granadier, for it was him that sent him to Gaffany, & he made use of *She*, in order that he might not be understood by the Corporal of the Guard, for fear of bringing him into a Scrape.
>
> **Q.** Was it about Mr. Newburgh at all that the word *She* was made use of?
>
> **A.** No it was not.

Ross thus denied that any soldier in Philadelphia had ever called Newburgh *she*, and this effectively settled the point. Curiously, Ross insisted that the man whom he had misgendered was a grenadier named Ewen. Ewen is a mysterious figure who does not appear again in the transcript, although his identification as a grenadier repeated a trope that Colonel Massey had observed earlier. Apparently, the red and blue jacket, leather straps, and miter-shaped cap of Britain's elite fighting men struck more than one infantryman as queer.[29]

Newburgh then questioned his two friends: Lieutenant Alexander Fowler and Ensign Nicholas Trist. Both subalterns were character witnesses. He had to be careful about examining them because Chapman had already accused them of conspiring against the captains; thus, too strong of a testimony from either man would only prove that his actions had aggravated divisions in the regiment. More important, Newburgh needed them to refute the long-standing rumor that he was a buggerer.

Appearing first, Fowler testified that he had "lived in the Same Gallary" with Newburgh and that "he has been very often in Company with him, daily almost." During that time, he had observed how the officers and soldiers in the Eighteenth Regiment "treated him with disrespect & contempt." He had advised Newburgh to return to Ireland to clear his name, and he added that the chaplain had been receptive to this suggestion because "he did not like America." However, Newburgh ultimately had decided to stay and fight for his reputation.[30]

Then Newburgh asked about his character. He did not inquire into charges of buggery directly, but Fowler's answer was coded in a language of morality and family honor.

Q. Wheather during their acquaintance he has ever observed him guilty of any immoral or indecent behaviour, unbecoming a Clergyman and a Gentleman?
A. He never did, he always found Mr. Newburgh's Company Polite, agreeable, & edyfying.
Q. Did he ever observe him to be fond of low Company?
A. He never did, quite the contrary.

Because Newburgh was a man of high morals and avoided men of questionable character, Fowler concluded that he was not a buggerer.[31]

Fowler offered his own character as proof of Newburgh's innocence, telling the court that if the chaplain were a buggerer, then he never would have been friends with him. He also cited Newburgh's litigiousness as proof of his unblemished character. Responding to questions from the court, Fowler insisted that he had never threatened to cut off relations with Newburgh if he did not sue Batt. Yet he had said that if the priest returned to "Ireland with out vindicating his Character, and he ever met him walking with his uncle Lord Mount florence there he would shun him as a mad dog." If he had let the accusations stand, then Fowler would have concluded that the charges were true, but since Newburgh was fighting the charges, he could not be a buggerer.[32]

Fowler's testimony also chipped away at the claims of seduction. Why had he assisted Gaffney, Newburgh asked; "Does he not believe that his motives for assisting Gaffany were intirely from Charity?" Fowler responded, "He thinks it could proceed from nothing else." But Chapman found this response unsatisfying, so he cross-examined Fowler about Newburgh's litigiousness and disobedience. Since the private's allegations against Hamilton and Shee were "malicious and ill founded," Chapman asked, did he not think that "it would have been more Charity, and more becoming a Divine" for Newburgh "to have advised him to drop a prosecution which was likely to prove his ruin?" Fowler did not have a good answer for this and opined that the chaplain "should not have troubled himself with Gaffany."[33]

In Fowler's version of events, he never thought that Newburgh was a buggerer. He did not understand everything about his friend, such as why he went to such lengths to help an unfortunate private, but he had been slow to judge him. Unlike the captains, who took Batt's stories at face value, Fowler let the chaplain plead his case and present testimonials from Ireland. These claims were subsequently verified by his upstanding behavior. Fowler concluded that Robert Newburgh was a man of good character, and thus took no notice of his appearance or deportment.

Ensign Trist took a somewhat different approach. Perhaps because he was of a lower rank, or perhaps because he was more honest, Trist revealed the difficulty of being friends with a reputed buggerer. Unlike Fowler, Trist had not stopped questioning Newburgh's character upon seeing testimonials of his

Baron Mountflorence

Source: British School (c.1760–65), John Cole, 1st Baron Mountflorence of
Florence Court (1709–67), National Trust, CMS_PCF_631071.

good behavior; rather, he monitored the chaplain's actions and
clothes for signs of transgression. Ultimately, he concluded that
Newburgh was innocent of the charges that the captains had
lodged against him.

In his August 17 testimony, Trist's initial answer to the
claim that the parson was a buggerer matched the responses
of most enlisted men: he had no opinion. Responding to Newburgh's questions about the meeting at Hamilton's quarters in
April, Trist affirmed that he had been satisfied with the testimonials Newburgh provided, although "he was Still of his for-

mer opinion" that it was a private dispute. He added that Captain Mawby and Major Hamilton had agreed with him, and he remained convinced that "the matter rested wholly between Mr. Batt and Mr. Newburgh, and that the regiment had not the Least to do with it."[34]

Yet Trist was also surprised that Newburgh did not present a manlier response to the accusations against him. Like Fowler, he had also advised Newburgh to confront Batt and told him to consider "how his friends would look, on his returning with Such a Load of Infamy on his Shoulders." He even internalized the rumors and wondered how he might respond if someone called *him* a buggerer. "If any man had dared to Load him with Such Infamy," Trist told the court, he would prosecute him "as far as the Laws of England would permit him, and after that was over, he would take him by the nose or Cane him."[35]

Trist was emphatic that Newburgh had never dressed like a macaroni. The officers on the court introduced the topic, asking whether Newburgh's dress was "unbecoming a Clergyman?" "Never that he saw," Trist replied, adding that "he has seen many a Clergyman Drest in the Same manner." He had observed Newburgh wear white silk stockings, "a Graish Bath coat, Bound with Black, and Black Buttons," and a "half Mourning coat, with Black buttons." But he had also seen "Hundreds" of clergymen wear such clothes, and he added that Newburgh's coats were "the like of which he has seen the Revd. Mr. White of Philadelphia weare." Newburgh then took over questioning Trist.

Q. As he has seen Mr. Newburgh almost every Day Did he ever See him in what might be called a fashionable Morning Maccaroni Dishabelle?

A. He cant say what they call a macerouney Disabill he never saw him Drest in any manner, but what he has seen other Clergyman.

Trist's response suggests that he was unfamiliar with macaronies, which is surprising given his education and worldliness. Yet a lack of knowledge did not hinder Trist's observations. He had monitored Newburgh's appearance and actions but found nothing inappropriate in what he saw.[36]

Trist's testimony also provides a counterpoint to Chapman's understanding of gender. According to Trist, Newburgh possessed a considerable wardrobe, and although it was all gray and black, it was far more elaborate than a simple cassock. Yet the clergyman's traditional garb was a thing of the past. Indeed, Trist had seen the Reverend William White dress as fashionably as Newburgh. White was the assistant minister at Christ Church and St. Peter's, and he represented a new direction for the Anglican priesthood and America. White was a Philadelphia native and only twenty-six years old. He had traveled to London for his ordination, and he returned wearing the latest fashions, including white silk stockings. Trist thus did not believe that such clothes were a cause for concern, so he dismissed Chapman's claims that effeminate attire revealed anything about Newburgh's character.[37]

Trist's testimony about White's appearance suggests that he had a familiarity with Americans that few other members of the Eighteenth Regiment shared. Following his marriage to Elizabeth House, he had begun to socialize with other Philadelphians, and this apparently included the minister at the city's largest Anglican church. To the captains, such knowledge of a colonist's attire was troublesome. Like his support of a reputed buggerer, Trist's acquaintance with White confirmed that he was a man of questionable loyalty.

✤ ✤ ✤

Following the testimonies from Fowler and Trist, Reverend Newburgh proceeded to question other officers and enlisted men. Specifically, he sought to use their testimony to discredit the claims that he had said that Batt offered him money to drop his civil suit and that he had claimed testimony was added to the court of enquiry without his knowledge. He also sought to put to rest the allegation that he had used alcohol and flattery to seduce Gaffney, or that he had any unclean intentions toward the private.

To respond to Gaffney's charges, Newburgh called Private William Osborne. Osborne had been Newburgh's servant during Gaffney's trial, so he had firsthand knowledge of the two men's interactions. Osborne also had a personal interest in depicting Newburgh's interactions with Gaffney as honorable. He knew that his former master had been accused of having sex with a servant back in Ireland, and as he occupied a similar position, he needed to convince everyone that he had never engaged in sexual relations with the chaplain.

Appearing before the court-martial on August 18, Osborne testified that he had been in Newburgh's room in Perth Amboy during Gaffney's visits but had never observed anything untoward pass between the two men.

Q. Could Gaffany Come into Mr. Newburgh's bed-room at 10 oClock at Night and after his being in bed without the deponents Knowledge?
A. No. he Could not.
Q. Was not the House shut up Immediately on Mr. Newburgh's going to Bed?
A. It was.

Osborne added that Gaffney had never been in Newburgh's room longer than an hour and that the latest he had seen the private with the chaplain was "About four or Five oClock in the evening." He even questioned Gaffney's knowledge of the house where Newburgh had lodged, stating that the chaplain "lay in the front room over the Parlour," not in the closet at the top of stairs as Gaffney had claimed.

Osborne had a high opinion of Newburgh, and so, like the subalterns, he served as a character witness. He testified that the chaplain was an upstanding officer who had never partaken toddy with privates, nor "Come home drunk or Intoxicated." Osborne also refuted claims that Newburgh was a macaroni. He was well acquainted with his master's personal effects, which prompted Newburgh to ask, "Is there among those Cloaths, any coat, either Body or Surtout, with a Crimson Collar?" "No," Osborne replied.[38]

It is difficult to know whether Osborne was telling the truth or whether he was covering for his master. His characterization of events was so different from what Gaffney and other enlisted men had stated that someone was clearly lying. It appears that the court was skeptical of Osborne's testimony and tended to believe Gaffney instead. Indeed, Osborne's favorable account of Newburgh raised other concerns among the officers on the court. Perhaps they worried that Newburgh was again introducing perjury into a legal proceeding, or they may have wondered why Osborne was so devoted to him.

Newburgh also took testimony from Captain John Shee. This was an odd choice since Shee was almost as sour on him as Chapman and Payne were. Yet he hoped to impeach Gaffney's testimony, so he asked the captain "to give a Character of Gaffaney." Shee responded that Gaffney had been "a Clean good Soldier, and a Soldier of Spirit, but Lately he has behaved a mutinous bad man." He also believed Gaffney to be "guilty of Perjury falshood & Ingratitude." In short, Shee confirmed that Gaffney could not be trusted.[39]

However, Shee also had a low opinion of Newburgh, and he was not shy about sharing this with the court. He had mostly stayed out of the controversies regarding Newburgh in the spring. He had rejected the priest's demands that the officers present certificates, sworn testimonials, and other actions to "Vindicate his Character," yet he also refused to join the other

captains in attacking Newburgh. Shee was older and more reserved than the other captains, and like Hamilton and Gage,
he preferred not to render an opinion on a sexual act that took
place long ago and far away. At the courts-martial in Perth Amboy and New York, he testified that what he had said "to
Mr. Newbourgh was that neaither Capt. Batt nor Capt. Payne,
nor any other Officers had accused him of Buggery."[40]

Shee explained that "He had no acquaintance with Mr. Newburgh" before Gaffney's trial, and his disapproval derived
solely from the legal aid the chaplain had provided to the private, as such acts were "highly unbecoming his Character, as
an Officer, a Gentleman and a Christian." Shee also was adamant that there had been no quid pro quo. He stated that when
he found out that the private expected a lighter sentence for
his testimony against Newburgh, he sent a corporal "to tell
Gaffaney that if promises had been made to him, that they were
made without the Smallest authority from the regt."[41]

Shee's testimony undermined several key parts of Newburgh's defense. Although he was called to demonstrate Gaffney's lack of integrity, he instead offered many examples of
Newburgh's low character. He had once stood apart from the
other captains in withholding his opinion of the chaplain, but
now Shee joined Batt, Chapman, Payne, and Mawby in declaring that Robert Newburgh no longer belonged in the army.

❖ ❖ ❖

Shortly after questioning Captain Shee, Robert Newburgh
"Closed the evidence" and brought his defense to an end. By
this point, the court-martial had been going for nearly two
weeks and after ten days of testimony, everyone was exhausted.
Newburgh asked the court for "Some time to Methodize his
defence," and the officers on the court gladly agreed. They
scheduled the tribunal to resume four days later.

On Monday, August 22, the court-martial reconvened at
9:00 a.m., but it sat for only a few minutes. Newburgh had a

letter delivered to the officers "Signifying his having been rendered Incapable thro' Sickness and other Causes, of Compleating his defence." He asked for another extension, which the court granted, delaying the case until Wednesday. This was not the first time that Newburgh had delayed the end of a trial. During his court of enquiry, he had postponed the conclusion by a week so that he could collect additional testimonials. This may have been his motive again, or perhaps he needed additional time to write his closing statement, which was quite lengthy. Yet by citing sickness, he reminded the court of popular connections between physical weakness and buggery, and that it was because of an illness in Sligo that he had been caught sleeping with his servant.[42]

Newburgh's defense was considerably shorter than Chapman's prosecution, consuming less than half the time. Some of the testimony that he presented was effective, but some witnesses undercut his case. Certainly, he deflected claims that he had perjured himself at Mawby's trial, changed his answers at the tailors' regimental court-martial, and engaged in ungentlemanlike conduct. However, he did not adequately put to rest charges that Batt had tried to bribe him, that he had lied about evidence being entered in the court of enquiry, and most important, that his legal assistance of Gaffney had not sown division in the regiment.

Throughout his case, Newburgh attempted to address the lingering allegations that he was a buggerer. Again, he was not methodical in this attempt but relied on character witnesses who claimed that he was too moral to engage in sodomy or that he did not possess the flamboyant clothes of a macaroni. Yet this was too timid an approach. By failing to make an adequate defense, Robert Newburgh stood before the court as a presumed buggerer. Nor was it a charge he would refute in his closing argument.

CHAPTER NINE

Nil Humanum a me alienum puto

ON WEDNESDAY, AUGUST 24, 1774, closing arguments began in the general court-martial of Robert Newburgh. Nearly a week had passed since the chaplain of the Eighteenth Regiment last examined witnesses, but his illness had delayed the conclusion of the trial. Following army protocol, Reverend Newburgh delivered his closing argument first, then Captain Chapman summed up the prosecution's case. The court also asked the deputy judge advocate to weigh in before it rendered a decision.[1]

The closing arguments could not have been more different: one was eloquent, the other was curt. Robert Newburgh practiced rhetoric before the court. He employed comparisons to illustrate his points, questioned the evidence, and appealed to the consciences of his judges. He also drew on the language of the Enlightenment, invoking reason and arguing that all people have equal rights. Conversely, Benjamin Chapman was plainspoken. He ridiculed his opponent's artful turns of phrase and insisted that truth was unadorned. He also respected the distinctions of rank, placing loyalty to king and country above individual rights.

Both men addressed the issue of whether the parson was a buggerer. Much as he had throughout the trial, Chapman reiterated that he was not prosecuting anyone for buggery, while simultaneously persecuting Newburgh as a buggerer. This clever feat was persuasive and prompted Newburgh to revise his strategy. While he was adamant that he was not guilty of any unnatural acts, he had to concede that the officers on the court thought he was. As this was an allegation he could not disprove, he embraced it. He asked why a man's preferences, demeanor, or clothes should affect his place in society, while reminding the court that it was the Christian's obligation to help those who were less fortunate. Robert Newburgh argued that all people deserved liberty and equality, even buggerers, and in so doing, made the case for homosexual rights more eloquently than anyone else in Revolutionary America.

❖ ❖ ❖

When Robert Newburgh attended Trinity College in the early 1760s, Ireland's preeminent institution of higher learning promoted rhetoric. Rhetoric is the art of persuasive speaking, and its practitioners use figures of speech and other techniques to convince listeners of an argument. "Mankind, however curious and lovers of truth, will seldom give admission to her," observed Trinity Professor of Oratory John Lawson. Instead, a speaker had to "employ all the charms and address of that to fix, conquer, and win over the distractions, prejudice and indolence of mankind." Although Lawson died the year that Newburgh entered Trinity, his lessons had an effect on the aspiring clergyman. When he delivered his closing argument, Newburgh used skilled rhetoric and elocution to argue for his innocence. Unlike his defense, Newburgh's close was well organized, thoughtful, and even inspiring.[2]

Newburgh began by laying seven documents before the court. He had presented many of these to the court of enquiry, and they served the same purpose here: to burnish his character. He also reviewed the six charges against him and refuted each one. It was clear that Newburgh sought to use his closing

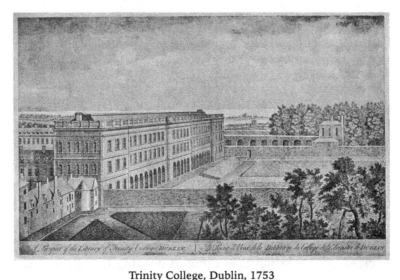

Trinity College, Dublin, 1753

Source: "Old Print of Library, 1753," in *The Book of Trinity College Dublin, 1591–1891* (Belfast: Ward and Co., 1892), 152.

argument to make two points. First, that the prosecution had provided insufficient testimonials and documents such that it was "impossible, without the Gift of Divination," to understand them. Second, that his rights had been violated. Since his arrest almost three months earlier, he had been "deprived of my Liberty" and was unable to properly prepare his defense.

From the outset, Newburgh addressed the question of whether he was guilty of buggery. He introduced Captain John Mawby's June affidavit, which had formally accused him of having sex with a man. This was the ideal moment to emphatically deny that he had committed a sexual crime, yet as was his wont, Newburgh once again avoided doing so. Instead, he made a legalistic argument that the evidence was inconclusive. "I am told I am charged with the Commission of a most unnatural Crime," he observed, "but am not told, when, where, or with whom." This was disingenuous, but it previewed his rhetorical skills.

Newburgh then proceeded to exploit the army's decision not to prosecute him for buggery. "Every Society is interested in the Suppression of Crimes," he continued, "and every Individual is bound by the obligations he is under to Society, rather to detect, and punish, than conceal, & favor Criminals." But the prosecution had chosen to ignore illegal sexual acts, so he shamed Chapman for not trying him for buggery. "I know not therefore, how the Gentleman can Justify permitting a man to go home in Peace, whom they had Reason to think guilty of a most unnatural Crime."

He went further. "An innocent man will never fly from his Accusers; I Never have, or ever will fly from mine." This was as close as Newburgh ever came to denying that he had engaged in same-sex relations, but again, his wording was cleverly vague. Rather than explaining why he was innocent, he attacked Chapman instead. The captain "certainly must have known whether he could have supported that Charge or not," he noted, adding that since the captain lacked evidence, "why did he draw it in such unfavourable Colours in the Proceedings of this Court?"[3]

While Newburgh brushed off the charge of buggery, he had a harder time disproving that he was a buggerer. He introduced Thomas Batt's letter from May 1773, which had started the entire affair. In response, Newburgh had obtained "Testimonials of my Character, and Reputation" from Irish clergy and other prominent men, and he read each one to the court. He had made this argument several times before, although it had never been persuasive. In spite of this, he insisted that because he was a man of good character, he could not be a buggerer.[4]

Newburgh descended to pathos at this point, lamenting the fact that once his reputation had been smeared, there was no way of salvaging it. "Too young to be hackneyd in the Ways of Men and bred and educated among Persons of too much Liberality of Sentiment and Generosity of Disposition," he had not anticipated that Batt's accusations would poison the Eighteenth Regiment against him. On his arrival in Philadelphia, he had been "received with coolness" by the captains, and this persisted for several months, culminating in the officers' meeting in Major Hamilton's room. In response to the testimonials he produced, "I found a general Silence prevail." Only the subalterns had stood up for him, and he contrasted the silence of the captains with the "manly and honest Declaration of Mr. Fowler" and Trist. Ultimately, he had no choice but to seek a court-martial. With that, Newburgh moved on to the charges against him.[5]

Chapman later remarked that this first part of Newburgh's closing argument continued "for the Space of 41 Minutes." Much of the evidence and arguments had appeared in previous trials, but the discussion of male-male intimacy had shifted over the past few months. In his civil trial, Newburgh had explained that he had slept with his servant for health reasons, but he did not repeat this point at his court-martial. But it was no longer sexual acts that concerned the army; it was his character.[6]

❖ ❖ ❖

Given that no one could prove that he had had sex with a man, Robert Newburgh's decision to ridicule the prosecution's lack of evidence on this point was a smart strategy. Yet he might have tried to argue an affirmative defense: that he had engaged in sodomy, but it did not matter. General Gage and Major Hamilton thought that Newburgh's sexual acts did not warrant his removal from the army, and perhaps the officers on the court felt the same way.

While homosexuality was roundly decried in the eighteenth-century Anglo Atlantic, a vocal minority disagreed. The lackluster enforcement of capital laws suggests that not everyone thought that a man deserved to die for sodomy; likewise, pamphlets and newspaper articles that condemned buggerers as unredeemable presented only one side of the argument. As philosophers like Denis Diderot began to speculate that certain acts and desires might be beyond an individual's control, they reflected the larger cultural belief that sodomites deserved sympathy. For some people, buggery was a personal failing that should be tolerated or at least ignored.[7]

During the reign of William III, "Hassan a Turk" submitted a petition to the king seeking a pardon. He had been "Condemn'd for Sodomy," and he laid out the case for why his life should be spared in spite his crime. Hassan explained that he had come to England without money and was thus unable to arrange a temporary marriage or "buy a Slave" for sex. However, he discovered "some Resemblance of the Recreations of the East practis'd by those Thy Infidells" and found "my satisfaction to my own Sex." Hassan pleaded with the king for mercy, insisting that sodomy was not a capital crime in his native land. Under "the Laws of the Successor of the Prophets," sex between men was not "imputed as Death."[8]

Hassan's petition is curious. Although it is unclear who Hassan was or what became of his request, the story continued to touch several English gentlemen for more than a century. Hassan's petition was translated by Sir William Hedges, an Anglo Irish merchant who served as governor of the East India Company in Bengal. Presumably, it was during his sojourn that Hedges learned Hassan's language, although he was living in London when he translated the document. The petition then found its way into the collection of Robert Harley, the earl of Oxford, who preserved a wide array of texts. Hedges and Oxford likely shared the British belief that Islamic lands were rife with sodomy, but neither man disparaged either Hassan or his petition. The appeal for tolerance may have been merely a curiosity to Oxford or maybe it resonated with a man who promoted religious toleration when he served in Parliament in the 1690s.[9]

Two years before Newburgh's court-martial, another king was asked to pardon a convicted sodomite. In July 1772, former British artilleryman Captain Robert Jones was tried in London for "that detestable and abominable vice, not to be named among Christians, called buggery." Jones stood accused of intercourse with a twelve-year-old boy, and after a short trial at the Old Bailey, was sentenced to hang. Although this was also pederasty, it solicited an array of opinions that paralleled the ongoing discourse of adult male-male relations.[10]

Captain Jones's case was widely covered in the Anglo Atlantic press, and it engendered the liveliest public debate on homosexuality until Oscar Wilde's trial a century later. Many writers saw the case as proof of England's rising immorality, and some mocked Jones with homophobic doggerel like the article which appeared in London and New London newspapers accused him of consorting with macaronies. But the captain also had his defenders. One writer claimed that Jones's valiant military service made such accusations unimaginable and cited his heroics in the 1762 siege of Havana as proof that he could not belong "to those vile miscreants who are a disgrace to human nature." Another wondered whether buggery should be tolerated: "A man may doubtless be addicted to this black crime, without being a ruffian, a murderer, and a cheat."[11]

Following Jones's conviction, a number of people called on George III to pardon him. One pamphleteer made the case that the only evidence against Jones was the testimony of the boy whom he had buggered. This violated English law, which required two witnesses to convict a man of sodomy. "I say, that no Crime is to be punished but upon full Proof," the author proclaimed. "The Crimes imputed to Capt. JONES" were no reason to abandon "the Law of a free Nation." If this conviction stood, then Britain could no longer condemn the Spaniards for "superstitious Tyranny" nor "the Portuguese with burning Jews alive." This argument was presented directly to the king, who carefully considered the evidence against the captain.[12]

Ultimately, King George pardoned the convicted buggerer. Although initial reports claimed that Jones was headed to America, he ultimately settled in France "with a *lovely Ganymede* (his footboy)." In response, the British press excoriated the king for not defending the laws and morals of the nation. Radical journalist and politician John Wilkes seized on Jones's pardon to attack George III and leveraged notoriety around the case to run for lord mayor of London.[13]

Robert Newburgh and the men of the Eighteenth Regiment certainly knew about Captain Jones and his trial. Being Anglo Irishmen themselves, they probably saw similarities between Jones's case and their own. They shared vitriolic attacks and impassioned defenses, questions of character and questions about whether a man should face punishment for buggery. In the debate surrounding Jones's case, some emphasized sympathy, human nature, and forgiveness; perhaps the men who sat in judgment of Newburgh had similar impulses.

To that end, at this point in his closing argument, Robert Newburgh pivoted toward an argument about rights and how personal preferences did not matter. Although he never admitted to having had sex with another man, he invoked enlightened tropes that mirrored an idea in Britain, Ireland, and America that there was nothing wrong with buggerers.

❖ ❖ ❖

Having disposed of allegations regarding his sexual acts, Reverend Newburgh moved on to actual charges that the British army had leveled against him. He methodically addressed each one, and his rhetoric soared as he claimed innocence against accusations of falsehood, seduction, and ungentlemanlike behavior. His metaphors had a humorous twist, and he was gentle in his denunciations. Unable to shake the perception that he was a buggerer, he drew upon the highest ideals of the Enlightenment to argue that he should be acquitted.

The Enlightenment is a vague term for the intellectual and philosophical changes of the eighteenth century. Inspired by men like John Locke, Baron de Montesquieu, and Voltaire, the Enlightenment marked a new appreciation for empiricism and the laws of nature. Such thinkers liberated themselves from the medieval confines of a God-centered universe, and as secularism emerged, some questioned divinely appointed inequality. Instead, the individual emerged as the most important political unit. Such liberal thought had a leveling effect; every man possessed equal rights and personal liberties. Robert Newburgh had learned these truths at Trinity, and now he applied them in his defense.[14]

He began with the allegation of perjury, specifically the charge that he had falsely claimed that Captain Mawby *had said my Testimonials were satisfactory to him in every Respect.*" He insisted that the entire affair had been a misunderstanding and thus irrelevant. On this point, he waxed philosophical on the nature of confusion. Individuals rarely used "the very self same Words," he observed, but rephrased statements according to personal taste. He then offered an illustration: "suppose I should happen to be present at a Quarrel between a Frenchman who spoke very bad English and a West Country Man," and afterward someone wanted to know what each man had said. In this instance, "can it be supposed," Newburgh asked, "it would be necessary for me to speak broken English when I told what the Frenchman said, or to express myself in the West Country Dialect, in declaring what I heard the other speak"?

He elaborated on this point as he moved on the second instance of the allegation: that he had complained that Mawby had put him "into a Room the most inconvenient in the Barracks."

Again, Newburgh argued that it had all been a misunderstanding and claimed that qualifiers like "most inconvenient" were
matters of personal preference.

> I can suppose that Captain Mawby may swear that the
> Rooms are inconvenient, and I may swear that they are
> convenient, and yet both of us be free from that horrid
> Crime; For Convenience being as I said before, a mere
> Matter of Opinion every one has a Right to call that
> convenient which he may think is so.

It was not perjury, but a difference of opinion! This was a fun-
damentally liberal argument. It also ran counter to military order. It was up to the commanding officer to determine where
each man slept, and a chaplain's opinion on the matter was irrelevant. But Newburgh disregarded this principle and suggested that he had the same rights as a captain.[15]

He then pressed the point, asking the court why his preference for a room mattered. "If neither the Garrison necessary
Houses or the Taylors were Objections to me, I cannot see why
others should object for me." Everyone was entitled to his own
opinion. "Tho I had no Right to use any Room without his Permission I certainly had a Right to like one Room better than
another without first having obtained his Licence for that Purpose." Here, Newburgh was more cautious in his assertion of
choice, as it raised questions of why he had wanted to be closer
to the outhouses and tailors. He did not want to confirm Chapman's innuendos.[16]

On the charge of prevarication, Newburgh dismissed changing his answer at the tailors' court-martial as another misunderstanding. Initially, he had been asked whether he knew the tailors, but later he was asked whether he *had any Conversation with
them relative to that Affair.* He answered yes to the first, but no to
the second; both answers were true. He even took the opportu-

nity to push back against the captains, again using a language couched in principles of liberty. "It would have been no more than fair, and what one man has a Right to expect from another" had the court asked him to clarify at the time what he meant.[17]

Perjury and prevarication were never the strongest charges, and with artful remarks, Newburgh put each one to rest. However, disproving that he had committed falsehood was more challenging. In response to the claim that he had said that testimony was added to the court of enquiry transcript without his knowledge, Newburgh's rhetorical skills failed him. Uncharacteristically, he attacked the captains. "I was permitted to read so far, and no farther. Why were such orders given. Why this Caution. Why this Secrecy," he asked.[18]

Newburgh had a better response to the second charge of falsehood. He read several pages of testimony from the trial to prove that Fowler, Trist, and Collins had never threatened to turn their back on him if he did not prosecute Batt. But he did not have a good answer for the third charge—that he had claimed Batt had bribed him to drop the civil suit. Again, he argued that it was all a misunderstanding. "In speaking on that Subject I Might have said that 300£ would not make me whole for the Injuries I had sustained by his Slander," he admitted. Unlike the choice of a room, however, bribery was a serious charge and could not be dismissed as a simple difference of opinion. As a result, Newburgh's comments about the court of enquiry transcript and his claims that Batt had bribed him remained unresolved before the court.[19]

❖ ❖ ❖

The heart of the army's case against Reverend Newburgh was that he had committed *"scandalous and indecent acts"* by encouraging Private Nicholas Gaffney to slander his superiors. Not surprisingly, it was in addressing these charges that Newburgh's defense rose to its most passionate level. He turned to religion, specifically, his duty as a chaplain to help the oppressed. Yet even in his appeals to God, he returned to liberal ideas, insisting that Christian love required equality.

Newburgh began by explaining that he had known neither the "unhappy Soldier" nor Captain Shee before Gaffney's court-martial. His decision to provide legal advice had not derived from "private Reasons or sinister Views"; rather, it was his duty to help a man in trouble.

> I had always been taught that Men, by Nature were entitled to equal Rights, and that it was my Duty as a Gentleman, and a Christian, to afford Relief to Distress, whether I found it in a Lord, or a Beggar, an officer, or a Soldier.

In explaining why he had helped Gaffney, Newburgh expanded on the theme of equality. Just as a man was entitled to his choice of words or opinion of rooms, every soldier deserved an effective defense, no matter his rank.[20]

Again, Newburgh pressed the point. Because Gaffney was a private, he was *more* deserving of legal assistance. "Had I assisted the Capt. instead of the Soldier, the Master, instead of the Servant, the man who had Power, instead of him who had none, There is Reason to presume, I should have escaped Reprehension, and perhaps been thanked." Yet it was his duty to subvert military hierarchy in this instance. "I shall never consider myself as acting a part inconsistent with the Character of a Clergyman a Gentleman or a Christian," he explained.[21]

Nowhere else in Newburgh's trials is his religiosity more evident nor his theology more obvious. At Trinity, he had learned a type of Anglicanism that had been inspired by the Irish Enlightenment. Like the Church of Ireland priests who solicited charity during *bliain an áir*, he believed in a common humanity and the responsibility of Christians to serve the less fortunate. This inspired an involvement that went beyond sympathy. Because all men had equal rights regardless of their station, a clergyman had a responsibility to help the lowly safe-guard their liberties even if this disrupted the social order.

Such beliefs were not unique to Newburgh. Throughout the Anglo Atlantic, Anglican priests denounced injustice. When British army chaplain Thomas Charles Heslop Scott discovered corruption in the Thirty-Fourth Regiment, he rebuked his commanding officer in his sermon. Other enlightened clergymen called for structural change, and in the American colonies, some critiqued imperial policies as unchristian. The Reverend John Lewis of South Carolina used the biblical story of Naboth's vineyard to denounce George III's rapacious tax policy. The Anglican priests in Philadelphia sympathized with ongoing colonial protests and, in June 1775, all six signed a letter defending Americans against "a Slavish Resignation of their Rights."[22]

Having explained his reason for assisting Gaffney, Newburgh told the court how the private had abused his kindness. "I was I confess deceived and disappointed," he asserted. Gaffney had exaggerated his case and duped him. Newburgh marveled "that a man of so black a Heart" should turn from disobeying Shee to denigrating him. He referred the court to the various times when Gaffney had lied, citing the contradictory testimonies of two privates. Yet he insisted his was bound by Christian duty to help a reprobate like Gaffney. "If we were to try the Merit of all who asked our Charity before we extended it, our Hands and Purses would seldom be opened." Although he regretted how things turned out, Newburgh would do it all again.[23]

As he wound down his closing argument, Newburgh returned to the scandalous rumors that Chapman and others had spread about him. He began by addressing the insinuation that he had immoral motives for assisting Gaffney. He reread the testimony of Private Osborne in order to prove "that Gaffney could not come into my Bed Room at 10 oClock at night." Likewise, he read testimony from other enlisted men to prove that he was not "addicted to swearing" and that he had not allowed "Gaffeney and other Soldiers, to take indecent Familiarities with me." He had not lusted after Gaffney or any other soldier in the regiment.[24]

He also asserted that Gaffney had misrepresented his opinion of Ensign McDermott's court-martial. He had asked Private William West about Kitty Shaw's age because "West had been to the trial and had seen the Girl." When the private informed him that the girl was younger than ten, Newburgh "observed that if her Conduct had been so very indecent there could be no great Criminality in Mr. McDermott being a little irritated." In other words, Newburgh claimed that he had not made light of having sex with a child; rather, he only stated that the incident could not be legally construed as rape because the girl was prepubescent.[25]

He then reflected on McDermott's case and pondered whether the ensign was also entitled to equal rights. "The popular Opinion ran at that time a good deal against Mr. McDermot," but given that the court had acquitted the ensign, "I was led by a desire of setting that Matter in its true Light to declare my Sentiments about it." In effect, Newburgh viewed McDermott the same way he had once viewed Gaffney: a man wrongly accused who needed a defender. Every person deserved to be treated fairly, especially those who had been wrongly accused.[26]

Finally, Newburgh addressed the claim that he was a macaroni. "I cant forbear observing that this Prosecution affords as noble an Instance of the true Bathos as any to be met with in Martinus Scriblerius." This was a reference to a popular novel about a man who finds himself subjected to an absurd set of circumstances.

> First I am Charged with a capital Crime, thence the Gentleman descends to perjury, thence to Prevarication, thence

to simple Falsehood, thence to giving Rum Toddy to some thirsty Soldiers, thence to uncivil Languge, thence to wearing a red Collar on a borrowed Coat, thence to leather Breeches and so quite away down to white Stockings.

In this one statement, Newburgh succinctly traced the case against him as well as how Chapman and the other captains connected buggery to disobedience, seduction, and appearance.[27]

He then mocked Chapman for criticizing his clothing. He wondered aloud what church the captain belonged to because he knew of no Christian denomination that "forbid its Teachers to wear white Stockings and Leather Breeches." Once again, Newburgh invoked liberal principles. A man's faith could not be observed by outward appearance, he contended, and insisted that "it is just as criminal in a Preacher to eat Bread and Butter as to put on a Bath Coat with black Buttons." A man's clothes were irrelevant to what was in his heart.[28]

Newburgh then offered a novel interpretation of character that ran contrary to the prevailing opinion. Eighteenth-century political thought held that a man's nature predicted his actions, thus Chapman and the other captains had insisted that they could tell that the parson was a buggerer because of his outward appearance. But Newburgh rejected such judgments as narrow-minded and not reflective of a man's true nature. Whether a minister wore "a Gown and Cassock" had been the subject of bitter debate in medieval times and had led to bloody wars. "But from the little Acquaintance I had gained with the World in this Age," he concluded, "I imagined all those old Prejudices were exploded, and that Man and Ministers were judged of, more by their Principles and Doctrines, than their Dress." This was the heart of liberalism and the very soul of the Enlightenment: the personal was *not* political. So long as a man did good work, it did not matter that he looked like a macaroni.[29]

Throughout his various cases, Robert Newburgh does not always come across in the most positive light. He vacillates between pitiless victim and an opportunistic manipulator. However, his closing argument embraced the best hopes of the Enlightenment with its promise of personal liberty and equal rights before the law. These came with the responsibility to be charitable to all people, regardless of rank, and the Christian had a special obligation to help the poor and oppressed. At times, he alluded to topics that many associated with homosexuality: preference for a room close to the necessaries, the defense of a man whom popular opinion convicted of sexual immorality, and the right to not be judged for flamboyant appearance. He never argued that a man had the right to be a buggerer or that what a person did in bed was irrelevant, but nevertheless, Newburgh's rhetoric anticipated the sexual liberalism of a later age.

❖ ❖ ❖

While rhetoric was prized at Trinity, most English universities rejected skilled oratory as a form of deceit practiced by demagogues. Instead, Oxford and Cambridge taught that plain speech was a more truthful form of communication. Benjamin Chapman was neither English nor a college graduate, but simplicity infused his closing remarks. His summary was short, direct, and unadorned. He rejected Robert Newburgh's claim that character could not be determined by outward appearance; indeed, Chapman's case was all about exposing Newburgh. He sought to prove that the chaplain's actions revealed low character.

The court reconvened at 9:00 a.m. on August 25. Captain Chapman began by acknowledging that he did not share Newburgh's rhetorical skills, although he thought that this was a good thing. "Truth needs no Ornament," he added in a jab at the chaplain's oratory, rather "She appears most lovely in her Native Purity." Chapman then took aim at Newburgh's closing argument, labeling it an "eloquent Harangue." He mocked Newburgh's legalism and suggested that the chaplain had pursued the wrong vocation. "In this page we find him preaching at a Conventicle; in the next, pleasing in a common Law Court"; but it was all theater designed to cover up his crimes.[30]

Chapman insisted that sexual offenses were "Matters wholly foreign from the Articles of Charge," and deferred any consideration of buggery to the judge advocate. With that, he moved on to the five charges on which he had presented evidence. He returned to the case of perjury at Mawby's court-martial, quoting the testimonies of Fowler and Trist to prove that it had not been an innocent misunderstanding. He again mocked Newburgh's use of rhetoric. The chaplain could not provide any evidence, so he relied on "a curious Display of fallacious argument and specious Reasoning" that ignored the evidence.[31]

The captain continued by turning to two examples of prevarication and falsehood. He centered on two points that Newburgh had not been able to put to rest: that he had claimed that Batt tried to bribe him, and that evidence had been added to the record of the court of enquiry. On the first charge, Chapman recounted testimony from the court-martial, and on the second, he told the court that if they would "look into those Proceedings, you will find no Traces of any of them." As before, the discrepancies between Newburgh's words and actions were proof of his lowly character. "Happy is the Man who can not be accused of having told more than three Falshoods," Newburgh had muttered earlier, a remark that Chapman found rich considering that "the greatest part of his time has been taken up in reconciling Contradictions, Collecting a Volume of Certificates to make a Character, and harassing Society under a Cloak of Charity."[32]

Chapman also reiterated the dangers of the legal assistance that Newburgh had offered Gaffney. He again relied on sexual innuendo to explain the chaplain's connection to the private. The testimonies of enlisted men had proved that the two "usually sat down together, Drank out of the same Bowl & conversed in the most familiar manner." Inevitably, these conversations became "loose and immoral," and included talk of McDermott's sexual crimes, which Chapman was astonished to hear Newburgh defend. He also returned to his insinuation that the chaplain's affections for the private were inappropriate if not immoral. Newburgh had "presented Gaffeney with a Snuff box, and as it was received from a Lady," it was logical that "it was accompanied with the friendly Expressions." Chapman did not explicitly accuse Newburgh of having sexual designs on Gaffney, but he heavily implied it. What was the purpose of this "this condescending Familiarity" he wanted to know? "A thousand might be Suggested exactly to the purpose."[33]

Further, Chapman rebutted Newburgh's claims that he had been motivated by charity, questioning whether he even knew the meaning of the word.

> *Charity* sent him to Gaffeney before they went to Amboy. *Charity* induced him to assist him in the manner already mentioned. *Charity* made him abuse Major Hamilton and the other officers in Serjt. Pyrah's Room. *Charity* made him prevail on Jeff, an Ignorant Soldier to accuse him of a Crime he could not prove, and which Subjected him to such Punishment on Mr. Newburgh's acquittal, that he Deserted to save himself.

Chapman had additional examples, so many in fact that he crossed some of them out in the handwritten copy of his closing argument.[34]

It was not charity, but seduction. Newburgh's "delusive Arts, & poisonous Persuasions" had led to "ignorant Soldiers Engaging in Seditious Combinations against their Officers."

Most disturbingly, Newburgh was a clergyman whom the soldiers were taught to look up to, "and whose Advice they consider as a Law." Newburgh did not offer legal help to Gaffney out of charity, but out of craven self-interest.

Seduction ultimately led to the collapse of the divinely appointed order of men. A chaplain had a duty "to inspire the Soldiery with Notions of Submission to their Officers," Chapman informed the court, but Newburgh had failed to support the regimental hierarchy; his leveling words had turned the enlisted men against the officers and led to "the utter Subversion of all Order, Discipline and Subordination." In sharp contrast to the Newburgh's call for equal rights, Chapman reminded the court that rank and deference were vital to the British army.[35]

Chapman's close was less than one quarter the length of Newburgh's, which he acknowledged as he concluded his remarks. At the end, he turned wistful as he remembered the last year of trials and intrigue that the clergyman had brought to the Eighteenth Regiment.

> When I reflect on the happy state of the Royal Irish, at the time of Mr. Newburgh's joining them, and the almost constant trouble and confusion, we have been since involv'd in on his Acct I confesses I can with difficulty suppress my resentment. For, Gentlemen I can with confidence affirm, that had we never seen Mr. N we should have been as happy as any Corps in the King's Service.

This was a convenient misremembering of history. The Eighteenth had been fraught with divisions long before Newburgh joined the unit, yet for Chapman, everything that was wrong with army life boiled down to the buggering priest.[36]

In many ways, Benjamin Chapman was not that different from Robert Newburgh. He was a native of Ireland and roughly the same age, about thirty. But when they were sixteen, the two men took very different paths: Newburgh went to college and

Chapman entered the army. The captain lacked the chaplain's erudition; he was plain-spoken and believed in the values of tradition and order. This is not to say that Chapman was un-enlightened. He no doubt understood Lockean contract theory and believed that all men possessed natural rights. However, he did not believe in an equality that undermined rank nor a liberalism that entitled a man to behave any way he wanted to. Especially at a moment when the British Empire was poised to be torn in two, he had no sympathy for a rebel. In this, Chap-man's close was more in keeping with the values and opinions of British officers who sat on the court.[37]

❖ ❖ ❖

Following Captain Chapman's closing argument, the judge advocate, Captain Stephen Payne Adye, "Desired permission to lay a few observations" before the court. Judge advocates of-ten argued weighty cases, but Adye told the court that he would have remained silent "had not Mr. Newburgh opened his de-fence with some complaints which I look upon myself as bound to explain." Specifically, Adye wanted to address Newburgh's comments on buggery. The court had no business deciding on this matter because "the Commission of an Unnaturall Crime it is not brought as a Charge against him." He also offered ad-ditional observations on perjury and other matters but having established that whether the parson was a buggerer was be-yond the purview of the court, Adye concluded his remarks.[38]

Newburgh then demanded a rebuttal. He wanted to re-spond to the closing remarks of Chapman and "beg'd the In-dulgence of the Court" to do so. The court agreed, but it only gave him until 1:00 p.m. to do so. The court also refused to allow him to present his remarks orally, permitting only a writ-ten version be submitted.[39]

Newburgh's second close did not match the flair of his first. He denounced "the very Gross Misrepresentations" that Chap-man had entered about Mawby's court-martial, and he scoffed

at the claim that he had "descended from the Dignity of a Clergyman and Gentleman." He also fended off the prosecution's
latest innuendo: "Mr. Chapmans Observations in the Circum-
stance of my giving that Paltry Snuff Box to Gaffny deserves not
your Attention or my Notice." He concluded by reiterating that
he was compelled to help Gaffney by Christian compassion.

> If the Ornamental Quality of Pity and Sympathy in the
> Misfortunes of Mankind be a Crime, I shall boast and
> Glory in the Character mine Enemys have struggled to as-
> sign me, and thank them for a Compliment their Malice
> never intended. *Nil Humanum a me alienum puto.*

Newburgh approximated *homo sum, humani nihil a me alienum puto,*
which means "I am a man, nothing human can be alien to me."[40]

Homo sum, humani nihil a me alienum puto first appeared in
the Roman play *Heauton Timorumenos* by Terence in 163 B.C.
Because Terence was once a slave, the phrase survived as a
statement of resilience and the mutual obligation of humans
to one another. It appears in the writings of Cicero and St. Augustine, and it was introduced to the eighteenth century in the
widely read London magazine *The Spectator.* Newburgh may
have come across the phrase in his studies at Trinity or in any
number of English, Irish, or American newspapers where the
words were invoked by advertisers and politicians with some
regularity. The phrase embodied the essence of the Enlightenment in which all people shared a common humanity.[41]

The words of Terence mirrored Newburgh's insistence that
he had the right to prefer one room over another, that all accused people deserved legal help, and that the clothes a person wore were irrelevant to his character. He made all of these
claims while standing accused of being a buggerer. Perhaps he
understood the connection; certainly, his accusers did.

It would be overly simplistic to claim that the Enlightenment facilitated an acceptance of homosexuality. Many of the

Terence

Source: The Comedies of Terence and the Fables of Phaedrus, trans.
Henry Thomas Riley (London: Bohn, 1853), frontispiece.

great thinkers of the eighteenth century remained opposed to
male-male intimacy: Montesquieu equated sodomy with witchcraft, while Voltaire worried about its negative effects on reproduction. Yet enlightened ideals had the revolutionary potential
for the acceptance of what was once seen as an abomination.

It was in the midst of the English Enlightenment that Util-
itarian philosopher Jeremy Bentham composed the first de-

fense of homosexuality in English. In his published and unpublished writings, Bentham dismissed biblical punishments for sodomy as outdated, and he rejected the notion that sex between two men was unnatural. Sexual desire and activities were a matter of personal preference, and no one should be punished for them. Bentham first sketched out these ideas in 1774, the same year as Newburgh's court-martial. In many ways, they were part of the same intellectual moment.[42]

Homo sum, humani nihil a me alienum puto was also well known among those who believed that the best way to achieve the sentiment was through revolution. The phrase appears in the writings of John Adams, Thomas Jefferson, and Benjamin Franklin while these men contemplated declaring independence. Once the Revolutionary War began, the words were repeated by those who believed that the highest ideals of America required equality. John Wilkes invoked the phrase before the House of Commons to denounce the Treason Act of 1777, which suspended the writ of habeas corpus for American rebels. A decade later, the words resurfaced in a Philadelphia newspaper to denounce "Negro Slavery."[43]

The American Revolution was the greatest manifestation of the Enlightenment in the Western Hemisphere. The colonists believed that the British government had negated their rights through taxation without representation, a standing army in peacetime, and restrictions on trade; claims that were ultimately incorporated in the Declaration of Independence. Thereafter, the founders created a republic of citizens rather than replicating Britain's monarchy and aristocracy. Each state wrote its own constitution, many of which included lists of rights guaranteed to all individuals. When the thirteen states unified into a single nation under the US Constitution, they enshrined American freedoms in the Bill of Rights.[44]

How far the promise of individual rights could go was raised during the Revolution and has been debated ever since.

Religious freedom was achieved as states pursued disestablishment and erected a "wall of separation" between church and state. African Americans argued that human bondage was inconsistent with liberty, and many European Americans agreed; all of the northern states moved to abolish the institution by 1804. Some revolutionaries proposed enfranchising women and educating the entire population. Nor did the demand for justice end with the Constitution. As the Civil War approached, abolitionists and suffragettes called on Americans to live up to the promise of the Declaration of Independence by granting full civil rights to all Americans. For this reason, some historians have marked American independence as a radical social revolution.[45]

Robert Newburgh's closing argument suggests that the revolutionary ideals of equal rights and a common humanity included homosexuals. Although none of the founders quoted Terence to promote buggery, Chapman and the other captains had already connected Newburgh's sexual acts to an assault on the social order and the patriotic tendencies of his supporters. Philosophically at least, the American Revolution contained the potential for sexual liberalism and an acceptance of all regardless of sexual acts and identities.[46]

Some historians take a less sanguine view of the creation of the United States. They note that despite enlightened rhetoric, the founders allowed racial slavery to persist for four score and seven years, while women of all races gained few political rights before the twentieth century. Power remained in the hands of capitalists, while economic inequality was addressed primarily through continental imperialism whereby the nation made war on Indigenous peoples and Mexicans so that Anglos could settle homesteads. For this reason, they unfavorably compare the timidity of the American Revolution to the more radical French and Haitian versions that followed. It is thus difficult to imagine a place for homosexual rights in the early republic.[47]

Yet hope outlasts oppression. Because the Enlightenment defined the Revolution, the nation that followed always contained the seeds of abolitionism, feminism, and social equality. For this reason, we should not be so quick to dismiss the revolutionary potential of Newburgh's closing argument. The same words that he used to defend himself recall those of the First Amendment, which historians have cited as instrumental to the gay rights movement of the twentieth century. As with race and gender, we can appreciate that the potential for inclusion for LGBTQ+ people was inherent in the creation of the United States even if equality was delayed by two centuries.[48]

❖ ❖ ❖

The general court-martial convened at 9:00 a.m. on August 26 to deliberate. After three weeks of testimony, thirty-three witnesses, and four closing arguments, the president and twelve officers had sufficient evidence to render a verdict. But there was no agreement on the facts of the case. Deliberations continued until 3:00 p.m., then the officers adjourned for the day.

On Saturday, August 27, 1774, the court announced its verdict. First, the officers found Robert Newburgh guilty of falsehood for "having declared that Capt. Batt had offered him three hundred pounds to drop his prosecution" and for having claimed that the court of enquiry "irregularly made several additions to their proceedings without his knowledge or consent." However, the court was unconvinced that "these crimes amount to a charge of vicious and immoral behaviour" and moved on.

Second, the court found Newburgh "guilty of an impropriety in his conduct, by suffering Soldiers, when in his presence, to lose the respect due to his station, and of improper behaviour by being unguarded in his expressions before them." Newburgh's improper relationship with Private Gaffney had sown division in the regiment, so the court suspended him for "six months from all Duty and pay as Chaplain to the 18th or Royal Regiment of Foot of Ireland." This meant that he would not receive a salary for six months. Although this was a harsh punishment, it could have been worse. The court could have cashiered Newburgh and expelled him from the army without compensation for his commission.

Third, the court addressed the rest of the case. "With respect to the remaining charges brought against the said Robert Newburgh, the Court is of opinion that they are ill founded, and some of them frivolous accusations." The thirteen officers had not been able to agree that the chaplain deserved to be punished for his testimony at Mawby's court-martial, disrespect for his commanding officer, or his macaroni appearance. As a result, the court "doth therefore acquit him of these several charges."[49]

Colonel Nesbitt signed the proceedings of the case and verdict, as did Captain Adye. Nesbitt then collected the transcript, thirty supporting documents, and closing arguments, and sent them all to the commander in chief for his approval.[50]

The verdict left everyone unhappy. Newburgh had not been vindicated, nor had he been convicted of most of the charges leveled against him. He would lose a considerable amount of pay, but he retained his chaplaincy. Above all, the question of his character remained unresolved. Because the court took Adye's advice and offered no opinion on whether the parson had committed buggery, the question of whether Robert Newburgh was a buggerer remained unresolved.

CHAPTER TEN

Many Circumstances Have Happened

THE DAY AFTER REVEREND NEWBURGH'S general court-martial concluded, Major General Frederick Haldimand dispatched a letter to the commander in chief. Writing from New York, Haldimand had little to say about the trial other than that the "Conseil de Guerre" had finally ended. Instead, he focused on more pressing concerns such as the "Deputés au Congrès," which had gathered in Philadelphia. A buggering chaplain was the least of his concerns.[1]

As Haldimand's letter traveled to Lieutenant General Thomas Gage in Boston, the American colonies crept toward revolution. On September 1, 1774, Gage dispatched more than two hundred British soldiers to seize the Massachusetts gunpowder supply in Middlesex County and transport it to Boston. The colonists were outraged by the confiscation of their communal property and organized mass meetings to protest what became known as the Powder Alarm. As tensions built, Gage mounted cannons on Boston Neck, while the Sons of Liberty began monitoring the governor's actions and sent warnings to the other colonies by way of Paul Revere.[2]

Meanwhile, delegates began to gather for the First Continental Congress. Massachusetts representative John Adams left Gage's colony in mid-August and spent a week in New York

City during Newburgh's court-martial. Before the trial ended, Adams departed for Philadelphia and attended the opening session at Carpenter's Hall on September 6. Several of Newburgh's associates joined Adams. George Ross, the brother of his lawyer, John Ross, sat as a delegate for Pennsylvania, while a fellow Anglican clergyman, the Reverend Jacob Duché, delivered the opening prayer.[3]

Buggery was not a topic of discussion at the First Continental Congress. Instead, the delegates voted resolutions that denounced the Coercive Acts and called for a continental boycott of all British goods. Yet the tensions that had appeared at Newburgh's court-martial surfaced nevertheless. For many delegates, loyalty to George III and deference to the traditional order were essential. Congress protested taxation without representation because it was inconsistent with "the principles of the English constitution," and it asked Gage to discipline redcoats in Boston in order to effect "a cordial & effectual reconciliation between Great-Britain & the colonies." Yet the delegates also invoked a language of "common rights," informing the king that their pursuit of a peaceful resolution did not abrogate their liberties "which cannot be legally taken from them, altered or abridged by any power whatever." It is difficult not to hear echoes of Captain Chapman's appeal to military hierarchy and Reverend Newburgh's claims of equal rights in Congress's declarations.[4]

Although Robert Newburgh's military trials ended in August 1774, his quest for justice continued. For the next eight months, he sought a pardon from Gage and continued his civil suit against Thomas Batt. However, the impending revolution complicated these efforts. Nor did the conclusion of the court-martial end the rifts among the Royal Irish. Instead, the captains and subalterns remained at odds, and their disagreements over the chaplain's character mapped onto political divisions. Nearly all of the men and women who had supported Newburgh became Patriots, while his accusers and opponents remained loyal subjects of George III. In many ways, this case of homosexuality foretold the American Revolution.

❖ ❖ ❖

Shortly after the court-martial ended, Robert Newburgh and other members of the Eighteenth Regiment returned to Philadelphia. Newburgh was incarcerated at the barracks in the Northern Liberties and remained confined for another month. According to army regulations, the case did not conclude until the commander in chief approved the court's decision. With powder alarms and colonial unrest, General Gage did not receive the trial transcript until September 9, and word of his approval did not reach Philadelphia until two weeks after that. As a result, Newburgh was "deprived of the invaluable Blessing of Liberty" until September 21.[5]

While he waited, Newburgh pondered his next move. He could have countersued. Because the court had not convicted him of buggery, he was well within his rights to file charges against Chapman and Payne for defamation and thus initiate another court-martial. That he chose not to surprised the judge advocate, who wondered at "His not prosecuting his accusers for the charges which were deemed *ill founded, frivolous* and *vexatious.*" Newburgh may have thought that his civil suit against Batt would settle the matter, or maybe he concluded that an army court would never render justice for him.[6]

Instead, he appealed his sentence. First, he wrote to Lieutenant Colonel John Wilkins, who was still the commanding officer of the Royal Irish. This was an odd choice since Newburgh had never met Wilkins or written to him before. It is probable that Fowler and Trist encouraged him to reach out to Wilkins as the letter reflected the regiment's long-standing divide between captains and subalterns. "I have had a Very Severe and Cruel persecution from Men I am, & shall ever remain unacquainted with," Newburgh wrote. Chapman and the other captains had exhibited "A Malevolence peculiar to themselves" that he still did not understand. Yet Newburgh remained defiant even in defeat, insisting that the court-martial had been necessary for "a Vindication of my Fame & Honor" as well as his "Innocence and Integrity." Somewhat undercutting this point, he enclosed a letter from Colonel Eyre Massey, the man who had first noted his flamboyant attire.[7]

But Wilkins was in London, and it took two months for Newburgh's letter to reach him. On November 2, the colonel wrote to Gage pleading for "our Chaplain the Reverend Mr. Newburgh." Apparently, the subalterns and their wives had also written to him, as Wilkins noted that "Other Gentlemen & Ladies his intimate Acquaintence both here & in America" had asked him to intervene. However, because two months had passed since he received Newburgh's letter, Wilkins assumed that the chaplain had already "Obtaind justice in the Military & Civil Law." It took another two months for Wilkins's reply to reach Gage in Boston.[8]

Wilkins also had his own problems. The charges of corruption that had driven him from Illinois in 1772 continued to haunt him. In December 1774, Gage announced that a court of enquiry would be held in England to adjudicate the matter. In response, Lieutenant Alexander Fowler wrote several impassioned pleas on Wilkins's behalf. He was remorseful for having sided against the colonel three years earlier, but now, "Thank God, I have a Heart susceptible of feeling and a Mind open to Conviction." Fowler remained loyal to Wilkins and enthusiastically awaited his return to America, believing that the men "will return to their Duty with chearfullness & Alacrity on Lieut. Colonel Wilkins Joining the Regiment."[9]

Newburgh also appealed to Gage. Having heard about colonial unrest in Massachusetts, he apologized "for presuming to trouble your Excellency at A Time when Concerns of the highest Consequence employ your Attention." But he was insistent that the sentence was unfair. "The Court has done me the Justice and Honor to acquit me of the Heinous Crimes alledgd against me," he explained, but the officers had suspended him for six months anyway. Newburgh thus asked Gage to commute his sentence. He cited the "very severe Distresses" of having his pay stopped as well as the requirement that he pay a deputy in his absence. He also referred to his chronic illness, claiming that "A very infirm State of Health have renderd my present Situation more Calamitous and Greivous."[10]

While Newburgh sent out appeals, the Eighteenth Regiment was on the move. As problems worsened in Boston, Gage pulled troops to Massachusetts. On September 1, he ordered Haldimand to "get the 18th to Jersey," and a week later, the Royal Irish departed for Perth Amboy and Elizabeth. Philadelphians marked the regiment's departure with respect and sadness. "Both officers and soldiers observed the strictest attention to good order and harmony," lauded the *Pennsylvania Journal*. Another newspaper echoed these sentiments and noted that the redcoats had "acquired the warmest Esteem and Admiration" of the colonists. A month after Newburgh's trial ended, Philadelphia had emptied of British soldiers for the first time in a decade.[11]

In New Jersey, the Eighteenth Regiment crowded into small barracks already occupied by parts of the Forty-Seventh, thus renewing a connection between the two regiments. The Royal Irish did not linger long in New Jersey but soon headed to New York City. Reverend Newburgh marched with the rest of the regiment and dispatched his appeal to Gage from the Upper Barracks, where he had been tried less than two months earlier. But Gage was obsessed with Boston. The Forty-Seventh Regiment soon departed for Massachusetts, and in mid-October, three companies of the Eighteenth followed, including those captained by Benjamin Chapman and John Shee.[12]

The fracturing of the Royal Irish brought about a change in leadership. Major Isaac Hamilton still commanded the regiment, but his continued illness had rendered him largely invalid. In his place, Captain Benjamin Charnock Payne assumed day-to-day command of the companies in New York. However, his highhanded ways once again sowed division in the ranks as, according to some, the captain acted "cruelly and tyrannically." Payne enforced a harsh discipline on the regiment and even admitted to striking "about a dozen Soldiers." When he drummed soldiers' wives out of the barracks, the number of deserters grew. According to more than one peeved soldier, it was Payne's harsh treatment that prompted Sergeant John Brogden to abandon the Royal Irish. It was highly unusual for a noncommissioned officer to desert, especially a sergeant like Brogden, who had managed the regimental infirmary in Philadelphia. Some even believed that Payne's cruelty extended up the chain of command. Surgeon's mate John L. Lynn claimed that the captain had offered him £100 to poison Major Hamilton.[13]

❖ ❖ ❖

The experience of defending Robert Newburgh deeply affected the subalterns. Neither Lieutenant Fowler nor Ensign Trist regretted siding with the chaplain, and they remained loyal to him long after the court-martial concluded. "A Friend to the Reverend Mr. Newburgh I have been, and his Friend I will continue," Fowler proclaimed nearly a year later. Yet the two men also realized that they were unwelcome in the British army, and both looked for a way out, even if this meant joining the gathering rebellion.[14]

Since marrying Elizabeth House, Nicholas Trist had harbored American sympathies. While the Eighteenth Regiment was still in Philadelphia, many delegates to the Continental Congress lodged in the boardinghouse run by Trist's mother-in-law, Mary Stretch House. Connecticut representative Silas

Deane frequently dined with the Trists, and he observed the ensign's inner turmoil. "The Officer here, is much to be pitied," Deane observed. "He loves this Country, he loves his Young Wife, who is very deserving, and who is a warm daughter of Liberty." Deane believed that Trist was torn between his desire to settle in America and his need to support his family. "Could he get rid of his Commission on any Terms, short of ruining himself he would gladly do it," Deane concluded.[15]

Alexander Fowler also sought a means to leave the British army. Having been disabled in Illinois, he had continued to suffer an impairment of the limbs throughout his time in Philadelphia. Despite his "hopes of obtaining a Radical Cure," Fowler concluded that he was unfit for service, and after he traveled with the regiment to New Jersey, he proposed "selling to Mr. Trist the eldest Ensign" his commission. But Gage denied the request. With a rebellion brewing, he refused to allow any officer to retire from active service.[16]

Unable to sell their commissions, Fowler and Trist took up residence in New York's Upper Barracks. Their wives joined them, and in February 1775, Elizabeth Trist bore a son: Hore Browse. The two families maintained their close friendship, with Alexander and Frances Fowler serving as godparents to Hore. They also prepared for life after the service, and Trist acquired a thousand acres near Manchac in southern Louisiana. The subalterns' questionable loyalty was well known and their rooms in the barracks dubbed "Whig's Corner."[17]

The two subalterns regularly came into conflict with their new commanding officer. "I wou'd advise you & Mr. Trist to always on your guard," John Lynn warned Fowler, who claimed that Captain Payne would "Murder you both, if he cou'd do it with impunity." Fowler later claimed that by the spring of 1775, Payne was "in a fever, and often out of his senses," brought on by the impending revolution. He insisted that "the *fevers* and *deliriums* of this t——, was occasioned by the shouts and acclamations of the people called by Mr. Payne the *Sons of Liberty*." The "very *echo of liberty* to Payne, was like the *echo of death*," Fowler concluded, labeling Payne a tyrant.[18]

As such language suggests, tensions among the officers now took on a political cast. An ensign saw Fowler "appear on their Regimental parade, in a very Intimate manner with Donald Campbell" who was "A Notorious Rebel." Trist was also seen talking to Campbell, and both men were widely believed to be in league with other New York "sons of Sedition," including Isaac Sears and Alexander McDougall. Payne claimed that Benjamin Franklin's son-in-law had heard Fowler proclaim "That he was determined to throw up his Commission rather than draw his Sword against the Injured Americans." News of the subalterns' politics even reached their friend and artilleryman Lieutenant Robert Collins, who had been deployed to Boston by this point. "Pray, my dear Fowler," Collins wrote, "take a friend's advice, and don't take notice, or even speak to any of the rebellious."[19]

Much as they had with Newburgh, the captains seized on rumors of a man's character to force him out of the army. Thomas Batt again took the lead, and much as he had once smeared Newburgh as a buggerer, he now called Fowler a Patriot. Certainly, Fowler noticed the connection and claimed that because Batt had "failed in making *a hole in the parson's coat*, by reporting him a b——," he was determined to chastise Fowler, "by reporting him a *rebel*." Fowler's subtle reference to Newburgh's clothing is revealing, as was his reaction to the charges. He denied that he was in league with the colonists, and he claimed to have dined with Donald Campbell only once. He even produced affidavits from Sears and McDougall claiming that they had "no acquaintance connection or correspondence directly or indirectly of any Kind whatsoever" with Fowler. But no one believed him. Perhaps his denial of charges was strategic in ways that echoed Newburgh's denial that he was a buggerer. But Batt was relentless, insisting that "Lieutenant Fowler was as violent a *Whig* as *Adams*."[20]

Robert Newburgh remained close to Fowler and Trist, and he probably resided with them at Whig's Corner in the Upper Barracks. He was no doubt privy to their rebellious tendencies and attempts to leave the British army. But it is unclear what Newburgh's politics were during this time or whether he considered joining the Revolution. He could have been torn between loyalty and patriotism like Fowler and Trist, although it would have been more difficult for him to envision life in a new country than it was for the subalterns. He was unmarried, and this precluded a need to acquire property and settle down. Moreover, his education and cosmopolitanism made rough-hewn America less appealing. Or perhaps desire played a role. Despite Americans' lack of interest in prosecuting buggerers, there were fewer opportunities for homosexual liaisons in New York and Philadelphia than there were in London and Dublin.

In early November 1774, General Gage finally responded to Newburgh's request for a pardon. He sent orders to Major Hamilton commuting Newburgh's sentence, thus reducing his suspension from six months to three. Gage ordered the chaplain to resume his duties, although he also told Hamilton, "As many Circumstances have happened that will prevent his being of my use to the Regiment, I shall have no Objection to his going Home." Despite being cleared of buggery, Robert Newburgh was still not welcome in the British army.[21]

Newburgh was ebullient at the news of his pardon, and he effusively thanked Gage for his compassion. Yet he found the general's order that he return to Ireland perplexing as he wanted to "Stay in America." He informed Gage that the chaplaincy was his vocation and "so I Trust in God I shall hereafter discharge my High Calling to the Advantage and Spiritual Profit of those entrusted to my Care." He also remained convinced that returning home would only prove his accusers correct. As before, the

British army found Newburgh too controversial to remain in his present capacity, but the chaplain refused to leave.[22]

Indeed, the commutation of his sentence did not end New-burgh's legal quest. Instead, he continued his civil action against Thomas Batt. In mid-December, he again wrote to Gage requesting leave for "A Suit at Law depending at Philadelphia which requires my Personal Attendance." Pressing his case, Newburgh insisted that Gage also excuse the two subalterns because "Lieut. Fowler and Ensign Trist of the Royall Regiment of Ireland, are Evidences in my Behalf." Gage had no objections to Newburgh's traveling to Philadelphia so long "as you prom-ise to provide a Clergyman to officiate in your absence." He was less enthusiastic about excusing Fowler and Trist, but the "Major cannot refuse them, if they are properly sub-pona'd ac-cording to Law."[23]

Despite Newburgh's hope that his commutation had cleared his name, Captain Payne had no interest in making amends. In March 1775, Newburgh wrote to Gage complain-ing that "Payne has given Directions" to the enlisted men who needed religious counsel "to apply to the Dissenting or any other Minister" instead of him. He was convinced that Payne was still "basely traducing my Character before even the Pri-vate Men of the Regiment" and cited a recent letter that Payne had sent to Colonel Massey "in which the Expressions are shocking and Indecent." The memory of his court-martial seven months earlier still preoccupied Newburgh's thoughts, and he was frustrated that although "that Court had deemed Ill Founded and Vexatious" the charges of buggery, he continued to be humiliated by Payne.[24]

Payne responded harshly to Newburgh's criticism. Several soldiers reported that the captain threatened them if they did not shun the chaplain. In an affidavit, Sergeant Brogden stated that Payne had told him that if he did not "deny his having re-ceived such order, that he (Capt. Payne) would break the deponent, and have him flogged." Gage had little interest in re-litigating the case, however. He told Newburgh to apply "for Redress to your Commanding Officer," and left the matter in Payne's hands.[25]

As winter turned to spring, the captains in the Eighteenth Regiment continued to press for Newburgh's removal. In a let-ter dated April 19, 1775, Payne wrote to Captain Shee in Bos-ton about a plan he had hatched with Major Hamilton. It called for dispatching the regiment's two most troublesome members to a place that evoked bad memories for the Royal Irish. Payne plotted to obtain:

> General Gages leave to send Newburgh to preach the Gos-pel to the two Companies in the Illinois. It is the only method we can devise of to get quit of this fellow, who's whole time is employ'd in Mischief. We applied to the Genl also with respect to Fowler, who's connections here with the most violent sons of Sedition, make it necessary he should be likewise removed.

Batt and Chapman may also have been part of this scheme. However, Gage, Shee, and the rest of the British army soon had bigger problems than a buggerer and his patriotic ally. On the same day that Payne composed his letter, the American Revo-lutionary War began.[26]

❖ ❖ ❖

Around 5 a.m. on April 19, 1775, Major John Pitcairn of the Royal Marines and about 250 British soldiers confronted Massachusetts Captain John Parker and 80 militiamen on Lex-ington Green. Pitcairn's men were part of a larger force that General Gage had ordered to march on Concord in order to cap-ture colonial munitions and, if possible, the leaders of the rebel-lion. In the dim light of dawn, someone discharged a musket, and the two sides exchanged fire. The results were deadly. Al-though only one British soldier was wounded, seven Americans

The Battle of Lexington

Source: François Godefroy and Nicolas Ponce, *Journée de Lexington*
(Paris: Ponce et Godefroy, 1784). Library of Congress, Rare Book and Special
Collections Division, 2004670001.

were killed. The battle at Lexington would prove to be only
the first battle in an eight-year-long war.[27]

The Eighteenth Regiment was central to the first battle of
the Revolution. Three companies commanded by Captain Shee
had arrived in Boston the previous October, where they hud-
dled inside a city crowded with British soldiers. Shee's men
were joined by six thousand other British troops including the
officers and enlisted men of the Forty-Seventh Regiment. This
meant that many participants in Newburgh's court-martial
quartered in the city, including the prosecutor, star witness, and
eleven members of the court. Gage reorganized the soldiers in
Boston into four battalions, placing the Forty-Seventh in the
first and the Eighteenth in the third.

When the British army set out on April 19, it included a grenadier company of the Royal Irish led by Shee. This company likely included Private John Tyrrell, who had testified at Newburgh's trial. After exchanging gunfire at Lexington, the grenadiers marched west to Concord, where they discovered a group of minutemen at the North Bridge ready to fight. A second battle ensued that proved far deadlier for the redcoats than Lexington.

After Concord, the British soldiers trudged back to Boston. As they did so, they were subjected to musket volleys and verbal abuse from the outraged colonists. During the day's march, Private John Russell was killed, and Captain Shee wounded. Although Shee's wounds were not life-threatening, they were severe enough that Lieutenant George Bruere had to assume temporary command of the grenadier company. Master tailor Private Samuel Lee was captured by Americans during the day's events, and later boasted that he was "the first prisoner in the Revolution." Lee, who had once testified that Payne had asked, "is not the Parson a *Bougre*," subsequently deserted the British army, married, and became a tailor in Concord.[28]

News of Lexington and Concord spread rapidly throughout the colonies and deeply affected the other members of the Eighteenth Regiment. In Philadelphia, Thomas Batt immediately sought to rescue his former comrades. According to his wife, Catherine, he "bought a Vessel, loaded it with wine and other kind of Necessaries to the amount of Two thousand pounds Sterling and went therewith to Boston." Fowler was skeptical of Batt's motivations and claimed that he headed to Boston to escape "a civil prosecution commenced against him by the *Rev. Mr. Newburgh for defamation*." Although Batt lost most of his shipment, he was warmly welcomed in Boston. Gage persuaded him to rejoin the British army and commissioned Batt senior captain of the Royal Fencible Americans.[29]

Events in Massachusetts also destabilized New York. When word of Lexington and Concord arrived on April 23, "the Town was immediately in an uproar," reported acting Governor Cadwallader Colden. Colonists raided the city's armory, seized supply ships, and organized military units. They also eyed the "100 Men of the royal Irish Regt" in the Upper Barracks. The quarters in New York lacked cannons and battlements, meaning that Newburgh and the other men of the regiment were "without Protection but in their Arms." As order broke down, the governor fretted that the soldiers would be massacred. "I am in continual Fear, that the Troops here may be drawn into some unlucky affair or other," Colden informed Gage.[30]

Fortunately, Congress intervened. On May 11, the Second Continental Congress convened in Philadelphia, and following a prayer by Reverend Duché, the delegates turned to events in New York. Unwilling to escalate matters, Congress resolved "that the troops be permitted to remain in the barracks, so long as they behave themselves peaceably and quietly." However, Congress warned that if the soldiers "commit hostilities or invade private property," then "the inhabitants should defend themselves and their property and repel force by force." It was ominous advice that foretold the future.[31]

Gage was sympathetic to the Eighteenth Regiment, and he initially proposed sending the Seventh from Quebec to New York City. However, on May 10, a group of Patriots seized Fort Ticonderoga on Lake Champlain, and this scuttled any rescue attempt. Meanwhile, Major Hamilton grew increasingly fearful of the colonists, informing Gage that New York "has been for some time past entirely ruled by an Armed Mob to the Amount of 4 or 5000, who stile themselves Sons of Liberty." The ranks of enlisted men began to deplete due to "the large Premiums and Encouragement that is publicly given them to Desert." Many of the seduced deserters became Patriots. Hamilton told Gage how a former lieutenant of the Sixtieth Regiment offered "to attack our Barracks, and get Possession of our Arms and Ammunition and Oblige the Men to join their Party." The former lieutenant was Donald Campbell, the man whom Alexander Fowler had admitted to dining with a few months earlier.[32]

As the situation grew dire in New York, Robert Newburgh finally decided that it was time to go home. According to Fowler, "Mr. Newburgh sailed for London the 13th" of May 1775. It is unclear why he took this opportunity to depart, especially after he had repeatedly refused to do so many times before. Maybe he did not wish to sail to Boston, or worse, be stranded in Illinois as Payne and others plotted. Or maybe Newburgh knew that if he remained with the Eighteenth, he would be pressed to join Fowler and Trist in renouncing his king and siding with the Sons of Liberty. Previously, he had resisted returning home out of fear that it would confirm allegations that he had had sex with his servant. Yet in his closing argument, he accepted that his reputation as a buggerer was permanently fixed, so he may have worried less about what others thought about him. Whatever the reason, in May 1775, Robert Newburgh left the Royal Irish Regiment for good.[33]

Shortly after Newburgh departed, Gage ordered the Eighteenth to evacuate New York. On June 6, Payne led fifty men across the city to the HMS *Asia* anchored in New York Harbor. Hamilton remained behind with the remaining twenty men, who were either sick or disabled including Fowler. At once, the peace that Congress had negotiated collapsed. As Payne marched the troops through New York, "they were surrounded by a Mob of several Hundreds," who offered the soldiers cash "to Desert and join them." More disturbingly, the Patriots "stopped the Baggage and Arms Chests, and after examining all the Bales, returned the Mens Cloathing and Officers Baggage, and kept the Arms." Many blamed Payne for this turn of events, claiming that he had negotiated with local leaders to surrender the soldiers' effects even though the mob was unarmed. Trist thought Payne acted "cowardly" and "very submissively."[34]

The New York contingent of the Royal Irish headed to Boston, but before they arrived, the regiment's three companies in Massachusetts faced a brutal conflict at Bunker Hill. On June 17, 1775, British forces launched an assault on provincial fortifications across the Charles River from Boston. Although the British won the battle, they suffered more than a thousand casualties. Once again, the Eighteenth was at the forefront of the conflict. Lieutenant William Richardson was injured, and more than a quarter of Royal Irish grenadiers were either killed or wounded in the battle. The regiment was a shell of its former self.[35]

❖ ❖ ❖

The Battle of Bunker Hill proved to be the breaking point for the Eighteenth Regiment. A month after Bunker Hill, General Gage granted Isaac Hamilton leave to retire from the regiment "as his health is much impaired, and by no Means able to do any duty." John Shee was promoted to major and became commanding officer. A few months later, Colonel Wilkins resigned his commission. Thereafter, General Sir John Sebright sought other men to command his regiment.[36]

Bunker Hill also marked a shift in the North American Establishment more broadly. Thomas Gage, who had convinced the king that he could bring the colonists to heel, found his reputation badly damaged by the fighting in New England. In August 1775, Gage was recalled as commander in chief and removed as governor of Massachusetts. Frederick Haldimand, who had served as acting commander when Newburgh first arrived in the colonies, also left North America in the summer of 1775. Haldimand would go on to serve as governor of Quebec, but Gage retired back to London, as other men prosecuted the war in America.[37]

As the Eighteenth Regiment waited in Boston, its propensity for litigation flared up once again. In July 1775, Alexander Fowler filed four charges against Benjamin Payne for the captain's leadership in New York. A general court-martial followed that lasted three weeks. Fowler argued that Payne had treated soldiers cruelly, uttered falsehoods, plotted to poison Hamilton, and allowed "an unarmed mob" to seize the troops' belongings as they left New York. He examined Nicholas Trist and Private John Green, and in so doing, painted a picture of a regiment coming apart at the seams: an invalid commanding officer, soldiers deserting en masse, and a captain driven mad by rebel taunts.[38]

The memory of Robert Newburgh haunted the trial. Fowler insisted that it was his friendship with Newburgh that "was the Cause of this strange Combination against me." At trial, Trist testified that Sergeant Brogden had deserted because Payne said "that he would break him" if he went to Newburgh for spiritual guidance. Private Osborne likewise told the court that Payne had beaten him for "carrying a letter from his Master Mr. Newburgh." Moreover, Fowler effectively used Newburgh's logic to justify his suit. He had been smeared by Payne's loose talk, and although he was accused of disloyalty rather than buggery, he had to file charges against Payne to defend his character.[39]

Fowler insisted that he was a loyal lieutenant, but Payne defended himself by attacking Fowler's loyalty to Great Britain. The court doubted the sincerity of Fowler's protestations. On August 18, 1775, the court cleared Payne of three of the four charges but found him guilty "of having propagated reports of Mr. Fowler's being connected with the sons of Sedition." The decision confirmed what everyone already suspected: Fowler was a rebel. In case anyone missed this point, the court directed "their opinion and Censure thereon be made known to the Royal Irish" by having it read to the regiment. Much as

Newburgh's strident defense had confirmed that he was a bug-gerer, Fowler's vigorous claims of loyalty marked him as a Patriot.[40]

As Private Gaffney had discovered the year before, an un-proven accusation often resulted in a retaliatory suit. Shortly after his court-martial ended, Payne accused Fowler of "exhib-iting Malicious, frivolous, wicked, and ill grounded Charges" against him, and a second trial ensued against the lieutenant. Again, Newburgh's character was central to the case. In his closing argument, Fowler portrayed himself as the victim of "a two years persecution" brought on by his friendship with the chaplain. He compared his predicament to that of Newburgh and McDermott; like men accused of buggery and child sexual abuse, he was the victim of malicious gossip. But the court was unsympathetic. It ruled against Fowler and ordered that he be cashiered and not allowed to sell his commission. The decision was unusually harsh and reflected the army's conclusion that Fowler was in league with the Americans. General Gage ap-proved the sentence, but he let Fowler sell his lieutenancy so as to not be entirely deprived of a livelihood. In October 1775, Alexander Fowler left the British army and became a civilian.[41]

While Fowler and Payne court-martialed each other, the Eighteenth Regiment continued to disintegrate. In August, Gage received orders for the men of the Royal Irish in Boston to be drafted into the Fifty-Ninth Regiment. Shortly thereaf-ter, the two companies in Illinois were absorbed by the Eighth Regiment. Those not reassigned left America in Decem-ber 1775, and in early March, a British newspaper reported that "the shattered remains of the 18th regiment of foot, which was engaged in action at Bunker's Hill, and reduced to only twenty-five men, arrived at Maidstone." After nine brutal years, the Royal Irish Regiment concluded its service in America.[42]

For the rest of the Revolutionary War, the Eighteenth Reg-iment remained in England, recruiting and rebuilding its ranks.

Some of the officers who survived the war in North America stayed with the unit, but most left. By the time the regiment headed to Gibraltar in 1783, only a few of the men who had been involved in Newburgh's trials were still part of the unit. A reconstituted Eighteenth fought valiantly in the Napoleonic Wars, serving in France, Egypt, and Jamaica. It resumed protecting the empire's frontier during the second half of the nineteenth century, serving in India, Afghanistan, and South Africa. The regiment was deployed to the western front during World War I, and it disbanded less than a decade later. With the creation of the Irish Free State in 1922, the Royal Irish Regiment became an oxymoron, and it was extinguished after nearly two and a half centuries of service. In 1992, a new Royal Irish Regiment was founded through an amalgamation of the Royal Irish Rangers and the Ulster Defence Regiment such that the name lives on today.[43]

❖ ❖ ❖

Once the Eighteenth Regiment left America, the principals involved in Newburgh's trials went their separate ways. The officers followed paths that mirrored their political allegiances and their sides in the chaplain's court-martial. The captains remained loyal to King George III and were promoted up the ranks of the British army, while the subalterns left the imperial service and established themselves as citizens of the United States.

The men who had prosecuted Newburgh had little doubt about their allegiance to the Crown or the British army. Thomas Batt left Boston for Nova Scotia, where he was promoted to the rank of major and tasked with raising loyal colonists to defeat the American rebellion. Batt's American wife and two sons joined him in Halifax, although their time together was short. Thomas Batt died at Fort Cumberland in June 1781. The man who had first circulated rumors of Newburgh's buggery died fighting to preserve Britain's hold on North America.[44]

Captains Benjamin Charnock Payne and Benjamin Chapman also fought for Britannia, although on opposite sides of the Atlantic. Payne stayed in America. After his questionable leadership in New York, he was reassigned to supplying the army. He commanded a wood-gathering expedition in Maine, and then headed to Antigua in search of rations. In May 1776, Payne was appointed assistant to the deputy quartermaster general, and served as deputy barrackmaster general in Philadelphia during the British occupation of the city in 1778. The next year, the man who had once joked that the parson was a buggerer was promoted to major and transferred to the Ninety-Ninth Regiment of Foot.

Chapman returned to England with the Royal Irish and helped recruit new soldiers for the unit. He was promoted to major in 1781 and accompanied the regiment to Gibraltar two years later. Chapman had always been ambitious, from his attempts to curry favor with Colonel Fanning to his plot to depose Wilkins; ultimately, these efforts were rewarded. The man who had prosecuted Newburgh's court-martial was named the regiment's commanding officer in 1787.

Both Payne and Chapman retired to England. Payne transferred to half-pay shortly before the Revolution ended and married Maria Beaufoy Durant. The couple spent a decade together before Payne died in 1793. Even at the end, the former captains were linked. Shortly after Payne's death, Chapman transferred to half-pay and married his friend's widow, who continued to be known as Mrs. Payne even after she married Chapman.[45]

Newburgh's other opponents followed similar paths. Captain John Mawby accompanied the Eighteenth Regiment back to England. He resigned his adjutancy in 1778 but remained with the Royal Irish, rising to the rank of major in Gibraltar. Ever the army patriarch, Mawby saw his son Sebright command the Royal Irish in Minorca in May 1800. Captain John Shee

The Royal Irish Regiment, 1840

Source: Michael Angelo Hayes, *The 18th (Royal Irish) Regiment of Foot: At the Storming of the Fortress of Amoy, August 26th 1841* (1840). Prints, Drawings and Watercolors from the Anne S. K. Brown Military Collection, Brown Digital Repository, Brown University Library.

transferred to the Seventy-Fifth Regiment where he was promoted to the rank of lieutenant colonel, serving until 1789, when he returned to Ireland with his second wife.[46]

In many ways, the captains exhibited the aspirational form of manhood that was typical of the eighteenth-century Anglo Atlantic. Each did his duty to king and country, then started a family. They were undoubtedly heterosexual and launched homophobic attacks against any man who did not live up to their expectations. It was not an unusual version of manhood at the time. It was sharply competitive and loyal, marked by violence and a changed empire.

Conversely, Newburgh's allies left the service before the Declaration of Independence was signed and became patriotic citizens of the United States. By the time he was forced out of the British army, Alexander Fowler had already made plans for a civilian life. Nine days before the battle at Lexington, he purchased a thousand acres in West Florida, and later, he acquired land in Virginia and Pennsylvania. With his wife, Frances, Fowler returned to England to clear his name. He sued General Gage and published the transcript of his case against Payne in an English newspaper. The couple then traveled to France before returning to America.[47]

Fowler's name appeared in the journals of the Continental Congress in February 1779, when he was elected one of two "auditors in the army." He continued to serve the US government in this capacity until the Revolutionary War ended, by which point he had moved to Pittsburgh, had at least two sons, and set up a dry goods store. His business failed, but Fowler was a proud citizen of the new republic. He was appointed brigadier general in the Pennsylvania militia and stood for public office as a member of Thomas Jefferson's Democratic-Republican Party. Shortly before his death in 1806, Fowler sought subscribers for his memoirs, which were titled *The Republican Beacon*. Although it appears that the book was never published, in a newspaper advertisement for it, Fowler reflected on why he had been cashiered from the Eighteenth Regiment: "altho' he suffered a political martyrdom, he had no cause to regret, for America became Independent, and he enjoyed the pleasing consolation of living and dying a Free Man."[48]

Nicholas Trist also left the British army and became a US citizen, but his path was less straightforward. He was promoted to lieutenant in May 1775 but resigned his commission three months later. Trist then headed to Louisiana to start a plantation near Manchac. His wife and son remained in Philadelphia until the Treaty of Paris finally ended the Revolution. In December 1783, Elizabeth and Hore headed west to rejoin Nicholas, rooming with the Fowlers in Pittsburgh and reaffirming a friendship that had once centered around their defense of

Robert Newburgh. Elizabeth Trist did not reach Manchac until July 1784, by which time her husband had died. She subsequently sold off the Louisiana property and returned to Philadelphia, where she befriended Thomas Jefferson, James Madison, and other national leaders. In 1823, Elizabeth Trist moved to Virginia and became a permanent guest of Jefferson's. When she died five years later, she was buried at Monticello in an unmarked grave. Trist's grandson, also named Nicholas, negotiated the Treaty of Guadalupe Hidalgo that ended the Mexican-American War in 1848.[49]

In contrast to the captains, the former subalterns exhibited a more distinctively American variety of manhood. Both Fowler and Trist headed west; with neither inheritances nor titles, they sought to make a living in the backcountry. Both entered growing sectors of the new nation's economy—Fowler became a merchant and Trist a planter—although both failed at these endeavors. They also married and fathered sons, and perhaps they instilled in them the vision of a more hopeful future. Both gravitated toward Republican politics as well. Fowler's ambition to become a US Congressman was thwarted by western Pennsylvania politicking. He wrote to President Jefferson for patronage, and cited Elizabeth Trist as a character witness. In the end, Fowler was a fierce proponent of liberty, outpaced only by Mrs. Trist in such opinions.[50]

Not all of Newburgh's confidantes became Jeffersonians. Robert Collins of the Royal Artillery remained loyal to the Crown and was promoted to captain lieutenant in 1779. Collins had chided Fowler for openly flirting with the Sons of Liberty, and that likely ended their friendship. He left the British army the following year and thereafter disappears from the historical record.[51]

Newburgh's fellow Anglican clergymen in Philadelphia danced on both sides of the loyalty divide. William Stringer remained loyal, even preaching a sermon based on Ezekiel

20:38: "I will purge out the rebels from among you and those that transgress." When the British evacuated Philadelphia for the second time in 1778, he went with them and lived out his life in London. Jacob Duché from Christ Church continued as chaplain to the Continental Congress until he publicly advised George Washington to abandon the American cause and had to flee to England. But Duché returned to Philadelphia after the war ended and became a US citizen. William White, who had once been compared to a macaroni, sided with the United States, and became the first presiding bishop of the Protestant Episcopal Church in America.[52]

We know little about what became of the enlisted men who interacted with Newburgh. Presumably, some were killed in the war like Private Russell, while others like Private Lee became Americans. Others went back to Ireland and England. It is unclear which path John Green or Nicholas Gaffney took. Like most men, they just fade away.

Robert Newburgh's life after the Eighteenth Regiment combined loyalty, independence, and obscurity. Having sailed for England in the spring of 1775, he returned to Ireland and reconnected with family scattered around the island. We do not know if the rumors of buggery persisted after three years or if he reconnected with the foster brother-cum-servant whom he had been accused of sleeping with. This would have been the ideal moment to retire from the army and settle down in an Irish parish. Perhaps rumors made this impossible, or maybe he preferred army life and the opportunities it presented for male-male intimacy.

Indeed, unlike Fowler, Trist, and Collins, Newburgh did not resign his commission, but traded it with Thomas Daliston, chaplain to the Fifteenth Regiment, in April 1776. A man named Thomas Newburgh also purchased an ensigncy in the same unit that same year. Newburgh was an unusual name for British officers in 1776, and so it is possible that this was a relative of Robert's, perhaps his brother Thomas Wrey, a nephew, or maybe even his foster brother. The Fifteenth Regiment was in America at the time, and so once again, Newburgh crossed the Atlantic to minister to redcoats. In July 1776, the Fifteenth Regiment was part of the British invasion of New York City, and a year later, it participated in the occupation of Philadelphia. Newburgh should have been present in both events, which would have returned him first to the Upper Barracks where his court-martial took place and then to the Philadelphia barracks where his legal problems began. The Fifteenth Regiment evacuated Philadelphia in 1778 and sparred with the Continental Army at Monmouth before sailing for the Caribbean. There, Newburgh ministered to men injured in the battles of St. Lucia, St. Vincent, and Grenada.[53]

On July 9, 1779, three days after the decisive British defeat at the Battle of Grenada, Newburgh sold his commission to William Chester and retired to half-pay. He was only thirty-six when he left the army. Thomas Newburgh also departed the Fifteenth Regiment at the same time, which further bolsters the case for a familial relationship. Once again, Robert Newburgh traded his chaplaincy, this time taking a position as a hospital chaplain at Belle-Île-en-Mer, a small island off the coast of Brittany. Belle-Île had briefly been held by Britain during the Seven Years' War, but since 1763, it had been a French territory. The British rendered it "Belleisle Garrison," and it was one of their overseas hospitals, like those in Germany, Portugal, and Havana.[54]

Belleisle was a sinecure that Newburgh profited from but did not reside at; his distinctive signature appears on Irish documents and correspondence for the next fifty years. In 1797, he witnessed a contract for his brothers, Broghill and Arthur, in County Cavan, and twenty years later, he addressed a letter from Londonderry. In September 1822, Newburgh wrote to George Canning, then MP for Liverpool and British foreign secretary (and later prime minister), on behalf of someone who sought a government position:

> in Complyance with the Request of A Person for whom I am much interested. There is an Establishment of A Water Guard to prevent Smuggling on this Coast. The Pay is very good, of Course the Object of many young Men. There is A Man whose Name is Carey Cook, A Protestant and I have known him and his Parents many years. He is very correct in morals and Behaviour, and wishes to be appointed in that Situation.

It is unclear who Carey Cook was or how Robert Newburgh knew his family. Even more curious is why this eighty-year-old had taken an interest in a young man. Certainly, the letter was a testament of character to help Cook find work, much like the recommendations that Newburgh had sought fifty years earlier to advance his own career. Yet, given the rumors that circulated, it is difficult to read his fawning praise of "A Person I am much interested" as entirely innocent.[55]

Three years later, on December 31, 1825, Robert Newburgh died, still listed as "Chaplain Newburgh" at "Belleisle Garrison." Officially, Newburgh ended his life exiled to France much like reputed buggerers Isaac Bickerstaff, Samuel Foote, and Robert Jones. The former chaplain's life after the Eighteenth Regiment took a different route than either the captains or the subalterns. He never married nor had children; he neither settled down in England nor pioneered a new life on the American frontier. Instead, Robert Newburgh's manhood was queer, and it followed a separate path.[56]

I Imagined All Those Old Prejudices Were Exploded

IN OCTOBER 2019, I was in Center City Philadelphia to give a talk about a recent book. It was a lovely lunchtime lecture, and afterward, I decided to enjoy the crisp, sunny afternoon. I set out walking from the place where the Declaration of Independence was signed and headed north about a mile to the City Archive.

By that point, I had tracked down most of Robert Newburgh's trial transcripts in Ann Arbor and London, but I was still missing his civil suit against Thomas Batt. I doubted that there ever had been a transcript of the proceedings, but I was hopeful there might be an entry in a ledger. Maybe it would give me some dates to work with. When I got to the City Archive, the very helpful staff informed me that those records were at City Hall. I wasn't sure whether they sincerely thought that this was the case or if they were just trying to get rid of me, but either way, I took their advice. Still enjoying the day, I walked down Spring Garden to Second Street. On this site, the massive Philadelphia barracks once stood. Here, Reverend Newburgh first sought justice in a military court. No trace of the barracks remains, only condos and abandoned bars. But I found a taxi to take me to my next destination. City Hall, of course, did not possess any eighteenth-century civil court records. I was not surprised, but I was disappointed. There was no trace of Newburgh left in Philadelphia. No archival evidence or physical reminder that in this city the British army had paused on the eve of the American Revolution to contemplate whether the parson was a buggerer.

Conceding defeat, I headed down Thirteenth Street in search of a gay bar, deciding that a cocktail would be a fitting way to end the day. As I sipped my martini at U Bar, I thought of how, as a historian, I was saddened I could not find a record of my subject. But I also reflected on how, as a gay man in 2019, I had opportunities that no Philadelphia buggerer had in 1774. So much had been lost yet so much gained in the two and a half centuries since Newburgh's trials.

❖ ❖ ❖

What are we to make of Robert Newburgh? On the one hand, his court-martial confirms our worst expectations of the past as overflowing with hatred and homophobia. Thomas Batt thought a rumor of buggery was sufficient for Newburgh to lose his position, while Captain Chapman cited his appearance as proof of sexual desires. And this revulsion was felt widely; enlisted men scorned Newburgh and the captains refused to associate with him, all because of what they had heard. The most sympathetic responses came from Lieutenant Fowler, who threatened to abandon Newburgh if he did not deny the charges, and General Gage, who wished the whole matter would just go away. Given the long history of discrimination against LGBTQ+ people, is any of this really surprising?

On the other hand, there are aspects of the trials that subvert such a pessimistic view of the past. Newburgh's response to the accusations against him is no doubt the most surprising. Many high-profile men accused of buggery in the eighteenth century quietly accepted public ridicule and fled to France, but

Newburgh faced his accusers and launched lawsuits. He also invoked a language of liberty and equality to argue for his innocence, even though such claims only confirmed suspicions about his character. The loyalty of the subalterns and their wives is also remarkable. They knew the rumors about what he might have done and had observed who he was, but they vigorously defended the chaplain anyway. We should find this surprising.

In the eighteenth century, homosexuality was a controversial topic, and people had different opinions about it. Some thought that buggerers should be put to death, and others simply laughed at them; some ignored them, and others wondered if their sexual acts should exclude them from civil society. This debate was integral to eighteenth-century Anglo Atlantic culture and is not wholly foreign in our own times. Although the discourse has changed, we continue to struggle over the inclusion of LGBTQ+ people in ways that echo Newburgh's 1774 court-martial.

We might also see Robert Newburgh and his trials as occurring at a moment of profound change in the history of male-male intimacy. The mollies and macaroni of the eighteenth century brought visibility to buggerers, and the Enlightenment at least raised the possibility that these men should not be persecuted. Jeremy Bentham scrutinized sodomy among the ancient Greeks, yet he "found no reason for punishing it at all." Sexual liberalism appealed to revolutionary France, and laws against sodomy were eliminated in the Code Napoléon. The Netherlands followed suit, constituting a deliberate effort to decriminalize buggery across Europe.[1]

By the middle of the nineteenth century, the notion that some men desired other men expanded from being a character trait to a defining aspect of one's identity. In the 1860s, Karl-Maria Kertbeny devised the term *homosexual* to pathologize same-sex desire, and his work was expanded on by Karl Ulrichs,

Richard von Krafft-Ebing, and Havelock Ellis. As these and other sexologists theorized about sexual desire, they argued that it was futile and even cruel for the state to punish men for acting on their natural urges. In the twentieth century, sexuality became an identity much like race or gender. Once the gay man was akin to an African American or a woman, he could demand an end to the laws that discriminated against him.[2]

Yet the push for homosexual acceptance also had its detractors. Sodomy was a capital crime throughout the British Empire in the 1770s, and it remained against the law in the United States, Great Britain, and Ireland for another two centuries. In much of Europe, the calls of sexologists to destigmatize buggery fell on deaf ears. With unification in 1871, Germany promulgated the anti-homosexual legal code known as Paragraph 175. Psychoanalysis pioneered by Sigmund Freud and others dismissed same-sex desire as a developmental stage that healthy heterosexuals grew out of. The repression of men who had sex with men intensified in the twentieth century as a host of laws and regulations were introduced to prevent homosexuals from attaining full citizenship.[3]

If we think of Newburgh's trials as a moment in the history of homosexuality, they share many similarities with the history of abolitionism and other efforts to achieve individual liberty. Criticism of slavery can be found throughout the eighteenth century, but it was only in the 1770s and 1780s that these ideas resulted in changes to the law. The *Somerset* decision of 1772 abolished enslavement in England, and this was followed less than a decade later in America by emancipation rulings and laws in the Northern states. Looking back, we can appreciate how this moment laid the groundwork for ending the slave trade and complete abolition, even though resistance to ending slavery continued for another century.[4]

Newburgh's trials thus compel us to recognize that LGBTQ+ people are not a recent addition to the history of the West; nor is the struggle for their rights something that only began with the Stonewall Riots of 1969. Men who desired men particularly—and queer individuals generally—were present in the eighteenth century even if what they were called and how they acted bears some distance from our own experience.

❖ ❖ ❖

We also cannot avoid placing Newburgh's trials in the context of the American Revolution. The captains had suspicions that a colonial rebellion was imminent, and they perceived this as a threat to the divine order. They found manifestations of colonial rebellion in the impudence of Private Gaffney and traitorous allegiances like Ensign Trist's marriage. They linked these fears to Newburgh and buggery, meaning that there was often little distance between the captains' views of revolution and homosexuality.

Conversely, the critique of imperial mismanagement and British morality that presaged American independence meant that those loyal to Newburgh were more likely to overlook the rumors. The subalterns were sympathetic to Newburgh's appeals for liberty and equality despite—or perhaps because—these were the same sentiments mouthed by the Patriots. Although Robert Newburgh was neither an American nor a revolutionary, his trials were part of the same historical process that produced the United States of America.

We might also see Newburgh's case as evidence of a divergence of British and American opinion about same-sex desire. Advocates for freedom and repression appeared on both sides of the Atlantic in the nineteenth century, but Britain generally sought to persecute buggerers while the United States tended to ignore them. In this way, the political divergence that appeared at Newburgh's court-martial was a harbinger of an British-American split on homosexuality.

In Great Britain, Bentham's defense of buggerers proved to be a fleeting impulse. Prosecutions for men who had sex with men increased notably after 1780. At the Old Bailey, there were only twenty-four indictments for sodomy and related offenses between 1756 and 1779, but thirty-five over the next decade and fourteen in 1798 alone. This continued into the nineteenth century such that in the 1840s, more than 150 men were committed each year for gross indecency between men and other sodomitical crimes. Executions for buggery averaged two per year from 1806 to 1835, which was far higher than death rates for other capital crimes.[5]

The increase in prosecutions was brought about in part by aggressive changes in the law. Since the sixteenth century, sodomy had been legally defined as requiring both penetration and emission, but in 1828, Parliament amended the law to stipulate that the ejaculation of semen was no longer required to convict a man of sodomy. The Larceny (England) Act of 1827 also expanded the definition of homosexual acts, declaring all attempts at buggery including "Solicitation, Persuasion, Promise, or Threat" of sodomy to be crimes deserving of capital punishment.[6]

In 1861, Parliament replaced execution for buggery with penal servitude of ten years to life, although this did little to hinder prosecutions. The infamous Labouchère Amendment of 1885 reiterated that any attempt "by any male person of any act of gross indecency with another male person" could result in imprisonment up to two years regardless of whether the incident took place "in public or private." A decade later, Oscar Wilde was convicted of sodomy under the Labouchère Amendment. His trial attracted worldwide attention, eclipsing the eighteenth-century trials of Captain Robert Jones and other suspected buggerers.[7]

Homosexuality in nineteenth-century Britain was a constant cycle of exposure and prosecution. The more visible buggerers became, the more they were prosecuted; and the more they were prosecuted, the more visible they became. Historians have speculated as to why Britain was so obsessed with male-male intimacy in the nineteenth century, often putting gender fears at the center of this. Growing political equality may have led to a demand for greater gender essentialism and inequality, and this made homosexuals particularly problematic. It was largely through appearing as respectable and masculine that homosexuals were able to gain acceptance in British society. In effect, they escaped prosecution by disappearing into the closet.[8]

Ireland largely emulated British treatment of homosexuals in the nineteenth century. The Irish press covered same-sex scandals much like the English. Three years before Robert Newburgh died, perceptions of the church and army as bastions of buggery resurfaced when the Anglican Bishop of Clogher was caught having sex with a British soldier. High-profile scandals involving British officials at Dublin Castle followed in the 1880s with considerable interest on both sides of the Irish Sea. Numerous Irishmen were prosecuted for attempted sodomy and similar crimes including Oscar Wilde.[9]

However, Ireland's quest to escape from the United Kingdom also affected how the Irish saw homosexuality. Irish nationalists resurrected the old canard that sodomy was an English import and used this cudgel to embarrass the imperialists. Nationalist newspapers liberally covered buggery prosecutions in England while insisting that the offense was negligible in Ireland. When three English railway workers accused a Dublin police magistrate of sodomy in 1845, the newspapers came to his defense, arguing for his innocence because such crimes were unimaginable to the Irish. Even Wilde received a sympathetic portrayal in the Irish press, which insisted that he had been singled out for prosecution only because of England's hatred of Ireland.[10]

The United States diverged from Britain's harsh repression of buggerers. Historians have repeatedly marveled at the

unwillingness of early Americans to emulate their British brethren when it came to homosexuality. Instead, there was a tacit
toleration and willful ignoring of male-male intimacy during the
colonial era that persisted into the nineteenth century. As the
trials of Robert Newburgh suggest, the ideals of the Enlightenment strengthened these tendencies such that the American
Revolution established a sexual liberalism that was absent in
England.[11]

Allegations of buggery appeared in the United States at its
beginning. At Valley Forge in early 1778, in the throes of the
American Revolutionary War, Continental Army Lieutenant
Frederick Gotthold Enslin was court-martialed "for attempting
to commit *sodomy*, with John Monhort a soldier." Monhort was
the unwilling recipient of Enslin's advances, which made the
case more serious than if the two men had been caught in fla-
grante delicto. Enslin attempted to deny the charges under oath,
but this only furthered the case against him. Ultimately, General
George Washington approved a sentence that drummed Enslin
out of the corps for both attempted sodomy and perjury.[12]

But Valley Forge was also where Frederich Wilhelm, Baron
von Steuben, joined the American Revolution and taught the
Continental soldiers how to drill like a proper army. Steuben
had been a captain in the Prussian army but was forced to flee
when rumors emerged that he had "taken familiarities with
young boys." Once he joined the American army, Steuben de-
veloped unusually intimate relationships with several aides-de-
camps. If Benjamin Franklin, who brought Steuben to America,
knew of the rumors, he did not care. Nor did Washington.[13]

The twin cases of Enslin and Steuben suggest that General
Washington and the US Army were content to tolerate buggerers so long as their buggery did not become disruptive. While
Washington's ambivalence mirrored Gage's, there was a notice-
able absence of officers among the Continental army who dog-
gedly pursued rumors and innuendos when a man's sexual ten-

dencies were revealed. If there were men like Chapman, Payne, and Batt in the American army, the corps never court-martialed Steuben or anyone else for sexual character alone.

The lack of interest in prosecuting homosexuality was consistent with the highest ideals of the new republic. Following independence, the Americans took several opportunities to reject the cruel and unusual punishment that Britons had imposed on men who had sex with men. When a congressional committee that included John Adams adopted rules and regulations for a US Navy, they conspicuously left sodomy out of the list of offenses. The committee borrowed most of the regulations from the Royal Navy, which explicitly named buggery as a crime; thus, the omission had to be intentional. Similarly, when Thomas Jefferson proposed a revision to the laws of Virginia in 1779, he advocated for sodomy to no longer be a capital crime, recommending castration instead. Seven years later, the Commonwealth of Pennsylvania put Jefferson's suggestion into effect and abolished the death penalty for "sodomy or buggery."[14]

While same-sex sex remained against the law in most states, Americans never prosecuted buggerers at rates comparable to Britain. In the country's largest city, New York, there were only twenty-two indictments for sodomy between 1796 and 1873, nearly all of which involved violence or sex with minors. Nor did Americans share Britons' taste for homosexual scandals. Although newspapers carried salacious gossip about how James Buchanan and William Rufus King were known as "Miss Nancy," this did not inhibit these men's election to the two highest offices in the land. Perhaps American lack of concern about same-sex relations helps to explain why Walt Whitman's homoerotic *Leaves of Grass* received not censure but praise.[15]

While the American Revolution alone does not explain the divergence of British and American opinions on homosexuality, the political division of the two nations crystalized these differences in profound ways. In the United States, the

Enlightenment's promise of freedom from governmental intrusion and individual rights became part of the nation's creed. Conversely, Britain, which did not have a revolution in the eighteenth century, was less bound by the Enlightenment's demand for laissez-faire governance and personal freedom.

During the twentieth century, however, the United States became a lot more British. While Britain's persecution of sodomites continued, destroying the life of Alan Turing despite his utility to the war effort against the Nazis, the US joined in a harsh rebuke of men who had sex with men. As the apparatus of the federal government increased in size and power, the nation became hostile to homosexual immigrants, welfare recipients, and soldiers. In the heyday of America's communist hysteria, men perceived to be gay were fired from the government and private industry out of fears that their sexual orientation rendered them traitors to a nation locked in a Cold War. Indeed, the push for gay rights in Britain and America during the second half of the twentieth century was largely one movement: Britain decriminalized sodomy in 1967 only two years before the Stonewall Riots in New York. In the 2010s, gay marriage arrived in the United Kingdom, the United States, and the Republic of Ireland virtually simultaneously.[16]

This is not to say that Robert Newburgh lived in an era of acceptance or even tolerance. He himself denied that he was a buggerer, and maybe he was telling the truth, but the persecution he faced was far worse than what most gay men face today. Yet this does not diminish the fact that when he was accused of buggery, he was able to access a rhetoric of rights and attract the support of friends that might not have been available to him had not the American Revolution been growing around him. In this way, the true significance of Newburgh's trials is not lost like the Philadelphia barracks or records from a civil case. At its creation, the United States inherently included a place for LGBTQ+ people.

ACKNOWLEDGMENTS

WRITING THIS BOOK HAS BEEN AN INCREDIBLY POWERFUL and personal experience. I thought I was well versed in the histories of homosexuality and the American Revolution, but it has caused me to think of both in new ways. Beyond its contribution to scholarship, however, I hope that *Vicious and Immoral* will offer hope to those who look to the past.

Many people have helped me research, write, and revise this book, and I am grateful to them all. Helmut Puff and Ann Little read early drafts of the manuscript and offered key insights that strengthened it. Maurizio Valsania offered prompt and helpful advice.

Daniel Polley and Collin Ganio translated sources from French and Latin, respectively, and provided valuable context.

Steve Baule knows the Eighteenth Regiment better than anyone and explained the intricacies of British courts-martial to me. Don Hagist corrected my misperception that Robert Newburgh was a lieutenant.

Three Eastern Michigan University graduate assistants transcribed hundreds of pages of courts-martial and tracked down numerous books and articles. The hard work of Daniel Bowlin, Isaac Klooster, and Justice Carlton made writing this book possible.

I benefited from conversations with Philip Abraham, Mary Bilder, John Carson, James Dator, Joe Dooley, Greg Dowd, Kristen Foster, Debbie Gershenowitz, Lorri Glover, Jessica Gregory, David Hancock, Kate Haulman, Rachel Hermann, Greta LaFleur, Scott Larson, Janet Lindman, Clare Lyons, Ben Marsh, Matthew McCormack, Adam McNeil, Laura Migliorino, Catherine Molineaux, Molly Nebiolo, Angel-Luke O'Donnell, Ami Pflugrad-Jackisch, Sandy Slater, and Matthew Spooner.

It was my pleasure to research this book at the British Library, the Historical Society of Pennsylvania, the National Library of Ireland, the

William L. Clements Library at the University of Michigan—Ann Arbor, and the UK National Archives at Kew.

Research for this project was funded by Eastern Michigan University, the James H. Brickley Endowment for Faculty Professional Development and Innovation at EMU, the Eccles Centre for American Studies at the British Library, and the Georgian Papers Programme at the Omohundro Institute of Early American History and Culture.

I presented preliminary versions of this research to meetings of the European Early American Studies Association, the Omohundro Institute of Early American History and Culture, the Michigan Early Atlantic Seminar, the American Philosophical Society, the Georgian Papers Programme, the British Library, and the Organization of American Historians.

Images for this book were provided by the British Library, the British Museum, the Brown University Library's Digital Repository, Hugh Evelyn Prints, the Library of Congress, the National Trust, and the Society of the Cincinnati. The maps were drawn by Jacqueline R. Alessi and include locations that George Boudreau and Karie Diethorn helped me figure out. I also thank Alexis Braun Marks for the use of the EMU Archives camera.

I am happy to have wonderful colleagues in the History Section at EMU, especially Ashley Johnson Bavery, Jim Egge, Jesse Kauffman, Mary-Elizabeth Murphy, and Steven Ramold. I am also blessed to be surrounded by wonderful friends and family, including George Boudreau, Joe Burman, Suzanne Davis and Collin Ganio, Damian Evilsizor, Dario Gaggio, Kit French, David Hancock, Anne Kirk, Gary Kotraba, Ann Little, Marcia McCrary, Beverly McCurdy, Gerald and Ann Mora, Marie Mora and Alberto Davila, Helmut Puff, Matthew Richardson and Doug Konja, Doug Ross and Larry Barker, Sinderella, JoAnn Kennedy Slater, and Elizabeth Taylor.

I am especially grateful to my agent, Christopher Rogers, for finding me a publisher, and for the exceptional work of the editors and staff at Johns Hopkins University Press, including Laura Davulis, Ezra Rodriguez, and Charles Dibble.

I could not have finished this book without the love and support of my friend Anthony Mora. Thank you, Anthony, for listening to me complain about this book for many years.

I am also indebted to Robert Newburgh. Sometimes I felt as though he was haunting me through this entire process. I hope that I have done justice to his story and that he would forgive me for making the most embarrassing and trying ordeal of his life into a book.

Finally, I dedicate this book to a person who has been my best friend for thirty years and who appreciates better than most the joys of Anglicanism and buggery: Daniel Polley.

NOTES

Abbreviations

AFC *Adams Family Correspondence*. Edited by L. H. Butterfield. 2 vols.
  Cambridge: Harvard University Press, 1963.

BL The British Library, London.

DAB *Dictionary of American Biography*. 20 volumes. New York: Scribner's
  Sons, 1928–1936.

DNB *Dictionary of National Biography*. Edited by Leslie Stephen and
  Sidney Lee. First edition. 63 volumes. London: Smith, Elder,
  1885–1900.

FCM Fowler Court-Martial. Proceedings of a General Court Martial,
  Boston, [August 1775]. Judge Advocate General's Office: Court
  Martial Proceedings and Board of General Officers' Minutes, 1775.
  WO 71/146, NAK.

FHP Frederick Haldimand Papers. Western Manuscripts, BL.

GGCM Gaffney and Green Courts-Martial. Proceedings of a General
  Court Martial, Perth Amboy, New Jersey, May 21–June 3, 1774.
  Judge Advocate General's Office: Court Martial Correspondence and
  Board of General Officers' Minutes, October 1773–October 1774
  Oct. WO 71/79, NAK.

GWP *The Papers of George Washington: Revolutionary War Series*. 29 volumes.
  Edited by David R. Hoth et al. Charlottesville: University of Virginia
  Press, 1985–2022.

JADA *Diary and Autobiography of John Adams*. Edited by L. H. Butterfield.
  2 volumes. Cambridge: Harvard University Press, 1961.

JCC *Journals of the Continental Congress, 1774–1789*. 33 volumes. Washington: US Government Printing Office, 1904–1937.

JHS *Journal of the History of Sexuality*, 1990–present.

MaCM Mawby Court-Martial. Proceedings of a General Court Martial, Perth Amboy, New Jersey [May 26–27, 1774]. Judge Advocate General's Office: Courts Martial Correspondence and Papers, 1771–1776. WO 72/7/34, NAK.

McCM McDermott Court Martial. Proceedings of a General Court-Martial, New Brunswick, New Jersey, October 4–16, 1773. Judge Advocate General's Office: Court Martial Correspondence and Board of General Officers' Minutes, October 1773–October 1774. WO 71/79, NAK.

MR 18th Foot 1st Battalion (1767–1780). General Muster Books and Pay Lists. WO 12/3501, NAK.

NAK The National Archives, Kew.

NCE Newburgh Court of Enquiry. Proceedings of the Court of Enquiry, Philadelphia, April 12–21, 1774. Enclosure in Haldimand to Gage, June 26, 1774. TGP-AS 120.

NCM Newburgh Court-Martial. Proceedings of a General Court Martial, New York, August 8–27, 1774. Judge Advocate General's Office: Court Martial Proceedings and Board of General Officers' Minutes, 1774. WO 71/145, NAK.

NJD *Documents Relating to the Colonial History of the State of New Jersey. New Jersey State Archives*. First series. Edited by William Whitehead et al. 42 volumes. Newark: Daily Journal et al., 1880–1949.

NLI National Library of Ireland, Dublin.

PA *Pennsylvania Archives*. Colonial Records and First to Ninth Series. 136 volumes. Harrisburg: Severns et al., 1838–1935.

PAMC *Minutes of the Provincial Council of Pennsylvania, From the Organization to the Termination of the Proprietary Government*. 10 volumes. Philadelphia: Severns, et al., 1838–52.

PASL *The Statutes at Large of Pennsylvania from 1682 to 1801*. Edited by James T. Mitchell and Henry Flanders. 17 volumes. Harrisburg, PA: Busch et al., 1896–1915.

PCM Payne Court-Martial: Proceedings of a General Court Martial, Boston, 28 July–10 August 1775, in Judge Advocate General's Office: Court Martial Proceedings and Board of General Officers' Minutes, 1775, WO 71/146, NAK.

TGP-AS Thomas Gage Papers, American Series. WLCL.

TGP-ES Thomas Gage Papers, English Series. WLCL.

TJP *The Papers of Thomas Jefferson*. Edited by Julian P. Boyd, et al. 45 volumes. Princeton: Princeton University Press, 1950–2021.

WLCL William L. Clements Library, University of Michigan. Ann Arbor, Michigan.

WMQ *William and Mary Quarterly*. 3d series. 1944-present.

WO War Office, NAK.

Note: Several pages in GGCM, FCM, NCM, and WO 72/7/31 are incorrectly numbered in the original versions. For clarity, I have given the page number stated on the document with sequential page number in brackets.

Notes

Prologue: The Parson Is a Buggerer

1. NCM, p. 1.
2. Jonathan Ned Katz, *The Invention of Heterosexuality* (New York: Dutton, 1995), 52–54.
3. Paul E. Kopperman, "Religion and Religious Policy in the British Army, c. 1700–96," *Journal of Religious History* 14 (1987): 390–405; Steven M. Baule, *Protecting the Empire's Frontier: Officers of the 18th (Royal Irish) Regiment of Foot during Its North American Service, 1767–1776* (Athens: Ohio University Press, 2014), 213–17.
4. Charles Upchurch, "Liberal Exclusions and Sex between Men in the Modern Era: Speculations on a Framework," JHS 19 (2010): 409–31; Jeremy Bentham, "Offences Against One's Self: Paederesty," ed. Louis Crompton, *Journal of Homosexuality* 3 (1977): 389–406. See also Louis Crompton, *Byron and Greek Love: Homophobia in 19th-Century England* (Berkeley: University of California Press, 1985), 38–57; Rictor Norton, *Mother Clap's Molly House: The Gay Subculture, 1700–1830* (London: GMP, 1992), 119–22.
5. The Revolution is also conspicuously absent from works such as Jonathan Ned Katz, *Gay/Lesbian Almanac: A New Documentary* (New York: Carroll and Graf, 1983); John D'Emilio and Estelle B. Freedman, *Intimate Matters: A History of Sexuality in America*, 2nd ed. (Chicago: University of Chicago Press, 1997); Richard Godbeer,

Sexual Revolution in Early America (Baltimore: Johns Hopkins University Press, 2002). It receives short shrift in works such as Clare A. Lyons, "Mapping an Atlantic Sexual Culture: Homoeroticism in Eighteenth-Century Philadelphia," *WMQ* 60 (2003): 119–54; Thomas A. Foster, *Sex and the Eighteenth-Century Man: Massachusetts and the History of Sexuality in America* (Boston: Beacon Press, 2006); Michael Bronski, *A Queer History of the United States* (Boston: Beacon Press, 2011), 26–32. On the lack of sources, see William Benemann, *Male-Male Intimacy in Early America: Beyond Romantic Friendships* (New York: Harrington Park Press, 2006), x.

6. Michael S. Foldy, *The Trials of Oscar Wilde: Deviance, Morality, and Late-Victorian Society* (New Haven: Yale University Press, 1997); Merlin Holland, *The Real Trial of Oscar Wilde* (New York: HarperCollins, 2004).

7. H. G. Cocks, *Nameless Offences: Homosexual Desire in the Nineteenth Century* (London: Tauris, 2010), 6. See also William G. Naphy, "Reasonable Doubt: Defences Advanced in Early Modern Sodomy Trials in Geneva," in *Judicial Tribunals in England and Europe, 1200–1700: The Trial in History*, vol. 1, ed. Maureen Mulholland and Brian Pullan with Anne Pullan, 129–46 (Manchester: Manchester University Press, 2005).

Chapter One: A Native of Ireland

1. [Thomas Newburgh], *Essays Poetical, Moral and Critical* (Dublin: M'Culloh, 1769), 266. See also Sara Cullen, *Books and Authors of County Cavan: A Bibliography and an Essay* (Cavan: Cavan County Council, 1965), xiv, 42.

2. Louisa Mure, *Recollections of By-Gone Days* (1883), 109. See also *Essays Poetical*, 223–46, 264, 269.

3. *Essays Poetical*, 263. See also Philip Greven, *The Protestant Temperament: Patterns of Child-Rearing, Religious Experience, and the Self in Early America* (Chicago: University of Chicago Press, 1977), 45–46, 282–86.

4. Newburgh Defense, WO 72/7/30, p. 18.

5. NCM, p. 74. See also [Thomas Newburgh,] *Particulars Relating to the Life and Character of the Late Brockhill Newburgh, Esq.* (1761), 3–4; DNB, s.v. "Newburgh, Neubourg, or Beaumont, Henry de"; Frank Barlow, *The Feudal Kingdom of England, 1042–1216*, 4th ed. (London: Longman, 1988), 180–81.

6. *Particulars of Brockhill Newburgh*, 4–8; Raymon Gillespie, ed., *Cavan: Essays on the History of an Irish County* (Dublin: Irish Academic Press, 1995); *Ballyhaise Agricultural College, 1906–2006: Including a History of Ballyhaise House and Estate from 1610* (Ballyhaise: Ballyhaise Agricultural College, 2006), 1–7; Brendan Scott, *Cavan, 1609–53: Plantation, War and Religion* (Dublin: Four Courts Press, 2007); Brendan Scott, ed., *Culture and Society in Early Modern Breifne/Cavan* (Portland, Ore.: Four Courts Press, 2009); R. J. Hunter, *The Ulster Plantation in the Counties of Armagh and Cavan, 1608–41* (Belfast: Ulster Historical Foundation, 2012).

7. Richard Mant, *History of the Church of Ireland, from the Revolution to the Union of the Churches of England and Ireland, January 1, 1801* (London: Parker, 1840); Donald Harman Akenson, *The Church of Ireland: Ecclesiatical Reform and Revolution, 1800–85* (New Haven: Yale University Press, 1971); T. W. Moody and W. E. Vaughan, eds., *A New History of Ireland: IV, Eighteenth-Century Ireland, 1691–1800* (Oxford: Oxford University Press, 1984), 31; Alan Acheson, *A History of the Church of Ireland, 1691–2001* (Dublin: Columba Press, 1997); James Kelly, ed., *The Cambridge History of Ireland: Volume III, 1730–1880* (Cambridge: Cambridge University Press, 2018), 206–9.

8. Moody and Vaughan, *New History of Ireland*, 34, 44, 82–83; Lawrence Henry Gipson, *The British Isles and the American Colonies: Great Britain and Ireland, 1748–54* (New York: Knopf, 1968), 185–238; James Douet, *British Barracks, 1600–1914: Their Architecture and Role in Society* (London: Stationery Office Books, 1997), 15, 29–34; Stephen Conway, *War, State, and Society in Mid-Eighteenth-Century Britain and Ireland* (Oxford: Oxford University Press, 2006), 140–41; Martyn J. Powell, "The Army in Ireland and the Eighteenth-Century Press: Antimilitary Sentiment in an Atlantic Context," *Éire-Ireland* 50 (2015): 138–72; Timothy D. Watt, "Taxation Riots and the Culture of Popular Protest in Ireland, 1714–40," *English Historical Review* 130 (2016): 1418–48; "Army Barracks of Eighteenth-Century Ireland," *Mapping State and Society in Eighteenth-Century Ireland*, School of History and Archives, University College Dublin, <www.barracks18c.ucd.ie/>.

9. *Particulars of Brockhill Newburgh*, 8. See also *Journals of the House of Commons of the Kingdom of Ireland*, 23 vols. (Dublin: House of Commons, 1763–65), 4: 4, 27, 38, 288, 470, 482, 686; 5: 2, 226; *Particulars of Brockhill Newburgh*, 18. The current Castleterra church,

Drung Parish, was built in 1820, incorporating parts of Brockhill Newburgh's "Family Gallery." Church of Ireland, "Castleterra, Ballyhaise," <www.gloine.ie/search/building/3057/castleterra>.

10. *Particulars of Brockhill Newburgh*, 13, 18; Charles Coote, *Statistical Survey of the County of Cavan, with Observations on the Means of Improvement* (Dublin: Graisberry and Campbell, 1802), 101. See also *Ballyhaise Agricultural College*, 15–19; Moody and Vaughan, *New History of Ireland*, 488; Gillian Darley, *Villages of Vision* (London: Architectural Press, 1975), 148; Jonathan Bardon, *The Plantation of Ulster: The British Colonisation of the North of Ireland in the Seventeenth Century* (Dublin: Gill Books, 2011), 322. Although Ballyhaise House was long thought to be designed by Richard Castle, recent work has established that the architect was Sir Edward Lovett Pearce. "Ballyhaise Agricultural College, Drumcrow (E.D. Ballyhaise), Ballyhaise, County Cavan," *National Inventory of Architectural Heritage*, Department of Culture, Heritage, and the Gaeltacht, <www.buildingsofireland.ie/buildings -search/building/40401620/ballyhaise-agricultural-college-drumcrow -e-d-ballyhaise-county-cavan>.

11. *Particulars Relating to Newburgh*, 23; W. Reynell, "Replies: High Sheriffs of Cavan," *Ulster Journal of Archaeology, Volume II* (Belfast: Ward, 1896), 143; Arthur Vicars, *Index to the Prerogative Wills of Ireland, 1536–1810* (Dublin: Ponsonby, 1897), 348; *Alumni Dublinenses: A Register of the Students, Graduates, Professors and Provosts of Trinity College in the University of Dublin (1593–1860)*, ed. George Dames Burtchaell and Thomas Ulick Sadleir, new ed. (Dublin: Thom, 1935), s.v. "Newburgh, Brockhill"; Papers Relating to the Families of Hutchins of Bantry, Co. Cork, Newburgh of Ballyhaise, Co. Cavan, and Tisdall, c1783–1863, MS 8685, NLI.

12. NCM, p. 76. See also John Burke, *A General and Heraldic Dictionary of the Peerage and Baronetage of the United Kingdom* (London: Colburn, 1826), s.v. "Enniskillen, Earl of"; James Edwin Cole, *The Genealogy of the Family of Cole* (London: Smith, 1867), 42–46, 50–53, 55–56; Edward McParland, "Florence Court, Co. Fermanagh," *Country Life* (1981): 1242–45, 1318–21; *Alumni Dublinenses*, s.v. "Cole, Henry"; Moody and Vaughan, *New History of Ireland*, 45.

13. Beaver H. Blacker, *Brief Sketches of the Parishes of Booterstown and Donnybrook, in the County of Dublin* (Dublin: Herbert, 1874), 273, 282; Francis Elrington Ball, *A History of the County Dublin, Part Second* (Dublin: Thom, 1903), 55; James Mills, *The Register of the Parish of*

S. Peter and S. Kevin, Dublin, 1669–1761 (Exeter: Pollard, 1911), 265; H. Bantry White, "An Old House at Donnybrook," *Journal of the Royal Society of Antiquaries of Ireland* 6th ser., 9 (1919): 149–52; Beatrice M. Doran, *Donnybrook: A History* (Dublin: History Press of Ireland, 2013).

14. P. W. Joyce, *A Smaller Social History of Ancient Ireland* (London: Longmans, Green, 1908), 286–87; Bronagh Ní Chonaill, "Foster-age: Child-Rearing in Medieval Ireland," *History Ireland* 5 (1997): 28–31; Peter Parkes, "Fosterage, Kinship, and Legend: When Milk Was Thicker Than Blood?" *Comparative Studies in Society and History* 46 (2004): 587–615; Lahney Preston-Matto, "Saints and Foster-age in Medieval Ireland: A Sanctified Social Practice," *Eolas: The Journal of the American Society of Irish Medieval Studies* 5 (2011): 62–78.

15. NCE, p. 17.

16. *Alumni Dublinenses*, s.v. "Newburgh, Robert"; Moody and Vaughan, *New History of Ireland*, 50.

17. David Dickson, *Arctic Ireland: The Extraordinary Story of the Great Frost and Forgotten Famine of 1740–41* (Belfast: White Row Press, 1997); L. M. Cullen, "The Irish Food Crises of the Early 1740s: An Eco-nomic Conjecture," *Irish Economic and Social History* 37 (2010): 1–23; Moody and Vaughan, *New History of Ireland*, 33–34; Kelly, *Cambridge History of Ireland*, 153–59, 210–13, 426–27.

18. *Particulars Relating to Newburgh*, 23–27; *Journals of the Commons*, 7: 387. See also Moody and Vaughan, *New History of Ireland*, 123–95; Kelly, *Cambridge History of Ireland*, 153–78, 213–18; *Ireland: Industrial and Agricultural* (Dublin: Browne and Nolan, 1902), 413–16; David Dickson, *New Foundations: Ireland, 1660–1800*, 2nd rev. ed. (Dublin: Irish Academic Press, 2000), 114.

19. Patrick Fagan, "The Population of Dublin in the Eighteenth Century with Particular Reference to the Proportions of Protestants and Catholics," *Eighteenth-Century Ireland* 6 (1991): 142; Moody and Vaughan, *New History of Ireland*, 57–66, 71–78; Kelly, *Cambridge History of Ireland*, 48–60.

20. NCM, pp. 42, 63; *Hibernia Curiosa: A Letter from a Gentleman in Dublin, to His Friend at Dover in Kent* (London: Flexney, 1769), 12; Esther K. Sheldon, *Thomas Sheridan of Smock-Alley, Recording His Life as Actor and Theater Manager in Both Dublin and London; and Including a Smock-Alley Calendar for the Years of His Management* (Princeton: Princeton University Press, 1967); Moody and Vaughan, *New*

History of Ireland, 44–45, 90; Michael Brown, *The Irish Enlightenment* (Cambridge: Harvard University Press, 2016), 212, 216–33, 270–76; Kelly, *Cambridge History of Ireland*, 465–75, 500–2.

21. Moody and Vaughan, *New History of Ireland*, 49–52. The Royal Barracks were renamed the Collins Barracks in 1922.

22. *Alumni Dublinenses*, s.v. "Newburgh, Robert."

23. Brown, *Irish Enlightenment*, 211; NCM, p. 85. See also NCE, 25; Kelly, *Cambridge History of Ireland*, 446–48; John William Stubbs, *The History of the University of Dublin, from Its Foundation to the End of the Eighteenth Century* (Dublin: Hodges, Figgis, 1889), 208; W. MacNeile Dixon, *Trinity College, Dublin* (London: Robinson, 1902); Sara Slinn, *The Education of the Anglican Clergy, 1780–1839* (Woodbridge: Boydell Press, 2017).

24. Brown, *Irish Enlightenment*, 73–85.

25. Quoted in Brown, *Irish Enlightenment*, 173. See also Katherine O'Donnell, "Burke and the Irish School of Oratory," *Studies in Burke and His Time* 21 (2007): 70–87.

26. Brown, *Irish Enlightenment*, 182, 211, 216, 245, 254–62, 285–87, 290–92; Moody and Vaughan, *New History of Ireland*, 105–22; David Hayton, "Anglo-Irish Attitudes: Changing Perceptions of National Identity among the Protestant Ascendancy in Ireland, ca. 1690–1750," *Studies in Eighteenth-Century Culture* 17 (1987): 145–57; Lesa Ní Mhunghaile, "Anglo-Irish Antiquarianism and the Transformation of Irish Identity, 1750–1800," in *Anglo-Irish Identities, 1571–1845*, ed. David A. Valone and Jill Marie Bradbury (Lewisburg: Bucknell University Press, 2008), 181–98; *Ireland and America: Empire, Revolution, and Sovereignty*, ed. Patrick Griffin and Francis D. Cogliano (Charlottesville: University of Virginia Press, 2021).

27. Stubbs, *History of the University*, 199. See also Louis Crompton, *Byron and Greek Love: Homophobia in 19th-Century England* (Berkeley: University of California Press, 1985), 85–98; Anna Clark, "Anne Lister's Construction of Lesbian Identity," JHS 7 (1996): 23–50; Charles Upchurch, *Before Wilde: Sex between Men in Britain's Age of Reform* (Berkeley: University of California Press, 2009), 50–52; Margaret C. Jacob, *The Secular Enlightenment* (Princeton: Princeton University Press, 2019), 247–48.

28. Blacker, *Brief Sketches*, 282. See also *Particulars of Brockhill Newburgh*, 25, 27; Blacker, *Brief Sketches*, 283; "List of Deaths for the Year 1762," *Gentleman's Magazine* (March 1762), 192; "List of Deaths for

the Year 1762," *Gentleman's Magazine* (May 1762), 310; Ball, *History of County Dublin*, 61; *Journals of the Commons*, 15: 373–97; *Dublin, Ireland, Probate Record and Marriage License Index, 1270–1858*, <www.ancestry.com>; "Flax Growers of Ireland, 1796—County Donegal," *Irish Flax Growers, 1796*, <www.failteromhat.com/flax1796.php>.

29. "List of Promotions for the Year 1762," *Gentleman's Magazine* (April 1762), 246; Kelly, *Cambridge History of Ireland*, 521.

30. NCM, pp. 46, 91[89].

31. *The Confession of Saint Patrick*, ed. and trans. D. R. Howlett (Liguori, Mo.: Triumph Books, 1994), 64. See also Brian Lacey, *Terrible Queer Creatures: Homosexuality in Irish History* (Dublin: Wordwell, 2008), 15–18.

32. Quoted in Lacey, *Terrible Queer Creatures*, 19. See also Lacey, *Terrible Queer Creatures*, 40–41, 51.

33. Quoted in *Medieval Handbooks of Penance: A Translation of the Principal Libri Poenitentiales and Selections from Related Documents*, ed. John T. McNeill and Helena M. Gamer (New York: Columbia University Press, 1938), 254. See also Lacey, *Terrible Queer Creatures*, 26–29.

34. *The Statutes at Large from Magna Charta to the End of the Eleventh Parliament of Great Britain, Anno 1761, [and Continued]*, ed. Danby Pickering, 46 vols. (Cambridge: Bentham, et al., 1762–1807), 25 Hen. VIII, c. 6; William Blackstone, *Commentaries on the Laws of England*, 16th ed., 4 vols. (London: Strahan, 1825), 4: 215. See also Barlow, *Feudal Kingdom of England*, 146–47; Crompton, *Byron and Greek Love*, 15–16; Upchurch, *Before Wilde*, 90–91; *Fleta: seu Commentarius Juris Anglicani*, ed. and trans. H. G. Richardson and G. O. Sayles (London: Quaritch, 1955); Jeffrey Weeks, *Coming Out: Homosexual Politics in Britain, from the Nineteenth Century to the Present* (London: Quartet, 1977), 12; John Boswell, *Christianity, Social Tolerance, and Homosexuality: Gay People in Western Europe from the Beginning of the Christian Era to the Fourteenth Century* (Chicago: University of Chicago Press, 1980); Rictor Norton, *Mother Clap's Molly House: The Gay Subculture in England, 1700–1830* (London: GMP, 1992), 15–22; *Sex and Sexuality in Anglo-Saxon England: Essays in Memory of Daniel Gilmore Calder*, ed. Carol Braun Pasternack and Lisa M. C. Weston (Tempe: Arizona State University Press, 2004); H. G. Cocks, *Nameless Offences: Homosexual Desire in the Nineteenth Century* (London: Tauris, 2010), 32–34; Peter Ackroyd, *Queer City: Gay London from the Romans to the Present Day* (London: Vintage, 2017), 41–42.

35. Cynthia B. Herrup, *A House in Gross Disorder: Sex, Law, and the 2nd Earl of Castlehaven* (New York: Oxford University Press, 1999), 11–12, 16–17; Lacey, *Terrible Queer Creatures*, 77–90.

36. Michael Kirby, "The Sodomy Offence: England's Least Lovely Criminal Law Export," in *Human Rights, Sexual Orientation and Gender Identity in the Commonwealth: Struggles for Decriminalization and Change*, ed. Corinne Lennox and Matthew Waites (London: Human Rights Consortium, 2013), 61–123; Averill Earls, "Unnatural Offenses of English Import: The Political Association of Englishness and Same-Sex Desire in Nineteenth-Century Irish Nationalist Media," JHS 28 (2019): 396–424; Lacey, *Terrible Queer Creatures*, 91–92. For more on homosexuality in Ireland, see Kelly, *Cambridge History of Ireland*, 231–54; *Reclaiming Gender: Transgressive Identities in Modern Ireland*, ed. Marilyn Cohen and Nancy J. Curtin (New York: St. Martin's Press, 1999); James Kim, "Goldsmith's Manhood: Hegemonic Masculinity and Sentimental Irony in *The Vicar of Wakefield*," *Eighteenth Century* 59 (2018): 21–44; Leanne Calvert, "'He Came to Her Bed Pretending Courtship': Sex, Courtship, and the Making of Marriage in Ulster, 1750–1844," *Irish Historical Studies* 42 (2018): 244–64.

37. Faramerz Dabhoiwala, *The Origins of Sex: A History of the First Sexual Revolution* (Oxford: Oxford University Press, 2012), 128–38. On cases of sodomy, see Netta Murray Goldsmith, *The Worst of Crimes: Homosexuality and the Law in Eighteenth-Century London* (Aldershot: Ashgate, 1998), 8–9; Upchurch, *Before Wilde*, 85; A. D. Harvey, *Sex in Georgian England: Attitudes and Prejudices from the 1720s to the 1820s* (New York: St. Martin's Press, 1994), 122–26.

38. Samuel Stevens quoted in Norton, *Mother Clap's Molly House*, 55. See also Randolph Trumbach, "London Sodomites: Homosexual Behavior and Western Culture in the 18th Century," *Journal of Social History* 11 (1977): 1–33; Harvey, *Sex in Georgian England*, 133–34; Randolph Trumbach, "The Birth of the Queen: Sodomy and the Emergence of Gender Equality in Modern Culture, 1660–1750," in *Hidden from History: Reclaiming the Gay and Lesbian Past*, ed. Martin Duberman, Martha Vicinus, and George Chauncey Jr. (New York: Meridian, 1989), 129–40.

39. Norton, *Mother Clap's Molly House*, 54–91. See also Tim Hitchcock, *English Sexualities, 1700–1800* (New York: St. Martin's Press, 1997),

58–75; Mike Rendell, *Sex and Sexuality in Georgian Britain* (Yorkshire: Pen and Sword, 2020), 127–39.

40. *Satan's Harvest Home: or the Present State of Whorecraft, Adultery, Fornication, Procuring, Pimping, Sodomy, And the Game at Flatts* (London: Dod, 1749), 50–52. See also *Sodom's Catastrophe, A Poem, with the Addition of Other Pieces of Poetry* (London: Robinson, 1748); *A New Historical Catechism* (London, 1750); Rev. Dr. Allen, *The Destruction of Sodom Improved, as a Warning to Great-Britain: A Sermon Preached on the Fast-Day, Friday, February 6, 1756, at Hanover-Street, Long-Acre* (London: Millar, 1756); Julie Peakman, *Amatory Pleasures: Explorations in Eighteenth-Century Sexual Culture* (London: Bloomsbury, 2016), 43–45, 56–57.

41. Jody Greene, "Public Secrets: Sodomy and the Pillory in the Eighteenth Century and Beyond," *The Eighteenth Century* 44 (2003): 203–32. See also Ackroyd, *Queer City*, 154–56.

42. Tobias Smollett, *Roderick Random*, ed. H. W. Hodges (London: Dent, 1927), 200. See also George E. Haggerty, "Smollett's World of Masculine Desire in *The Adventures of Roderick Random*," *The Eighteenth Century* 53 (2012): 317–30; Norton, *Mother Clap's Molly House*, 116–33; Crompton, *Byron and Greek Love*, 12–62.

43. Norton, *Mother Clap's Molly House*, 44–49, 159–84; Lacey, *Terrible Queer Creatures*, 104–108; Harvey, *Sex in Georgian England*, 124–29, 136–41.

44. Lacey, *Terrible Queer Creatures*, 91–99, 107–8; "John Atherton, Bishop of Waterford and Lismore," in Western Manuscripts, Add MS 4221, f. 39, BL; "A True and Amazeing Relation of the Notorious Uncleaness Incest Sodomy and Murther committed by Doctor John Atherton Lord Bishop of Waterford in the Kingdome of Ireland," in Western Manuscripts, Sloane MS 1818, ff. 177–88, BL; *The Life and Death of John Atherton, Lord Bishop of Waterford and Lysmore, within the Kingdom of Ireland* (London, 1641); *Bishop Atherton's Case Discuss'd in a Letter to the Author of a Late Pamphlet, Intitl'd* The Case of John Atherton, Bishop of Waterford in Ireland, Fairly Represented (London: Curll, 1711); Peter Marshall, *Mother Leakey and the Bishop: A Ghost Story* (Oxford: Oxford University Press, 2007).

45. James B. Leslie, *Armagh Clergy and Parishes* (Dundalk: Tempest, 1911), 212; James B. Leslie, *Clogher Clergy and Parishes* (Enniskillen: Ritchie, 1929), 221, 264. See also Stubbs, *History of University*, 207;

Donald M. Scott, *From Office to Profession: The New England Ministry, 1750–1850* (Philadelphia: University of Pennsylvania Press, 1978), 60–61.

46. Craddock Certificate, WO 72/7/3. See also NCE, p. 22; Coote, *Statistical Survey of Cavan*, 15.

47. NCE, p. 24. See also Samuel Eliot Morison, *The European Discovery of America: The Northern Voyages, A.D. 500–1600* (New York: Oxford University Press, 1971), 13–31.

48. Leslie, *Armagh Clergy and Parishes*, 214; Moody and Vaughan, *New History of Ireland*, 35, 84–91; Gipson, *British Isles*, 214–15; Christopher J. Fauske, *Jonathan Swift and the Church of Ireland, 1710–24* (Dublin: Irish Academic Press, 2002).

49. Fowler to Gage, June 15, 1775, TGP-AS 130.

50. David L. Jacobson, "The King's Four Churches: The Established Churches of America, England, Ireland, and Scotland in the Early Years of George II," *Anglican and Episcopal History* 59 (1990): 181–201; Acheson, *History of Church*, 76–81, 100–5; William Gibson, *Church, State, and Society, 1760–1850* (New York: St. Martin's Press, 1994); Peter M. Doll, *Revolution, Religion, and National Identity: Imperial Anglicanism in British North America, 1745–95* (Cranbury, N.J.: Associated University Presses, 2000); Brent S. Sirota, "The Church of England, the Law of Nations, and the Leghorn Chaplaincy Affair, 1703–13," *Eighteenth-Century Studies* 48 (2015): 283–306.

51. Newburgh Defense, WO 72/7/30, p. 18; Exshaw to Newburgh, April 9, 1774, WO 72/7/27. See also Cole Certificate, WO 72/7/5; Leslie, *Armagh Clergy and Parishes*, 324.

52. Newburgh Defense, WO 72/7/30, p. 18; Patten Testimony, WO 72/7/25. See also Gipson, *British Isles*, 193.

53. NCE, pp. 2–4, 8–11.

54. Comings to Newburgh, June 24, 1773, WO 72/7/10; Moody and Vaughan, *New History of Ireland*, 52, 86; Conway, *War, State, and Society*, 68–69; Kelly, *Cambridge History of Ireland*, 531.

55. Newburgh Defense, WO 72/7/30, p. 12. See also NCE, p. 10; Steven M. Baule, *Protecting the Empire's Frontier: Officers of the 18th (Royal Irish) Regiment of Foot during Its North American Service, 1767–76* (Athens: Ohio University Press, 2014), 85–87.

56. Sebright to Montgomery, November 23, 1772, WO 72/7/6. See also MR, 229; *A List of the General and Field-Officers, as They Rank in the*

Army (London: Millan, 1773), 72. On Cavendish, see Burke, *General and Heraldic Dictionary*, s.v. "Waterpark, Baron."

57. "From the London Gazette, Nov. 24," *Caledonian Mercury* (Edinburgh), November 30, 1772. See also Anthony P. C. Bruce, *The Purchase System in the British Army, 1660–1871* (London: Royal Historical Society, 1980), 31.

58. Sebright to Newburgh, December 22, 1772, WO 72/7/7. See also Gage to Barrington, June 15, 1766, TGP-ES 7; Alan J. Guy, *Oeconomy and Discipline: Officership and Administration in the British Army, 1714–63* (Manchester: Manchester University Press, 1985), 90–101; Baule, *Protecting the Empire's Frontier*, 43–44, 56–57, 63.

59. Scott to Haldimand, May 20, 1779, FHP 21732, f. 323; Scott to Haldimand, December 1779, FHP 21732, f. 428.

60. Scott to Haldimand, January 28, 1782, FHP 21734, f. 339. See also *Dictionary of Canadian Biography*, University of Toronto and Université Laval, <www.biographi.ca/en/index.php>, s.v. "Stuart, John."

61. Stuart to Blacket, [1783–84], FHP 21838, f. 338. See also Myna Trustram, *Women of the Regiment: Marriage and the Victorian Army* (Cambridge: Cambridge University Press, 1984); Stephen Brumwell, *Redcoats: The British Soldier and War in the Americas, 1755–63* (Cambridge: Cambridge University Press, 2002), 122–27.

62. Massey to Wilkins, October 15, 1772, WO 72/7/9. See also DNB, s.v. "Massey, Eyre"; Cecil C. P. Lawson, *A History of the Uniforms of the British Army*, 5 vols. (London: Davies, et al., 1940–67), 1: 31. Massey later became the first baron Clarina.

63. Moody and Vaughan, *New History of Ireland*, 31, 44, 52; Kelly, *Cambridge History of Ireland*, 76; Conway, *War, State, and Society*, 253–60; Brown, *Irish Enlightenment*, 237–38; Rosemary Sweet, "Provincial Culture and Urban Histories in England and Ireland during the Long Eighteenth Century," *Proceedings of the British Academy* 108 (2002): 223–40.

64. Batt to Newburgh, May 4, 1773, WO 72/7/1.

65. MR, pp. 1, 19, 43, 67, 79, 89, 105, 131, 135, 155, 165, 195, 203, 221, 233; Baule, *Protecting the Empire's Frontier*, 104–8.

66. Batt to Gage, June 30, 1775, TGP-AS 130; Batt to Newburgh, May 4, 1773, WO 72/7/1.

67. Newburgh Defense, WO 72/7/30, p. 7; Comings to Newburgh, June 24, 1773, WO 72/7/10. See also Irish Clergy Certificate for Newburgh, WO 72/7/23.

68. Newburgh Defense, WO 72/7/30, p. 9.

69. Sebright to Newburgh, [May 1773?], WO 72/7/8.

Chapter Two: The Happy State of the Royal Irish

1. GGCM, pp. 286–87.

2. GGCM, p. 289. See also James Neal Primm, *Lion of the Valley: St. Louis, Missouri* (Boulder: Pruett, 1981); *French St. Louis: Landscape, Contexts, and Legacy*, ed. Jay Gitlin, Robert Michel Morrissey, and Peter J. Kastor (Lincoln: University of Nebraska Press, 2021).

3. Richard Cannon, *Historical Record of the Eighteenth or the Royal Irish Regiment of Foot* (London: Parker, Furnivall, and Parker, 1848); G. le M. Gretton, *The Campaigns and History of the Royal Irish Regiment from 1684 to 1902* (Edinburgh: Blackwood and Sons, 1911); G. E. Boyle, "The 18th (or Royal Irish) Regiment of Foot in North America, 1767–75," *Journal of the Society for Army Historical Research* 2 (1923): 63–68; R. G. Harris, *The Irish Regiments, 1683–1999*, revised by H. R. G. Wilson (Staplehurst: Spellmount, 1999), 107–19; Cecil C. P. Lawson, *A History of the Uniforms of the British Army*, 5 vols. (London: Davies, et al., 1940–67), 1: 52; Steven M. Baule, *Protecting the Empire's Frontier: Officers of the 18th (Royal Irish) Regiment of Foot during Its North American Service, 1767–76* (Athens: Ohio University Press, 2014), 2–12.

4. A tenth company was subsequently added to the regiment. Reid to Gage, July 11, 1767, TGP-AS 67; MR, pp. 1–18; Baule, *Protecting the Empire's Frontier*, 92–94, 199–223; *A List of the General and Field-Officers, as They Rank in the Army* (London: Millan, 1773), 72; Colton Storm, "The Notorious Colonel Wilkins," *Journal of the Illinois State Historical Society* 40 (1947): 7–22.

5. Wilkins to Penn, June 16, 1768, in Wilkins to Gage, June 16, 1768, TGP-AS 78. See also PA 8th ser., 8: 6771–73; John Gilbert McCurdy, *Quarters: The Accommodation of the British Army and the Coming of the American Revolution* (Ithaca: Cornell University Press, 2019), 146.

6. Baule, *Protecting the Empire's Frontier*, 17. See also Robert G. Carroon, ed., *Broadswords and Bayonets: The Journals of the Expedition under the Command of Captain Thomas Stirling of the 42nd Regiment, Royal Highland Regiment (The Black Watch) to Occupy Fort Chartres in the Illinois Country, August 1765 to January 1766* (Springfield: Society of Colonial Wars in the State of Illinois, 1984).

7. GGCM, p. 261. See also GGCM, pp. 312–14, 318; Gage to Barrington, May 15, 1768, TGP-ES 12; Gage to Hamilton, September 23, 1771, TGP-AS 106; Gage to Hillsborough, July 1, 1772, TGP-ES 21; *Collections of the Illinois State Historical Library: British Series*, ed. Clarence Walworth Alvord and Clarence Edwin Carter, 3 vols. (Springfield: Illinois State Historical Library, 1915–21), 3: 415–16; Baule, *Protecting the Empire's Frontier*, 16–19, 94–97; Jacob F. Lee, *Masters of the Middle Waters: Indian Nations and Colonial Ambitions along the Mississippi* (Cambridge: Harvard University Press, 2019), 139–46; David MacDonald and Raine Waters, *Kaskaskia: The Lost Capital of Illinois* (Carbondale: Southern Illinois University Press, 2019), 27–33.

8. GGCM, p. 304, p. 294. See also GGCM, pp. 277, 283, 293, 296, 300, 305, 308, 309, 312–13, 341, 353.

9. Baule, *Protecting the Empire's Frontier*, 94–95. See also Walter S. Dunn Jr., *The New Imperial Economy: The British Army and the American Frontier, 1764–68* (Westport: Praeger, 2001); Gage to Wilkins, February 5, 1773, TGP-AS 117.

10. Complaints of the Officers of the Royal Irish against Lieutenant Colonel Wilkins, October 26, 1772, enclosure in Gage to Hamilton, April 20, 1773, TGP-AS 118. See also Gage to Barrington, May 5, 1773, TGP-ES 22.

11. Baule, *Protecting the Empire's Frontier*, 95–99; Gage to Barrington, October 1, 1771, TGP-ES 21; Gage to Hamilton, April 20, 1773, TGP-AS 118; Gage to Wilkins, May 12, 1773, TGP-AS 118; Gage to Haldimand, August 5, 1773, FHP 21665, ff. 159–60; Gage to Haldimand, September 1, 1773, FHP 21665, ff. 170–71.

12. Fowler to Gage, February 2, 1775, TGP-AS 125. See also Baule, *Protecting the Empire's Frontier*, 111; MR, pp. 15, 23, 179, 183, 197; Chapman to Hutcheson, October 28, 1773, FHP 21730, ff. 358–59; Extract of a Letter from Captain Chapman to Captain Kemble, enclosure in Gage to Wilkins, February 5, 1773, TGP-AS 117.

13. Chapman Closing Argument, WO 72/7/31, p. 13. See also Chapman to Gage, January 28, 1773, TGP-AS 116; Baule, *Protecting the Empire's Frontier*, 111.

14. Baule, *Protecting the Empire's Frontier*, 104–5, 128–29; MR, pp. 1, 19, 43, 67, 105, 165, 195; PCM, pp. 5–7, 35–36, 41–42, 46–47, 57–60.

15. An Extract of a Letter Just Received from Lieut. Hutchins of the 60th Regiment Dated Pensacola, August 7, 1772, enclosure in Gage to Hamilton, April 20, 1773, TGP-AS 118.

16. PCM, exhibits 17 and 18; Fowler to Haldimand, July 30, 1773, FHP 21730, f. 186; Baule, *Protecting the Empire's Frontier*, 162–64; MR, pp. 47, 57, 81, 95, 101, 119, 145, 157, 179.

17. Fowler to Gage, February 2, 1775, TGP-AS 125; FCM, exhibit 5.

18. FCM, exhibit 2, p. 6; Fowler to Gage, September 22, 1774, TGP-AS 123; FCM, exhibit 4. See also PCM, p. 140; exhibit 12; FCM, exhibit 2, p. 8; exhibit 4.

19. FCM, exhibit 7, pp. 3, 5, 6.

20. Baule, *Protecting the Empire's Frontier*, 95, 163–66.

21. PCM, p. 27. See also Baule, *Protecting the Empire's Frontier*, 176–77; MR, pp. 159, 177, 191; Gerard Gawalt, *Elizabeth House Trist: An Undaunted Woman's Journey through Jefferson's World* (North Charleston: CreateSpace, 2017), 3.

22. Hillsborough to Gage, December 4, 1771, TGP-ES 21.

23. Baule, *Protecting the Empire's Frontier*, 81–82.

24. Gage to Barrington, July 25, 1775, TGP-ES 30; PCM, p. 135; Baule, *Protecting the Empire's Frontier*, 82–83, 89.

25. GGCM, pp. 287–88; Baule, *Protecting the Empire's Frontier*, 19–20, 123; Gage to Barrington, September 2, 1772, TGP-ES 23; Gage to Edmonstone, December 17, 1772, TGP-AS 116; Edmonstone to Gage, December 24, 1772, TGP-AS 116; Edmonstone to Gage, January 28, 1773, TGP-AS 116; Gage to Hamilton, February 11, 1773, TGP-AS 117; Gage to Haldimand, June 3, 1773, FHP 21665, ff. 133–35.

26. MR, pp. 213–28.

27. Patrick McRobert, *A Tour through Part of the North Provinces of America: Being, a Series of Letters Wrote on the Spot, in the Years 1774 and 1775* (Philadelphia: Historical Society of Pennsylvania, 1935), 30. See also Evarts B. Greene and Virginia D. Harrington, *American Population before the Federal Census of 1790* (New York: Columbia University Press, 1932), 118n; Carl Van Doren, *Benjamin Franklin* (New York: Viking, 1938); Benjamin L. Carp, *Rebels Rising: Cities and the American Revolution* (New York: Oxford University Press, 2007); Daniel P. Johnson, *Making the Early Modern Metropolis: Culture and Power in Pre-Revolutionary Philadelphia* (Charlottesville: University of Virginia Press, 2022), 174–75.

28. "Philadelphia, January 26, 1769," in *Boston News-Letter and New-England Chronicle*, February 9, 1769. See also "Philadelphia, January 8," in *Pennsylvania Gazette*, January 8, 1767; "Arrivals," in

Pennsylvania Gazette, August 13, 1767; PA 7: 6154; J. Thomas Scharf
and Thomas Westcott, *History of Philadelphia, 1609–1884,* 3 vols.
(Philadelphia: Everts, 1884), 2: 987; Steven Rosswurm, *Arms,
Country, and Class: The Philadelphia Militia and the "Lower Sort" during
the American Revolution* (New Brunswick: Rutgers University Press,
1987), 18–30; Billy G. Smith, *The "Lower Sort": Philadelphia's
Laboring People, 1750–1800* (Ithaca: Cornell University Press, 1990),
38, 170–71.

29. *Burnaby's Travels through North America: Reprinted from the Third Edition
of 1798,* ed. Rufus Rockwell Wilson (New York: Wessels, 1904), 90;
PA 8th ser., 8: 6704; PA 8th ser., 8: 7099. See also PASL 7: 161–62;
PA 1st ser., 3: 62; PA 8th ser., 6: 4825, 4858, 4879, 5082; 7: 5658,
5662, 5788, 5916, 5921, 6034–35, 6047, 6068, 6085, 6102, 6127,
6135, 6140–41, 6288, 6421, 6450, 6518, 6557, 6563, 6586; 8:
6722, 6726, 6876, 6886, 6894, 6899, 7003, 7014, 7022, 7027,
7128, 7133, 7145, 7151, 7283, 7290, 7299, 7304, 7385, 7391,
7568, 7587; Wilkins to Gage, February 7, 1768, TGP-AS 73; Gage to
Wilkins, February 20, 1768, TGP-AS 74; Scharf and Westcott,
History of Philadelphia, 2: 1011–12; *Travels in North America in the Years
1780, 1781 and 1782 by the Marquis de Chastellux,* trans. and ed.
Howard C. Rice Jr., 2 vols. (Chapel Hill: University of North
Carolina Press, 1963), 1: 130; John F. Watson, *Annals of Philadelphia,
in the Olden Time,* ed. Willis P. Hazard, 3 vols. (Philadelphia: Stuart,
1884), 1: 415–16; 2: 168; John Russell Young, *Memorial History of
the City of Philadelphia from Its First Settlement to the Year 1895,* 2 vols.
(New York: New-York History Co., 1895–98), 1: 284–85; Pierre
Nicole, "A Survey of the City of Philadelphia and Its Environs
Shewing the Several Works Constructed by His Majesty's Troops,
under the Command of Sir William Howe, Since Their Possession
of that City 26th September 1777, Comprehending Likewise the
Attacks against Fort Mifflin on Mud Island, and until It's Reduction,
16th November 1777," in Geography and Map Division, Library of
Congress, Washington, D.C.; Anne H. Cresson, "Biographical
Sketch of Joseph Fox, Esq., of Philadelphia," *Pennsylvania Magazine
of History and Biography* 32 (1908): 175–99.

30. GGCM, pp. 269, 272–73, 276, 281–83, 302, 306–7, 320–23; PCM,
p. 9; NCM, p. 44.

31. PCM, exhibit 6, p. 3; "Twenty Shilling Reward," *Pennsylvania
Gazette,* May 17, 1773.

32. GGCM, p. 336[337], p. 259.
33. MR, p. 223. See also GGCM, 275, 332, 334; MR, p. 141.
34. Maxwell to Gage, May 1, 1771, TGP-AS 102; PAMC 10: 16. See also PASL 8: 241–42; PAMC 9: 684–85, 718; 10: 17–20; PA 1st ser., 4: 395–98.
35. "Cork, July 5," *Pennsylvania Packet*, September 13, 1773; "Run Away," *Pennsylvania Gazette*, September 22, 1773.
36. "Philadelphia, August 20, 1773," *Pennsylvania Packet*, August 23, 1773.
37. John Trenchard and Thomas Gordon, *Cato's Letters: Or, Essays on Liberty, Civil and Religious, and Other Important Subjects*, ed. Ronald Hamowy (Indianapolis: Liberty Fund, 1995), 690. See also John Philip Reid, *In Defiance of the Law: The Standing Army Controversy, the Two Constitutions, and the Coming of the American Revolution* (Chapel Hill: University of North Carolina Press, 1981); Reginald C. Stuart, "'Engines of Tyranny': Recent Historiography on Standing Armies during the Era of the American Revolution," *Canadian Journal of History* (19) 1984: 183–99; Dennis Rubini, "Sexuality and Augustan England: Sodomy, Politics, Elite Circles and Society," *The Pursuit of Sodomy: Male Homosexuality in Renaissance and Enlightenment Europe*, ed. Kent Gerard and Gert Hekma, 349–81 (New York: Haworth Press, 1989); G. Dean Sinclair, "Homosexuality and the Military: A Review of the Literature," *Journal of Homosexuality* 56 (2009): 701–18; John Gilbert McCurdy, *Citizen Bachelors: Manhood and the Creation of the United States* (Ithaca: Cornell University Press, 2009), 164–65.
38. Quoted in Rictor Norton, *Mother Clap's Molly House: The Gay Subculture in England, 1700–1830* (London: GMP, 1992), 45; quoted in Rictor Norton, ed., "The Women's Complaint to Venus, 1698," in *Homosexuality in Eighteenth-Century England: A Sourcebook*, <www.rictornorton.co.uk/eighteen/complain.htm>.
39. 22 Geo. II, c. 33. See also Arthur H. Gilbert, "Buggery and the British Navy, 1700–1861," *Journal of Social History* 10 (1976): 72–98; Jeffrey Weeks, *Coming Out: Homosexual Politics in Britain, from the Nineteenth Century to the Present* (London: Quartet, 1977), 12–13; B. R. Burg, *Sodomy and the Pirate Tradition: English Sea Rovers in the Seventeenth Century Caribbean* (New York: New York University Press, 1983); A. D. Harvey, *Sex in Georgian England: Attitudes and Prejudices from the 1720s to the 1820s* (New York: St. Martin's Press,

1994), 126; Stephen Brumwell, *Redcoats: The British Soldier and the War in the Americas, 1755–63* (Cambridge: Cambridge University Press, 2002), 121; Seth Stein LeJacq, "Buggery's Travels: Royal Navy Sodomy on Ship and Shore in the Long Eighteenth Century," *Journal for Maritime Research* 17 (2015): 103–16.

40. Quoted in Norton, *Mother Clap's Molly House*, 171. See also *A List of the General and Field-Officers, as They Rank in the Army* (London: Millan, 1754), 77; *A List of the General and Field-Officers, as They Rank in the Army* (London: Millan, 1759), 150; Peter A. Tasch, *The Dramatic Cobbler: The Life and Works of Isaac Bickerstaff* (Lewisburg: Bucknell University Press, 1971); Harvey, *Sex in Georgian England*, 136–37; Brian Lacey, *Terrible Queer Creatures: Homosexuality in Irish History* (Dublin: Wordwell, 2008), 104–5.

41. *Love in the Suds; A Town Ecologue* (London: Wheble, 1772), 9, 6. See also "Isaac Bickerstaff," *Caledonian Mercury* (Edinburgh), August 10, 1776.

42. Newburgh to Gage, October 16, 1774, TGP-AS 124. See also NCM, p. 97[95].

43. Exshaw to Newburgh, April 9, 1774, WO 72/7/27.

44. Weekes Testimony, WO 72/7/24. See also MaCM, p. 6.

45. NCM, p. 52. See also Hamilton, Orders Regarding Newburgh, WO 72/7/20; Baule, *Protecting the Empire's Frontier*, 217–19; Horace Wemyss Smith, *Life and Correspondence of the Rev. William Smith, D.D.*, 2 vols. (Philadelphia: Ferguson Brothers, 1880), 1: 411; *The Works of William Smith, D.D. Late Provost of the College and Academy of Philadelphia*, 2 vols. (Philadelphia: Maxwell and Fry, 1803), 2: 155–251.

46. Kevin J. Dellape, *America's First Chaplain: The Life and Times of the Reverend Jacob Duché* (Bethlehem: Lehigh University Press, 2013); Norris Stanley Barratt, *Outline of Old St. Paul's Church, Philadelphia, Pennsylvania* (Philadelphia: Colonial Society of Pennsylvania, 1917), 49–53, 81, 86–95.

47. MaCM, pp. 5–6. See also Thomas Simes, *The Military Medley: Containing the Most Necessary Rules and Directions for Attaining a Competent Knowledge of the Art: To Which Are Added an Explanation of Military Terms, Alphabetically Digested*, 2nd ed. (London: Simes, 1768), 197; Alan J. Guy, *Oeconomy and Discipline: Officership and Administration in the British Army, 1714–63* (Manchester: Manchester University Press, 1985), 94–95.

48. NCM, p. 19; NCE, p. 9; Watson, *Annals of Philadelphia*, 406–7.
49. Newburgh Defense, WO 72/7/30, p. 19; NCM, p. 61.
50. NCM, p. 84, 85; MaCM, p. 9. See also Trist to Jefferson, July 24, 1786, TJP 10: 166–170.
51. NCM, p. 63. See also "For a Fortnight Only," *Pennsylvania Packet*, November 1, 1773; "Positively the Last Week," *Pennsylvania Packet*, November 10, 1773; Watson, *Annals of Philadelphia*, 409; "America's First Theatre," *Theatre Magazine* 16 (1912): 16.
52. Clare A. Lyons, *Sex among the Rabble: An Intimate History of Gender and Power in the Age of Revolution, Philadelphia, 1730–1830* (Chapel Hill: University of North Carolina Press, 2006).
53. PCM, p. 47. See also Baule, *Protecting the Empire's Frontier*, 170–172, 188–191, 210–213; Brumwell, *Redcoats*, 122–27; Paul E. Kopperman, "The British High Command and Soldiers' Wives in America, 1755–83," *Journal of the Society for Army Historical Research* 60 (1982): 14–34; Myna Trustram, *Women of the Regiment: Marriage and the Victorian Army* (Cambridge: Cambridge University Press, 1984); Holly A. Mayer, *Belonging to the Army: Camp Followers and Community during the American Revolution* (Columbia: University of South Carolina Press, 1996); Alexander V. Campbell, *The Royal American Regiment: An Atlantic Microcosm, 1755–72* (Norman: University of Oklahoma Press, 2010), 148–50, 203–7; Serena Zabin, *The Boston Massacre: A Family History* (Boston: Houghton Mifflin Harcourt, 2020), 3–16. John Mawby senior is alternatively listed as captain and captain lieutenant in the muster rolls. For simplicity, I have chosen to refer to him as Captain Mawby. See MR 173–74, 181–82, 201–2, 213–14, 229–30, 245–46, 261–62, 281–82, 293–94, 309–10.
54. GGCM, p. 311; PCM, p. 58. See also Lyons, *Sex among the Rabble*, 110–12; Randolph Trumbach, *Sex and the Gender Revolution, Volume One: Heterosexuality and the Third Gender in Enlightenment London* (Chicago: University of Chicago Press, 1998), 199–201.
55. N. A. M. Rodger, *The Wooden World: An Anatomy of the Georgian Navy* (New York: Norton, 1996), 81. See also G. A. Steppler, "British Military Law, Discipline, and the Conduct of Regimental Courts Martial in the Later Eighteenth Century," *English Historical Review* 102 (1987): 859–886; Steven Baule and Don Hagist, "The Regimental Punishment Book of the Boston Detachments of the Royal Irish Regiment and the 65th Regiment, 1774–75," *Journal of the Society for Army Historical Research* 88 (2010): 5–18; Susan Gane,

"Common Soldiers, Same-Sex Love and Religion in the Early Eighteenth-Century British Army," *Gender & History* 25 (2013): 637–51.

56. James G. Cusick, "Slanders and Sodomy: Studying the Past through Colonial Crime Investigations," *Florida Historical Quarterly* 93 (2015): 415–45.

57. McCM, p. 3. See also McCM, p. 25. Michael Langley, *The Loyal Regiment (North Lancashire): The 47th and 81st Regiments of Foot* (London: Cooper, 1976), 5–13; Paul Knight, *A Very Fine Regiment: The 47th Foot during the American War of Independence, 1773–83* (Warwick: Helion, 2022), 31–60.

58. McCM, pp. 5–6.

59. McCM, p. 37. See also McCM, pp. 21, 38, 61.

60. McCM, pp. 116, 18, 106. See also McCM, pp. 62–64, 98–99, 112, 117, 121; *A List of the General and Field-Officers, as They Rank in the Army* (London: Millan, 1774), 101; *A List of the General and Field-Officers, as They Rank in the Army* (London: Millan, 1775), 70; Gage to Hillsborough, April 24, 1770, TGP-ES 17; Gage to Dartmouth, May 13, 1775, TGP-ES 29; Richard Cannon, *Historical Record of the Sixteenth, or, the Bedfordshire Regiment of Foot* (London: Parker, Furnivall, and Parker, 1848).

61. NCM, 40. See also McCM, p. 1.

62. NCM, p. 63; MaCM, p. 8. See also DNB, s.v. "Fanning, Edmund."

Chapter Three: Mr. Newburgh Would Cruise up His Gut

1. NJD 29: 86. See also Gage, Circular to Governors, [June 4, 1773], TGP-AS 118; John Richard Alden, *General Gage in America: Being Principally a History of His Role in the American Revolution* (Baton Rouge: Louisiana State University Press, 1948), 192–94; DNB, s.v. "Haldimand, Sir Frederick."

2. Cecil C. P. Lawson, *A History of the Uniforms of the British Army*, 5 vols. (London: Davies, et al., 1940–67), 2: 97; "Extracts from the Journal of Miss Sarah Eve (Concluded)," *Pennsylvania Magazine of History and Biography* 5 (1881): 203. See also "On Wednesday Last," *Pennsylvania Gazette*, November 24, 1773; R. G. Harris, *The Irish Regiments, 1683–1999*, revised by H. R. G. Wilson (Staplehurst: Spellmount, 1999), 108.

3. NJD 29: 105. See also Lawson, *History of the Uniforms*, 2: 30, 101.

4. "Philadelphia, October 18," *Pennsylvania Gazette*, October 20, 1773. See also Joseph Cummins, *Ten Tea Parties: Patriotic Protests That History Forgot* (Philadelphia: Quirk Books, 2012), 59–72; Benjamin L. Carp, *Defiance of the Patriots: The Boston Tea Party and the Making of America* (New Haven: Yale University Press, 2011).

5. PASL 3: 202. See also Clare A. Lyons, "Mapping an Atlantic Sexual Culture: Homoeroticism in Eighteenth-Century Philadelphia," WMQ 60 (2003): 119–154; Jen Manion, *Liberty's Prisoners: Carceral Culture in Early America* (Philadelphia: University of Pennsylvania Press, 2015), 158–60, 169–78.

6. Mary Beth Norton, *Founding Mothers and Fathers: Gendered Power and the Forming of American Society* (New York: Knopf, 1996), 211–217, 240–41, 257–60; Jane Kamensky, *Governing the Tongue: The Politics of Speech in Early New England* (New York: Oxford University Press, 1997), 27–28, 148–49. See also David Thomas Konig, *Law and Society in Puritan Massachusetts: Essex County, 1629–92* (Chapel Hill: University of North Carolina Press, 1979); Peter Charles Hoffer, *Law and People in Colonial America*, rev. ed. (Baltimore: Johns Hopkins University Press, 1998).

7. "Great Clackton in Essex, Feb. 24, 1756," *Ipswich Journal* (Ipswich, England), April 17, 1756. See also Roger Thompson, *Sex in Middlesex: Popular Mores in a Massachusetts County, 1649–99* (Amherst: University of Massachusetts Press, 1986), 174–186; John M. Murrin, "'Things Fearful to Name': Bestiality in Colonial America," *Pennsylvania History* 65 (1998): 8–43; Kirsten Fischer, *Suspect Relations: Sex, Race, and Resistance in Colonial North Carolina* (Ithaca: Cornell University Press, 2002), 131–58; Helmut Puff, *Sodomy in Reformation Germany and Switzerland, 1400–1600* (Chicago: University of Chicago Press, 2003), 107–23; Thomas A. Foster, *Sex and the Eighteenth-Century Man: Massachusetts and the History of Sexuality in America* (Boston: Beacon Press, 2006), 31–32, 67–68, 140–41; John Smolenski, *Friends and Strangers: The Making of a Creole Culture in Colonial Pennsylvania* (Philadelphia: University of Pennsylvania Press, 2010), 73–74, 131.

8. NCE, p. 3.

9. NCE, p. 3.

10. Alan Bray, *Homosexuality in Renaissance England* (London: Gay Man's Press, 1982), 50, 54; Netta Murray Goldsmith, *The Worst of Crimes: Homosexuality and the Law in Eighteenth-Century London* (Aldershot:

Ashgate, 1998), 34–37, 71, 93; Randolph Trumbach, "The Transformation of Sodomy from the Renaissance to the Modern World
and Its Great Sexual Consequences," *Signs: Journal of Women in
Culture and Society* 37 (2012): 832–48.

11. Quoted in Jonathan Ned Katz, *Gay/Lesbian Almanac* (New York:
Harper and Row, 1983), 114. See also Michael J. Rocke, "Sod-
omites in Fifteenth-Century Tuscany: The View of Bernadino of
Siena," *The Pursuit of Sodomy: Male Homosexuality in Renaissance and
Enlightenment Europe*, ed. Kent Gerard and Gert Hekma, 7–31 (New
York: Haworth Press, 1989); Richard Godbeer, "'The Cry of
Sodom': Discourse, Intercourse, and Desire in Colonial New
England," WMQ 52 (1995): 259–86; Stephen Robertson, "Shifting
the Scene of the Crime: Sodomy and the American History of
Sexual Violence," JHS 19 (2010): 223–42;.

12. Rictor Norton, *Mother Clap's Molly House: The Gay Subculture in
England, 1700–1830* (London: GMP, 1992), 23; Cynthia B. Herrup,
A House in Gross Disorder: Sex, Law, and the 2nd Earl of Castlehaven (New
York: Oxford University Press, 1999), 70–77. See also Alan Bray,
"Homosexuality and the Signs of Male Friendship in Elizabethan
England," *History Workshop* 29 (1990): 1–19; Carolyn Steedman,
Master and Servant: Love and Labour in the English Industrial Age
(Cambridge: Cambridge University Press, 2007).

13. NCM, p. 25. See also NCM, pp. 25–26, 81.

14. Newburgh, Denial of Charges, WO 72/7/11; NCM, p. 25.

15. NCM, pp. 25–26.

16. JADA 2: 187; JCC 10: 349. See also JCC 3: 423; 4: 194; 5: 844;
Harmon Pumpelly Read, *Rossiana: Papers and Documents Relating to
the History and Genealogy of the Ancient and Noble House of Ross of
Ross-Shire, Scotland, and Its Descent from the Ancient Earl of Ross*
(Albany: Read, 1908), 165–77; *Colonial Families of Philadelphia*, ed.
John W. Jordan, vol. 2 (New York: Lewis, 1911), 1250–51; Joseph F.
Foster, *George Bryan and the Revolution in Pennsylvania* (University
Park: Pennsylvania State University Press, 1994).

17. NCE, p. 4, 7.

18. Michel Foucault, *The History of Sexuality, Volume I: An Introduction*,
trans. Robert Hurley (New York: Random House, 1978), 39. See
also G. S. Rousseau, "The Pursuit of Homosexuality in the
Eighteenth Century: 'Utterly Confused Category' and/or Rich
Repository," *'Tis Nature's Fault: Unauthorized Sexuality during the*

Enlightenment, ed. Robert Parks Maccubbin, 132–68 (Cambridge: Cambridge University Press, 2010); Julie Peakman, *Amatory Pleasures: Explorations in Eighteenth-Century Sexual Culture* (London: Bloomsbury, 2016), 21.

19. Martin Nesvig, "The Complicated Terrain of Latin American Homosexuality," *Hispanic American Historical Review* 81 (2001): 689–729; Zeb Tortorici, "'Heran Todos Putos': Sodomitical Subcultures and Disordered Desire in Early Colonial Mexico," *Ethnohistory* 54 (2007): 35–67; Zeb Tortorici, "Against Nature: Sodomy and Homosexuality in Colonial Latin America," *History Compass* 10 (2012): 161–78; Mike Rendell, *Sex and Sexuality in Georgian Britain* (Yorkshire: Pen and Sword History, 2020), 126–39.

20. T. W. Moody and W. E. Vaughan, eds., *A New History of Ireland: IV, Eighteenth-Century Ireland, 1691–1800* (Oxford: Oxford University Press, 1984), 161; W. A. Hart, "Africans in Eighteenth-Century Ireland," *Irish Historical Society* 129 (2002): 19–32. See also Robert Richmond Ellis, "Reading through the Veil of Juan Francisco Manzano: From Homoerotic Violence to the Dream of a Homoracial Bond," *PMLA* 113 (1998): 422–35; Thomas A. Foster, *Rethinking Rufus: Sexual Violations of Enslaved Men* (Athens: University of Georgia Press, 2019).

21. Richard Mant, *History of the Church of Ireland, from the Revolution to the Union of the Churches of England and Ireland, January 1, 1801* (London: Parker, 1840), 600–604; Alan Acheson, *A History of the Church of Ireland, 1691–2001* (Dublin: Columba Press, 1997), 67, 74–75; Brian Lacey, *Terrible Queer Creatures: Homosexuality in Irish History* (Dublin: Wordwell, 2008), 91–99, 106–8.

22. *An Address from the Ladies of the Provinces of Munster and Leinster, to Their Graces the Duke and Duchess of D——t, Lord G—, and Caiaphas the High Priest* (London: Pro-Patria, 1754), 15.

23. Tortorici, "Heran Todos Putos," 55; Anna Clark, *Scandal: The Sexual Politics of the British Constitution* (Princeton: Princeton University Press, 2003), 44; Anderson Hagler, "Archival Epistemology: Honor, Sodomy, and Indians in Eighteenth-Century New Mexico," *Ethnohistory* 66 (2019): 515–35.

24. NCE, p. 10.

25. Quoted in Theo van der Meer, "Sodomy and Its Discontents: Discourse, Desire, and the Rise of a Same-Sex Proto-Something in

the Early Modern Dutch Republic," *Historical Reflections / Réflexions Historiques* 33 (2007): 52. See also Derek Neal, "Disorder of Body, Mind or Soul: Male Sexual Deviance in Jacques Despar's Commentary on Avicenna," in *The Sciences of Homosexuality in Early Modern Europe*, ed. Kenneth Borris and George Rousseau (New York: Routledge, 2008), 42–56; George E. Haggerty, "Smollett's World of Masculine Desire in *The Adventures of Roderick Random*," *The Eighteenth Century* 53 (2012): 319.

26. NCE, p. 17. It is possible that John Patten was John Patton Sr. (1745–1804), who emigrated from Sligo to Berks County, Pennsylvania, and fought with distinction with the Continental Army. PA, 2nd ser., 14: 247.

27. Thomas Coombe, *The Harmony Between the Old and New Testaments Respecting the Messiah* (Philadelphia: Dunlap, 1774). See also John F. Watson, *Annals of Philadelphia, in the Olden Time*, ed. Willis P. Hazard, 3 vols. (Philadelphia: Stuart, 1884), 163, 569; J. Thomas Scharf and Thomas Westcott, *History of Philadelphia, 1609–1884*, 3 vols. (Philadelphia: Everts, 1884), 1: 112, 139, 156–57, 267.

28. Mawby Defense, WO 72/7 p. 4. See also MaCM, p. 4.

29. NCM, p. 5. It could have been earlier. Alexander Fowler testified that Newburgh moved into the Philadelphia barracks in October or November 1773. However, Newburgh noted that he began to reside in the barracks at "the latter end of December." See MaCM, p. 3; NCM, p. 76.

30. NCM, p. 6; Mawby Defense, WO 72/7, p. 2.

31. NCM, p. 9; Mawby Defense, WO 72/7, p. 2.

32. Moncrieff to Nesbitt, [July 1773?], FHP 21730, ff. 187–88; Memorial of the Subalterns and Officers of the Garrison of Halifax, n.d., FHP 21732, ff. 184–85; NCM, p. 6.

33. NCM, p. 9.

34. NCM, pp. 73–74.

35. NCM, p. 6.

36. Nelson Waite Rightmyer, "Churches under Enemy Occupation: Philadelphia, 1777–78," *Church History* 14 (1945): 33–60.

37. NCM, pp. 75–76.

38. Officers' Testimony, WO 72/7/29. See also Pay List of December 1773, Royal Artillery Musters, WO 10/138, NAK; NCE, p. 15.

39. NCM, p. 89[91].

40. NCE, p. 16.

41. MaCM, pp. 1–2. The correspondence between Newburgh and Mawby has been lost.
42. Mawby Defense, WO 72/7, p. 2.
43. NCM, p. 60. See also PCM, pp. 33–34; Scott to St. Leger, October 13, 1781, FHP 21734, ff. 242–46.
44. NCM, pp. 60–61.
45. Cummins, *Ten Tea Parties*, 72–77.

Chapter Four: A Man of Infamous Character

1. GGCM, p. 236, 241, 243.
2. John Boswell, *Christianity, Social Tolerance, and Homosexuality: Gay People in Western Europe from the Beginning of the Christian Era to the Fourteenth Century* (Chicago: University of Chicago Press, 1980), 284n47, 290–91n62; Dirk Jaap Noordam, "Sodomy in the Dutch Republic, 1600–1725," in *The Pursuit of Sodomy: Male Homosexuality in Renaissance and Enlightenment Europe*, ed. Kent Gerard and Gert Hekma (New York: Haworth Press, 1989), 218; Rictor Norton, *Mother Clap's Molly House: The Gay Subculture in England, 1700–1830* (London: GMP, 1992), 123; Clare A. Lyons, "Mapping an Atlantic Sexual Culture: Homoeroticism in Eighteenth-Century Philadelphia," WMQ 60 (2003): 119–54.
3. "Yesterday before Sir John Fielding," *Derby Mercury* (Derby, England), June 30, 1775; "Bristol, June 21," *Jackson's Oxford Journal* (Oxford, England), June 28, 1760.
4. "Boston," *Virginia Gazette*, April 5, 1770; quoted in Patrick Spero, *Frontier Rebels: The Fight for Independence in the America West, 1765–76* (New York: Norton, 2018), 98.
5. Macdonnell and Blackader's Charges against Pierrieke, March 2, 1781, FHP 21734, f. 36.
6. Stephen Brumwell, *Redcoats: The British Soldier and the War in the Americas, 1755–63* (New York: Cambridge University Press, 2002), 76–77; Serena Zabin, *The Boston Massacre: A Family History* (Boston: Houghton Mifflin Harcourt, 2020), 61–64.
7. Jody Greene, "Public Secrets: Sodomy and the Pillory in the Eighteenth Century and Beyond," *The Eighteenth Century* 44 (2003): 203–32.
8. MR, pp. 191, 211, 217, 243, 249; *A List of the General and Field-Officers, as They Rank in the Army* (London: Millan, 1767), 82; *A List of the General and Field-Officers, as They Rank in the Army* (London:

Millan, 1771), 72; Steven M. Baule, *Protecting the Empire's Frontier: Officers of the 18th (Royal Irish) Regiment of Foot during Its North American Service, 1767–76* (Athens: Ohio University Press, 2014), 128–29.

9. PCM, exhibit 18, p. 2. See also PCM, pp. 5–7, 26, 29, 35–36, 46–47, 57–58.

10. PCM, pp. 148, 66.

11. PCM, p. 132, 45, 148. See also PCM, pp. 50, 132.

12. GGCM pp. 235–36.

13. Laurence Stern, *The Life and Opinions of Tristram Shandy, Gentleman*, book VII, chapter XXV. See also Ira D. Gruber, *Books and the British Army in the Age of the American Revolution* (Chapel Hill: University of North Carolina Press, 2010).

14. GGCM, p. 239.

15. GGCM, pp. 236–37. See also NCM, pp. 59–60.

16. GGCM, p. 235. See also GGCM, p. 249; NCM, pp. 11, 20, 59–60; PCM, pp. 63–64, 68–70.

17. NCM, p. 12.

18. NCM, p. 74.

19. NCE, pp. 4–5. Parr was commissioned justice of peace in 1761 and held this position until the Revolution. He may have been a Loyalist as it does not appear that he held any position in the state government. John Hill Martin, *Martin's Bench and Bar of Philadelphia* (Philadelphia: Welch, 1883), 34–35; William E. Nelson, "Government by Judiciary: The Growth of Judicial Power in Colonial Pennsylvania," *SMU Law Review* 59 (2006): 3–53.

20. NCM, p. 74, 79. There may have been another meeting a day earlier. See NCM, p. 3, 17, 20, 63.

21. Newburgh Defense, WO 72/7/30, p. 20; NCM, p. 3.

22. NCM, p. 17.

23. NCM, p. 97[99].

24. Mawby Defense, WO 72/7, p. 2; NCE, p. 1.

25. *The Works of Aurelius Augustine, Bishop of Hippo*, ed. Marcus Dods, trans. J. R. King, vol. III (Edinburgh: Clark, 1872), Chapter IV—6.

26. Jane L. McIntyre, "Character: A Humean Account," *History of Philosophy Quarterly* 7 (1990): 193–206; Richard H. Dees, "Hume on the Characters of Virtue," *Journal of the History of Philosophy* 35 (1997): 45–64; Andrew S. Trees, *The Founding Fathers and the Politics of Character* (Princeton: Princeton University Press, 2004); Craig

Bruce Smith, *American Honor: The Creation of the Nation's Ideals during the Revolutionary Era* (Chapel Hill: University of North Carolina Press, 2018); Harro Maas, "Monitoring the Self: François-Marc-Louis Naville and His Moral Tables," *History of Science* 58 (2019): 117–41. On sensibility, see Christopher Nealon, *Foundlings: Lesbian and Gay Historical Emotion before Stonewall* (Durham: Duke University Press, 2001); William Benemann, *Male-Male Intimacy in Early America: Beyond Romantic Friendships* (New York: Harrington Park Press, 2006), 49–50; Sarah Knott, *Sensibility and the American Revolution* (Chapel Hill: University of North Carolina Press, 2009).

27. Fraser to Haldimand, June 18, 1780, FHP 21787, f. 147; Barbut to Haldimand, April 5, 1781, FHP 21734, f. 87; Maxwell to Haldimand, April 6, 1781, FHP 21734, f. 89; Mathias to Haldimand, December 21, 1781, FHP 21734, f. 284.

28. Batt to Newburgh, May 4, 1773, WO 72/7/1. See also NCE, p. 18.

29. Stuart to Haldimand, November 27, 1782, FHP 21818, f. 326.

30. Romans 5:4; 2 Corinthians 8:2.

31. George Mosse, *The Image of Man: The Creation of Modern Masculinity* (New York: Oxford University Press, 1996), 60–61; Charles Upchurch, *Before Wilde: Sex between Men in Britain's Age of Reform* (Berkeley: University of California Press, 2009), 190–91.

32. Marilyn Morris, *Sex, Money, and Personal Character in Eighteenth-Century British Politics* (New Haven: Yale University Press, 2014), 45–58.

33. NCE, p. 1.

34. Compare NCE to Proceedings of a Court of Inquiry, Carleton Island, December 2, 1783, FHP 21787, ff. 350–52; Scott to Haldimand, June 3, 1782, FHP 21734, ff. 471–72.

35. NCE, p. 5.

36. NCE, pp. 6–7. See also Bernard Burke, *Genealogical and Heraldic History of the Landed Gentry of Great Britain and Ireland*, vol. 2 (London: Harrison, Pall Mall, 1879), s.v. "Tottenham of Tottenham Green Woodstock."

37. NCE, pp. 4, 8.

38. NCE, pp. 8–10.

39. NCE, p. 11.

40. NCE, p. 16.

41. NCE, p. 16–17.

42. Haldimand to Gage, June 26, 1774, TGP-AS 120.

43. Officers' Testimony, WO 72/7/29.

Chapter Five: Assisted Privately by Some Miscreant

1. GGCM, pp. 270–71.
2. GGCM, p. 258. See also GGCM, pp. 344–45.
3. GGCM, p. 273.
4. Adye to Gould, August 26, 1774, WO 71/145; GGCM, p. 260.
5. GGCM, p. 264.
6. GGCM, pp. 325, 324, 335, 260, 264; FCM, exhibit 3, pp. 31–32[33–34].
7. GGCM, pp. 274, 329, 332–33.
8. Hamilton to Haldimand, May 7, 1774, enclosure in Haldimand to Gage, June 26, 1774, TGP-AS 120. See also Adye Observations, WO 72/7/32, p. 5; Hamilton to Haldimand, May 26, 1774, FHP 21670, ff. 143–44; Adye to Moncrieff, May 28, 1774, FHP 21670, f. 146.
9. GGCM, p. 237.
10. NCM, p. 37. See also NCM, pp. 83, 94[96]; William A. Whitehead, *Contributions to the Early History of Perth Amboy and the Adjoining Country* (New York: Appleton, 1856), 256–58; Evarts B. Greene and Virginia D. Harrington, *American Population before the Federal Census of 1790* (New York: Columbia University Press, 1932), 112nn.
11. GGCM, p. 234; Richard Cannon, *Historical Record of the Twenty-Third, or, the Royal Welsh Fusiliers; Containing an Account of the Formation of the Regiment in 1689 and of Its Subsequent Services to 1850* (London: Parker, Furnivall, and Parker, 1850), 73–89; Francis Duncan, *History of the Royal Regiment of Artillery; Compiled from the Original Records*, 2 vols. (London: Murray, 1872–73), 1: 251–63; Michael Langley, *The Loyal Regiment (North Lancashire): The 47th and 81st Regiments of Foot* (London: Cooper, 1976), 5–13.
12. GGCM, p. 234.
13. PCM, p. 69.
14. GGCM, p. 235. See also PCM, pp. 36, 61.
15. GGCM, p. 236.
16. GGCM, p. 238.
17. GGCM, p. 242.
18. GGCM, p. 243.
19. GGCM, p. 248.
20. GGCM, p. 247.
21. GGCM, p. 252.
22. GGCM, p. 254.

23. GGCM, p. 257. See also Moncrieff to Hamilton, June 8, 1774, WO 72/7/16.
24. MaCM, p. 1.
25. MaCM, p. 1.
26. MaCM, pp. 2–3.
27. MaCM, p. 6.
28. MaCM, p. 7.
29. MaCM, pp. 7–8.
30. MaCM, p. 9.
31. "Jenny Cromwell's Complaint against Sodomy, 1692/3," Harley MS 7315, ff. 224, 226, BL. See also Peter Ackroyd, *Queer City: Gay London from the Romans to the Present Day* (London: Vintage, 2017), 97–100.
32. *Sodom and Onan, A Satire Inscrib'd to [Samuel Foote], Esqr., alias the Devil upon Two Sticks* (London, 1776), 17–18. See also Anna Clark, *Scandal: The Sexual Politics of the British Constitution* (Princeton: Princeton University Press, 2003); Matthew J. Kinservik, *Sex, Scandal, and Celebrity in Late Eighteenth-Century England* (New York: Palgrave Macmillan, 2007), 170–78, 183–92.
33. GGCM, pp. 257, 259.
34. GGCM, pp. 259, 262.
35. GGCM, pp. 274–75.
36. GGCM, pp. 277, 285.
37. GGCM, pp. 258, 302, 309, 311.
38. GGCM, p. 320.
39. GGCM, p. 324.
40. GGCM, p. 335[336].
41. GGCM, pp. 345–46.
42. GGCM, pp. 350–52.
43. GGCM, p. 354.
44. GGCM, pp. 343–44.

Chapter Six: A Patriotick American

1. Dartmouth to Gage, April 9, 1774, TGP-ES 24; John Richard Alden, *General Gage in America: Being Principally a History of His Role in the American Revolution* (Baton Rouge: Louisiana State University Press, 1948), 194–204; Alan Valentine, *Lord North*, 2 vols. (Norman: University of Oklahoma Press, 1967), 1: 309–23; David Ammerman, *In the Common Cause: American Response to the Coercive Acts of*

1774 (Charlottesville: University of Virginia Press, 1974), 1–10; Peter Whiteley, *Lord North: The Prime Minister Who Lost America* (London: Hambledon Press, 1996), 137–45.

2. GGCM, p. 344; Gage to Lloyd, May 30, 1774, TGP-AS 119; Moncrieff to Hamilton, June 8, 1774, WO 72/7/16; Haldimand to Gage, June 10, 1774, TGP-AS 119; Gage to Haldimand, July 22, 1774, FHP 21665, ff. 277–78.

3. Jeff to Judge Advocate, May 27, 1774, WO 72/7/19.

4. "Deserted," *Pennsylvania Packet*, August 22, 1774; NCM, p. 30; PCM, p. 70.

5. NCM, p. 30.

6. Newburgh to Haldimand, June 4, 1774, TGP-AS 119; NCM, pp. 30–31.

7. Hamilton Charges, enclosure in Haldimand to Gage, June 26, 1774, TGP-AS 120.

8. Newburgh to Haldimand, May 29, 1774, enclosure in Haldimand to Gage, June 26, 1774, TGP-AS 120.

9. Nesbitt to Moncrieff, May 29, 1774, enclosure in Haldimand to Gage, June 26, 1774, TGP-AS 120.

10. Moncrieff to Hamilton, May 30, 1774, enclosure in Haldimand to Gage, June 26, 1774, TGP-AS 120. See also Moncrieff to Newburgh, May 30, 1774, enclosure in Haldimand to Gage, June 26, 1774, TGP-AS 120.

11. Hamilton Orders, WO 72/7/20; Newburgh to Hamilton, June 1, 1774, WO 72/7/21.

12. NCM, p. 5; Mawby to Newburgh, June 5, 1774, WO 72/7/28. See also Accusations against Newburgh, enclosure in Hamilton to Gage, June 7, 1774, TGP-AS 119.

13. MR, p. 273.

14. Quoted in Mary Beth Norton, *1774: The Long Year of Revolution* (New York: Knopf, 2020), 94; *American Archives*, 4th ser., 6 vols. (Washington: Clarke and Force, 1837), 1: 365. See also Richard Alan Ryerson, *The Revolution Is Now Begun: The Radical Committees of Philadelphia, 1765–76* (Philadelphia: University of Pennsylvania Press, 1978); Steven Rosswurm, *Arms, Country, and Class: The Philadelphia Militia and "Lower Sort" during the American Revolution, 1775–83* (New Brunswick: Rutgers University Press, 1987); Peter Thompson, *Rum Punch and Revolution: Taverngoing and Public Life in Eighteenth-Century Philadelphia* (Philadelphia: University of Pennsyl-

vania Press, 1999); George W. Boudreau, *Independence: A Guide to Historic Philadelphia* (Yardley, Pa.: Westholme, 2012).

15. JCC 1: 20. See also Norton, *1774*, 128–29; Kevin J. Dellape, *America's First Chaplain: The Life and Times of the Reverend Jacob Duché* (Bethlehem: Lehigh University Press, 2013), 72–74.

16. The figures are in Pennsylvania currency. PA 8th ser., 8: 7128. See also PA 8th ser., 8: 6704, 6876, 7015, 7099–100; PASL 8: 241–42; Alexander Graydon, *Memoirs of His Own Time*, ed. John Stockton Littell (Philadelphia: Lindsay and Blakiston, 1846), 51–54; "Philadelphia Society before the Revolution," *Pennsylvania Magazine of History and Biography* 11 (1887): 276–87. On events in Boston, see Hiller B. Zobel, *The Boston Massacre* (New York: Norton, 1970); Eric Hinderaker, *Boston's Massacre* (Cambridge: Harvard University Press, 2017); Serena Zabin, *The Boston Massacre: A Family History* (Boston: Houghton Mifflin, 2020).

17. *Portrait of a Patriot: The Major Political and Legal Papers of Josiah Quincy Junior*, ed. Daniel R. Coquillette and Neil Longley York, vol. 6 (Boston: Colonial Society of Massachusetts, 2014), 207; "Philadelphia, July 25," *Pennsylvania Packet or, the General Advertiser*, July 25, 1774. See also "This Day Is Published," *Pennsylvania Packet*, July 4, 1774; Norton, *1774*, 152–53.

18. Hamilton to Gage, August 2, 1774, TGP-AS 122; Hamilton to Moncrieff, July 11, 1774, enclosure in Haldimand to Gage, July 17, 1774, TGP-AS 121. See also Harmon Pumpelly Read, *Rossiana: Papers and Documents Relating to the History and Genealogy of the Ancient and Noble House of Ross of Ross-Shire, Scotland, and Its Descent from the Ancient Earl of Ross* (Albany: Read, 1908), 165–67; John Gilbert McCurdy, *Quarters: The Accommodation of the British Army and the Coming of the American Revolution* (Ithaca: Cornell University Press, 2019), 226.

19. Trist to Hamilton, July 26, 1774, enclosure in Hamilton to Gage, July 30, 1774, TGP-AS 121; Hamilton to Gage, July 30, 1774, TGP-AS 121. See also Gerard Gawalt, *Elizabeth House Trist: An Undaunted Woman's Journey through Jefferson's World* (North Charleston: CreateSpace, 2017), 1–5.

20. Steven M. Baule, *Protecting the Empire's Frontier: Officers of the 18th (Royal Irish) Regiment of Foot during Its North American Service, 1767–76* (Athens: Ohio University Press, 2014), 177.

21. Lord to Gage, August 5, 1774, TGP-AS 122. See also Hamilton to
    Moncrieff, June 30, 1774, FHP 21665, f. 259; Woody Holton, *Forced
    Founders: Indians, Debtors, Slaves, and the Making of the American
    Revolution in Virginia* (Chapel Hill: University of North Carolina
    Press, 1999), 34, 162–63.

22. Haldimand to Gage, June 21, 1774, FHP 21665, f. 275. See also
    Gage to Haldimand, July 14, 1774, FHP 21665, ff. 271–72; Hal-
    dimand to Gage, 18 August 1774, FHP 21665, ff. 296–97.

23. Jon Butler, *Becoming America: The Revolution before 1776* (Cambridge:
    Harvard University Press, 2000). See also Ned C. Landsman, *From
    Colonials to Provincials: American Thought and Culture, 1680–1760*
    (Ithaca: Cornell University Press, 1997).

24. John Shy, *Toward Lexington: The Role of the British Army in the Coming
    of the American Revolution* (Princeton: Princeton University Press,
    1965); Pauline Maier, *From Resistance to Revolution: Colonial Radicals
    and the Development of American Opposition to Britain, 1765–76* (New
    York: Knopf, 1972); Edmund S. Morgan and Helen M. Morgan, *The
    Stamp Act Crisis: Prologue to Revolution*, 3rd ed. (Chapel Hill: Univer-
    sity of North Carolina Press, 1995); Benjamin L. Carp, *Rebels Rising:
    Cities and the American Revolution* (New York: Oxford University
    Press, 2007); Benjamin L. Carp, *Defiance of the Patriots: The Boston Tea
    Party and the Making of America* (New Haven: Yale University Press,
    2011).

25. Bernard Bailyn, *The Ideological Origins of the American Revolution*,
    enlarged ed. (Cambridge: Harvard University Press, 1992), 94–143;
    Pauline Maier, *American Scripture: Making the Declaration of Independence*
    (New York: Random House, 1997).

26. John D'Emilio and Estelle B. Freedman, *Intimate Matters: A History
    of Sexuality in America*, 2nd ed. (Chicago: University of Chicago
    Press, 1997), 1. See also John Demos, *A Little Commonwealth: Family
    Life in Plymouth Colony* (New York: Oxford University Press, 1970),
    192; Lawrence Stone, *The Family, Sex, and Marriage in England,
    1500–1800* (New York: Harper and Row, 1977), 65; Laurel Thatcher
    Ulrich, *Good Wives: Image and Reality in Northern New England,
    1650–1750* (New York: Knopf, 1982), 146–64; Robert V. Wells,
    "The Population of England's Colonies in America: Old English
    or New Americans?" *Population Studies* 46 (1992): 85–102; Henry A.
    Gemery, "The White Population of the Colonial United States,

1607–1790," in *A Population History of North America*, ed. Michael R. Haines and Richard H. Steckel (Cambridge: Cambridge University Press, 2000), 143–90; Jennifer L. Morgan, *Laboring Women: Reproduction and Gender in New World Slavery* (Philadelphia: University of Pennsylvania Press, 2004).

27. *The Journal of Esther Edwards Burr, 1754–57*, ed. Carol F. Karlsen and Laurie Crumpacker (New Haven: Yale University Press, 1984), 105, 83.

28. Richard Godbeer, "'The Cry of Sodom': Discourse, Intercourse, and Desire in Colonial New England," WMQ 52 (1995): 259–86. See also Jonathan Ned Katz, *Gay/Lesbian Almanac: A New Documentary* (New York: Carroll and Graf, 1983); Colin L. Talley, "Gender and Male Same-Sex Erotic Behavior in British North America in the Seventeenth Century," JHS 6 (1996): 385–408; William N. Eskridge Jr., *Dishonorable Passions: Sodomy Laws in America, 1861–2003* (New York: Viking, 2008), 16–19, 388–407; Michael Bronski, *A Queer History of the United States* (Boston: Beacon Press, 2011), 5–18.

29. Lois Green Carr and Russell R. Menard, "Immigration and Opportunity: The Freedman in Early Colonial Maryland," in *The Chesapeake in the Seventeenth Century: Essays on Anglo-American Society*, ed. Thad W. Tate and David L. Ammerman (Chapel Hill: University of North Carolina Press, 1979), 232. See also PASL 2: 8; 3: 202; William Benemann, *Male-Male Intimacy in Early America: Beyond Romantic Friendships* (New York: Harrington Park Press, 2006), 9–16.

30. *Long before Stonewall: Histories of Same-Sex Sexuality in Early America*, ed. Thomas A. Foster (New York: New York University Press, 2007), 19–77; Benemann, *Male-Male Intimacy*, 1–9; Bronski, *Queer History*, 2–5. On Native Americans, see Will Roscoe, *Changing Ones: Third and Fourth Genders in Native North America* (New York: St. Martin's Press, 1998); Mark Rifkin, *When Did Indians Become Straight?: Kinship, the History of Sexuality, and Native Sovereignty* (New York: Oxford University Press, 2011); Roger M. Carpenter, "Womanish Men and Manlike Women: The Native American Two-spirit as Warrior," in *Gender and Sexuality in Indigenous North America, 1400–1850*, ed. Sandra Slater and Fay A. Yarbrough, 146–64 (Columbia: University of South Carolina Press, 2011); Gregory D. Smithers, *Reclaiming Two-Spirits: Sexuality, Spiritual Renewal and Sovereignty in Native*

America (Boston: Beacon, 2022). On Africans and African Americans, see Stephen O. Murray and Will Roscoe, *Boy-Wives and Female-Husbands: Studies in African Homosexualities* (New York: St. Martin's Press, 1998); Marc Epprecht, *Heterosexual Africa?: The History of an Idea from the Age of Exploration to the Age of AIDS* (Athens: Ohio University Press, 2008); Alan Taylor, *The Internal Enemy: Slavery and War in Virginia, 1772–1832* (New York: Norton, 2013), 254; Thomas A. Foster, *Rethinking Rufus: Sexual Violations of Enslaved Men* (Athens: University of Georgia Press, 2019), 85–112.

31. Quoted in Thomas A. Foster, *Sex and the Eighteenth-Century Man: Massachusetts and the History of Sexuality in America* (Boston: Beacon Press, 2006), 166. See also Clare A. Lyons, "Mapping an Atlantic Sexual Culture: Homoeroticism in Eighteenth-Century Philadelphia," WMQ 60 (2003): 119–54.

32. "Extracts of Some Letters Received by the Last Vessels from London," *Pennsylvania Packet*, October 10, 1774; "The Ancient Destruction of Sodom and Gomorrah," *Hartford Courant*, August 9, 1774. See also "Boston, (Thursday) September 29," *Hartford Courant*, October 3, 1774; "Extracts of Some Letters Received by the Last Vessels from London," *South Carolina Gazette*, October 25, 1774; "Mr. Pinckney," *Virginia Gazette*, December 13, 1775.

33. Susan E. Klepp, *Revolutionary Conceptions: Women, Fertility, and Family Limitation in America, 1760–1820* (Chapel Hill: University of North Carolina Press, 2009), 8, 25–31.

34. TJP 1: 423; quoted in David Brion Davis, *Inhuman Bondage: The Rise and Fall of Slavery in the New World* (Oxford: Oxford University Press, 2006), 146; "To His Excellency Thomas Gage Governor" (1774), in *Collections of the Massachusetts Historical Society*, 5th ser., vol. 3 (Boston: Massachusetts Historical Society, 1877), 434; AFC 1: 370. See also Bailyn, *Ideological Origins*, 22–54; Gordon S. Wood, *The Radicalism of the American Revolution* (New York: Random House, 1991); Ira Berlin, *Many Thousands Gone: The First Two Centuries of Slavery in North America* (Cambridge: Harvard University Press, 1998); Rhys Isaac, *Landon Carter's Uneasy Kingdom: Revolution and Rebellion on a Virginia Plantation* (New York: Oxford University Press, 2004); Elaine Forman Crane, "Abigail Adams, Gender Politics, and *The History of Emily Montague*: A Postscript," WMQ 64 (2007): 839–44; Douglas R. Egerton, *Death or Liberty: African Americans and Revolutionary America* (Oxford: Oxford University Press, 2009),

46–60; Woody Holton, *Abigail Adams* (New York: Free Press, 2009); Sheila L. Skemp, *First Lady of Letters: Judith Sargent Murray and the Struggle for Female Independence* (Philadelphia: University of Pennsylvania Press, 2009); Rosemarie Zagarri, *Revolutionary Backlash: Women and Politics in the Early American Republic* (Philadelphia: University of Pennsylvania Press, 2011); Kate Masur, *Until Justice Be Done: America's First Civil Rights Movement, from the Revolution to Reconstruction* (New York: Norton, 2021).

35. Newburgh to Haldimand, June 4, 1774, TGP-AS 119. See also Newburgh to Haldimand, June 14, 1774, TGP-AS 120; Haldimand to Gage, June 16, 1774, FHP 21665, f. 247.

36. Newburgh to Gage, June 13, 1774, TGP-AS 120. See also David Hackett Fischer, *Liberty and Freedom: A Visual History of America's Founding Ideas* (New York: Oxford University Press, 2005), 3–13; DNB, s.v. "Cavendish, Sir William."

37. Hamilton to Gage, June 7, 1774, TGP-AS 119.

38. Newburgh to Gage, June 25, 1774, TGP-AS 120; Gage to Haldimand, June 26, 1774, TGP-AS 120. See also Gage to Haldimand, June 12, 1774, TGP-AS 120; Gage to Hamilton, June 26, 1774, TGP-AS 120; Gage to Newburgh, June 26, 1774, TGP-AS 120; Haldimand to Gage, June 26, 1774, TGP-AS 120; Thomas Gage, Orderly Books, 1766–74, New-York Historical Society, New York, N.Y., July 13, 1774; *Letters and Diary of John Rowe, Boston Merchant, 1759–62, 1764–79*, ed. Anne Rowe Cunningham (Boston: Clarke, 1903), 270–81.

39. Gage to Haldimand, August 7, 1774, TGP-AS 122.

40. Gage to Haldimand, September 1, 1774, TGP-AS 122.

41. Newburgh to Hamilton, July 30, 1774, WO 72/7/22. See also Gage to Haldimand, July 13, 1774, FHP 21665, f. 267.

42. NCM, p. 50.

43. NCM, p. 57.

44. Haldimand to Gage, July 28, 1774, FHP 21665, f. 285; Newburgh to Hamilton, August 2, 1774, WO 72/7/26. See also NCM, p. 100[102]; Haldimand to Newburgh, August 1, 1774, FHP 21665, ff. 289–90.

45. Newburgh to Hamilton, July 30, 1774, WO 72/7/22; PCM, p. 60.

46. Newburgh to Gage, August 7, 1774, TGP-AS 122; Gage to Haldimand, August 18, 1774, FHP 21665, f. 298. See also Gage to Newburgh, August 20, 1774, TGP-AS 122.

47. NCM, p. 95[93]. See also DAB, s.v. "Bowden, John"; James B. Bell, "Anglican Clergy in Colonial America Ordained by Bishops of London," *Proceedings of the American Antiquarian Society* 83 (1973): 103–60.

48. Joseph S. Tiedemann, *Reluctant Revolutionaries: New York City and the Road to Independence, 1763–76* (Ithaca: Cornell University Press, 1997), 13–41; Jill Lepore, *New York Burning: Liberty, Slavery, and Conspiracy in Eighteenth-Century Manhattan* (New York: Knopf, 2005).

49. Gage, Orderly Books, January 14, 1767, February 24, 1767, April 29, 1767, July 9, 1767, March 21, 1768, April 8, 1768; Stephen Jenkins, *The Greatest Street in the World: The Story of Broadway, Old and New, from the Bowling Green to Albany* (New York: Putnam's Sons, 1911), 84–93; I. N. Phelps Stokes, *The Iconography of Manhattan Island, 1498–1909*, 6 vols. (New York: Dodd, 1915–28), 1: 339–41; Tiedemann, *Reluctant Revolutionaries*, 109–11, 147–49.

50. Tiedemann, *Reluctant Revolutionaries*, 183–200; Leopold S. Launitz-Schürer Jr., *Loyal Whigs and Revolutionaries: The Making of the Revolution in New York, 1765–76* (New York: New York University Press, 1980), 114–19.

51. JADA 2: 103. See also AFC 1: 108.

Chapter Seven: The Advocate of an Injured Man

1. Haldimand to Gage, August 7, 1774, FHP 21665, f. 292.

2. NCM, p. 1. See also Hamilton to Chapman, August 4, 1774, WO 72/7/18.

3. Chapman Closing Argument, WO 72/7/31, p. 13.

4. NCM, pp. 1–2.

5. NCM, p. 2.

6. PCM, p. 70. See also PCM, p. 63; MR, p. 283; "Deserted," *Pennsylvania Packet*, August 8, 1774.

7. NCM, pp. 2, 5.

8. NCM, pp. 8, 10.

9. NCM, p. 13.

10. NCM, p. 15.

11. NCM, p. 16.

12. NCM, p. 17.

13. NCM, p. 22.

14. NCM, p. 25.

15. NCM, p. 26.

16. NCM, p. 28.
17. NJD 3: 415–16n; William B. Reed, *Life and Correspondence of Joseph Reed*, 2 vols. (Philadelphia: Lindsay and Blakiston, 1847).
18. NCM, p. 27.
19. NCM, p. 29. See also NCM, p. 89[91]; Zephyr Teachout, *Corruption in America: From Benjamin Franklin's Snuff Box to* Citizens United (Cambridge: Harvard University Press, 2014).
20. NCM, pp. 29–30.
21. NCM, p. 30–31.
22. *The Statutes at Large; Being a Collection of All the Laws of Virginia, from the First Session of the Legislature in the Year 1619*, ed. William Waller Hening, 13 vols. (New York: Bartow, et al., 1819–23), 3: 563. See also Richard B. Morris, *Government and Labor in Early America* (New York: Harper and Row, 1946), 414–32.
23. Gage to Barrington, September 13, 1766, TGP-ES 8; Pomeroy to Gage, May 1, 1769, TGP-AS 85; *King v. Dyer*, July 5, 1774, and *King v. Dunnivan*, July 24, 1774, TGP-AS 123. See also Füser to Gage, July 4, 1768, TGP-AS 78; "Extract of a Letter from a Gentleman at Windsor (Nova-Scotia) to a Gentleman in Halifax, dated August 22, 1774," in *Boston Evening-Post*, September 12, 1774; John Shy, *Toward Lexington: The Role of the British Army in the Coming of the American Revolution* (Princeton: Princeton University Press, 1965), 172–76, 361–63.
24. Cathy N. Davidson, *Revolution and the Word: The Rise of the Novel in America* (New York: Oxford University Press, 1986), 91–150; Rodney Hessinger, "'Insidious Murderers of Female Innocence': Representations of Masculinity in the Seduction Tales of the Late Eighteenth Century," *Sex and Sexuality in Early America*, ed. Merril D. Smith (New York: New York University Press, 1998), 262–82; Richard Godbeer, *Sexual Revolution in Early America* (Baltimore: Johns Hopkins University Press, 2002), 264–98.
25. *Papers of John Adams*, ed. Robert J. Taylor, et al., 19 vols. (Cambridge: Harvard University Press, 1977–2018), 2: 305, 344; Pauline Maier, *From Resistance to Revolution: Colonial Radicals and the Development of American Opposition to Britain, 1765–76* (New York: Knopf, 1972); Jay Fliegelman, *Prodigals and Pilgrims: The American Revolution against Patriarchal Authority, 1750–1800* (Cambridge: Cambridge University Press, 1982); Andrew Jackson O'Shaughnessy, *The Men Who Lost America: British Leadership, the American Revolution, and the Fate of the*

Empire (New Haven: Yale University Press, 2013), 98–103,
187–92; Hugh McIntosh, "Constituting the End of Feeling:
Interiority in the Seduction Fiction of the Ratification Era," *Early
American Literature* 47 (2012): 321–48; Serena Zabin, *The Boston
Massacre: A Family History* (Boston: Houghton Mifflin Harcourt,
2020), 80–83. On seduction, see Toni Bowers, "Seduction Narra-
tives and Tory Experience in Augustan England," *Eighteenth Century*
40 (1999): 128–54; Andrea L. Hibbard and John T. Parry, "Law,
Seduction, and the Sentimental Heroine: The Case of Amelia
Norman," *American Literature* 78 (2006): 325–55; Katie Barclay,
"Emotions, the Law and the Press in Britain: Seduction and
Breach of Promise Suits, 1780–1830," *Journal for Eighteenth-Century
Studies* 39 (2016): 267–84.

26. Historians have documented fears of homosexual seduction in
medieval Italian art and twentieth-century German laws, but little
has been written about its place in Anglo Atlantic. See Jennifer V.
Evans, "Decriminalization, Seduction, and 'Unnatural Desire' in
East Germany," *Feminist Studies* 36 (2010): 553–77; Dennis Ro-
mano, "A Depiction of Male Same-Sex Seduction in Ambrogio
Lorenzetti's *Effects of Bad Government* Fresco," JHS 21 (2012): 1–16.
On status and buggery, see Robert Oresko, "Homosexuality and
the Court Elites of Early Modern France: Some Problems, Some
Suggestions, and an Example," *The Pursuit of Sodomy: Male Homo-
sexuality in Renaissance and Enlightenment Europe*, ed. Kent Gerard and
Gert Hekma, 105–28 (New York: Haworth Press, 1989).

27. NCM, pp. 44–45.

28. A. D. Harvey, *Sex in Georgian England: Attitudes and Prejudices from the
1720s to the 1820s* (New York: St. Martin's Press, 1994), 132; Theo
van der Meer, "Sodomy and Its Discontents: Discourse, Desire, and
the Rise of a Same-Sex Proto-Something in the Early Modern
Dutch Republic," *Historical Reflections / Réflexions Historiques* 33
(2007): 41–67; Brian Lacey, *Terrible Queer Creatures: Homosexuality in
Irish History* (Dublin: Wordwell, 2008), 119.

29. NCM, p. 32.

30. NCM, p. 35.

31. Batt to Gaffney, [July 1774], WO 72/7/13.

32. NCM, p. 53; Batt to Gaffney, July 26, 1774, WO 72/7/12.

33. Gaffney to Batt, [July 1774], 72/7/15. See also Gaffney to Batt,
[July 1774], 72/7/14.

34. Batt to Gage, June 19, 1775, TGP-AS 130; Batt to Gage, August 11, 1775, TGP-AS 133.

35. NCM, pp. 37–39.

36. Scott to Haldimand, January 28, 1782, FHP 21734, ff. 338–40. See also Blake to Haldimand, November 3, 1778, FHP 21732, f. 155; Fisher to Mabane, July 11, 1781, FHP 21734, f. 160.

37. Alan Acheson, *A History of the Church of Ireland, 1691–2001* (Dublin: Columba Press, 1997), 96–100.

38. NCM, pp. 81–82.

39. *B. and M. Gratz, Merchants in Philadelphia, 1754–98: Papers of Interest to Their Posterity and the Posterity of Their Associates*, ed. William Vincent Byers (Jefferson City: Stephens, 1916), 14–17, 47, 66, 71–72, 88–89, 108–10, 118, 139–43; Anna Edith Marks, "William Murray, Trader and Land Speculator in the Illinois Country" (B.A. thesis, University of Illinois, 1919). I have been unable to establish who Mr. Laugher (or Lougher) was.

40. NCM, pp. 82–83.

41. NCM, p. 45.

42. John Boswell, *Christianity, Social Tolerance, and Homosexuality: Gay People in Western Europe from the Beginning of the Christian Era to the Fourteenth Century* (Chicago: University of Chicago Press, 1980), 187–93; Mark D. Jordan, *The Invention of Sodomy in Christian Theology* (Chicago: University of Chicago Press, 1997); Theo van der Meer, "Sodomy and the Pursuit of a Third Sex in the Early Modern Period," in *Third Sex, Third Gender: Beyond Sexual Dimorphism in Culture and History*, ed. Gilbert Herdt (New York: Zone Books, 1996), 137–212; H. G. Cocks, *Visions of Sodom: Religion, Homoerotic Desire, and the End of the World in England, c. 1550–1850* (Chicago: University of Chicago Press, 2017); Dyan Elliott, *The Corrupter of Boys: Sodomy, Scandal, and the Medieval Clergy* (Philadelphia: University of Pennsylvania Press, 2020).

43. Rictor Norton, *Mother Clap's Molly House: The Gay Subculture in England, 1700–1830* (London: GMP, 1992), 159–64; Harvey, *Sex in Georgian England*, 126–30.

44. *Mars Stript of His Armour: Or, the Army Displayed in All Its True Colours* (London: Serjeant [1765]), 60–61; [Henry Brooke], *A Fragment of the History of Patrick* (London, 1753), 34. On chaplains, see *Cuthbertson's System for the Complete Interior Management and Oeconomy of a Battalion of Infantry*, new ed. (Bristol: Rouths and Nelson, 1776),

131; *Advice to the Officers of the British Army: With the Addition of Some Hints to the Drummer and Private Soldier*, 6th ed. (London: Richardson, 1783); Parker C. Thompson, *From Its European Antecedents to 1791: The United States Army Chaplaincy* (Washington: Department of the Army, 1978); Sylvia R. Frey, *The British Soldier in America: A Social History of Military Life in the Revolutionary Period* (Austin: University of Texas Press, 1981), 116–17; Paul E. Kopperman, "Religion and Religious Policy in the British Army, c.1700–96," *Journal of Religious History* 14 (1987): 390–405; Janet Moor Lindman, "'Play the Man . . . for Your Bleeding Country': Military Chaplains as Gender Brokers during the American Revolutionary War," in *New Men: Manliness in Early America*, ed. Thomas A. Foster (New York: New York University Press, 2011), 236–55; Michael Snape, *The Royal Army Chaplains' Department, 1796–1953* (Woodbridge: Boydell Press, 2008), 15–25; Matthew McCormack, *Embodying the Militia in Georgian England* (Oxford: Oxford University Press, 2015), 59–60. On homosexuality and the Enlightenment, see Jon Thomas Rowland, *"Swords in Myrtle Dress'd" Toward a Rhetoric of Sodom: Gay Readings of Homosexual Politics and Poetics in the Eighteenth Century* (Teaneck: Fairleigh Dickinson University Press, 1998), 41–44; Michael Brown, "Farmer and Fool: Henry Brooke and the Late Irish Enlightenment," in *The Laws and Legalities of Ireland, 1689–1850*, ed. Sean Patrick Donlan and Matthew Brown (New York: Routledge, 2011), 301–24; Michael Brown, *The Irish Enlightenment* (Cambridge: Harvard University Press, 2016), 311–12.

45. Eric Josef Carlson, *Marriage and the English Reformation* (Oxford: Blackwell, 1994), 3–8, 52–65; William L. Sachs, *Homosexuality and the Crisis of Anglicanism* (Cambridge: Cambridge University Press, 2009); Timothy Jones, "The Stained Glass Closet: Celibacy and Homosexuality in the Church of England to 1955," JHS 20 (2011): 132–52; Adam Connell and Julia Yates, "'Then You Will Know the Truth, and the Truth Will Set You Free': An Interpretative Phenomenological Analysis of the Career Experiences of Gay Clergy in the Church of England," *Sexuality and Culture* 25 (2021): 482–502.

Chapter Eight: What Is Now Termed a Maccaroni

1. Richard Meanwell, *Meanwell's Town and Country Almanack and Ephemeris for the Year of Our Lord 1774* (New York: Hodge and Shober, 1774), 22.

2. NCM, p. 37. See also Pay List for April 1774, Royal Artillery Musters, WO 10/138, NAK.
3. NCM, pp. 41–42.
4. NCM, pp. 43–44.
5. NCM, pp. 47, 52, 50.
6. NCM, pp. 54–55.
7. NCM, p. 59. The entire passage is underlined in the original.
8. NCM, pp. 61–63.
9. NCM, p. 63.
10. Fashion Institute of Technology, "Fashion History Timeline," State University of New York, <www.fashionhistory.fitnyc.edu/1770 -1779>. Thanks to Ann Little for this citation.
11. James Arthur Miller, "Philander Chase and the Frontier," *Historical Magazine of the Protestant Episcopal Church* 14 (1945): 168–84; Marion J. Hatchett, "A Sunday Service in 1776 or Thereabouts," *Historical Magazine of the Protestant Episcopal Church* 45 (1976): 369–85; William Gibson, "'Pious Decorum': Clerical Wigs in the Eighteenth-Century Church of England," *Anglican and Episcopal History* 65 (1996): 145–61.
12. NCM, p. 63–64.
13. NCM, p. 64.
14. NCM, pp. 65–66. See also *The Cambridge History of Ireland: Volume III, 1730–1880*, ed. James Kelly (Cambridge: Cambridge University Press, 2018), 489–516. The merchant was William West. See Paul A. W. Wallace, "Historic Hope Lodge," *Pennsylvania Magazine of History and Biography* 86 (1962): 115–42.
15. NCM, p. 67. See also Hamilton to Chapman, August 4, 1774, WO 72/7/18.
16. NCM, pp. 67, 69.
17. "Origin of the Word Macaroni," *Virginia Gazette*, February 11, 1773. See also "Extract of a Letter from Exeter, October 23," *Virginia Gazette*, January 7, 1773; "From the *Macaroni Magazine* for October 1772," *Virginia Gazette*, February 11, 1773. This account of the word's origins has been challenged by Peter McNeil. See Peter McNeil, *Pretty Gentlemen: Macaroni Men and the Eighteenth-Century Fashion World* (New Haven: Yale University Press, 2018), 49–55.
18. NCM, p. 64. See also McNeil, *Pretty Gentlemen*, 13–32, 83–92; Gerald Howson, *The Macaroni Parson: A Life of the Unfortunate Dr. Dodd* (London: Hutchinsons, 1973); John Money, "The Masonic

Moment; Or, Ritual, Replica, and Credit: John Wilkes, the Maca-
roni Parson, and the Making of the Middle-Class Mind," *Journal of
British Studies* 32 (1993): 358–95; Philip Carter, "An 'Effeminate' or
'Efficient' Nation? Masculinity and Eighteenth-Century Social
Documentary," *Textual Practice* 11 (1997): 429–43; Anna Clark,
"The Chevalier d'Eon and Wilkes: Masculinity and Politics in the
Eighteenth Century," *Eighteenth-Century Studies* 32 (1998): 19–48;
Amelia Rauser, "Hair, Authenticity, and the Self-Made Macaroni,"
Eighteenth-Century Studies 38 (2004): 101–17; William Benemann,
Male-Male Intimacy in Early America: Beyond Romantic Friendships (New
York: Harrington Park Press, 2006), 50–54; Kate Haulman, *The
Politics of Fashion in Eighteenth-Century America* (Chapel Hill: Univer-
sity of North Carolina Press, 2011), 135–39.

19. *The Macaroni: A Comedy* (London: Nicoll and Bell, 1773), 5, 70. See
also *Dictionary of Irish Biography*, s.v. "Hitchcock, Robert."

20. John Cooke, *The Macaroni Jester, and Pantheon of Wit* (London: Cooke,
1773), 58, 13, 79, 103.

21. McNeil, *Pretty Gentlemen*, 151–79; "London, July 25," *New London
Gazette*, October 16, 1772. See also Dominic Janes, *Oscar Wilde
Prefigured: Queer Fashioning and British Caricature, 1750–1900* (Chicago:
University of Chicago Press, 2016), 25–54.

22. Randolph Trumbach, "The Birth of the Queen: Sodomy and the
Emergence of Gender Equality in Modern Culture, 1660–1750," in
Hidden from History: Reclaiming the Gay and Lesbian Past, ed. Martin
Duberman, Martha Vicinus, and George Chauncey Jr. (New York:
Meridian, 1989), 129–40; Randolph Trumbach, *Sex and the Gender
Revolution, Volume One: Heterosexuality and the Third Gender in
Enlightened London* (Chicago: University of Chicago Press, 1998), 7;
David Valentine, *Imagining Transgender: An Ethnography of a Category*
(Durham: Duke University Press, 2007); Charles Upchurch, *Before
Wilde: Sex between Men in Britain's Age of Reform* (Berkeley: University
of California Press, 2009), 86; Julie Peakman, *Amatory Pleasures:
Explorations in Eighteenth-Century Sexual Culture* (London: Blooms-
bury, 2016), 25; Mike Rendell, *Sex and Sexuality in Georgian Britain*
(Yorkshire: Pen and Sword History, 2020), 147–52.

23. "The City Macaronies Drinking Asses Milk, at the Lacteum, in
St. George's Fields," *Virginia Gazette*, April 15, 1773; "The Follow-
ing Is Substance of a Debate," *Virginia Gazette*, July 1, 1773. See also
"The Groom of a Noted Jockey," *Maryland Gazette*, February 20,

1772; "Cupid Turned Auctioneer," *South Carolina Gazette*, March 22, 1773; "A Parody on Hamlet, Addressed to the Macaronies," *Virginia Gazette*, December 16, 1773.

24. "To the Printer of the *Pennsylvania Packet*," *Pennsylvania Packet*, November 23, 1772; "On the Decay of English Customs and Manners," *Virginia Gazette*, December 29, 1774. See also "Extract of a Letter from Dublin," *Virginia Gazette*, June 18, 1772; "A Correspondent from Chatham," *Virginia Gazette*, January 7, 1773.

25. McNeil, *Pretty Gentlemen*, 180–83; Dror Wahrman, *The Making of the Modern Self: Identity and Culture in Eighteenth-Century England* (New Haven: Yale University Press, 2004), 60–65; Matthew McCormack, *Embodying the Militia in Georgian England* (Oxford: Oxford University Press, 2015), 59–65.

26. GWP 3: 266–67; TJP 14: 544; J. A. Leo Lemay, "The American Origins of 'Yankee Doodle,'" WMQ 33 (1976): 435–64; Eran Zelnik, "Yankees, Doodles, Fops, and Cuckolds: Compromised Manhood and Provincialism in the Revolutionary Period, 1740–81," *Early American Studies* 16 (2018): 514–44.

27. NCM, p. 64.

28. DAB, s.v. "Fanning, Edmund"; Paul David Nelson, *William Tryon and the Course of Empire: A Life in British Imperial Service* (Chapel Hill: University of North Carolina Press, 1990); Marjoleine Kars, *Breaking Loose Together: The Regulator Rebellion in Pre-Revolutionary North Carolina* (Chapel Hill: University of North Carolina Press, 2002).

29. NCM, pp. 69–70.

30. NCM, pp. 72–73.

31. NCM, p. 74.

32. NCM, p. 76.

33. NCM, pp. 75, 78.

34. NCM, pp. 79–80.

35. NCM, pp. 80–81.

36. NCM, pp. 83–84.

37. John N. Norton, *The Life of the Rt. Rev. William White, D.D., Bishop of Pennsylvania, and Presiding Bishop of the Protestant Episcopal Church in the United States*, 2nd ed. (New York: General Protestant Episcopal Sunday School Union and Church Book Society, 1860).

38. NCM, pp. 94–95[96–97].

39. NCM, p. 96[98].

40. NCM, pp. 96–97[98–99].
41. NCM, pp. 97–99[99–101]
42. NCM, p. 100[102].

Chapter Nine: Nil Humanum a me alienum puto

1. NCM, p. 100[102].
2. Quoted in Michael Brown, *The Irish Enlightenment* (Cambridge: Harvard University Press, 2016), 173.
3. Newburgh Defense, WO 72/7/30, pp. 3–5.
4. Newburgh Defense, WO 72/7/30, p. 12.
5. Newburgh Defense, WO 72/7/30, pp. 19–20.
6. Chapman Closing Argument, WO 72/7/31, p. 1.
7. Julie Peakman, *Amatory Pleasures: Explorations in Eighteenth-Century Sexual Culture* (London: Bloomsbury, 2016), 32.
8. "The Petition of Hassan a Turk," Harley MS 7315, f. 235, BL.
9. DNB, ss.v. "Hedges, Sir William," "Harley, Robert, first Earl of Oxford"; "To the Renowned Beigh W. H.," Harley MS 7315, ff. 236–37, BL. See also *Islamic Homosexualities: Culture, History, and Literature* (New York: New York University Press, 1997); Greta LaFleur, *The Natural History of Sexuality in Early America* (Baltimore: Johns Hopkins University Press, 2018), 63–102.
10. Quoted in Rictor Norton, ed., "The Trial of Robert Jones, 1772," *Homosexuality in Eighteenth-Century England: A Sourcebook*, <www .rictornorton.co.uk/eighteen/jones2.htm>. See also Timm Hitchcock, et al., *The Old Bailey Proceedings Online, 1674–1913* (www .oldbaileyonline.org, version 7.0, 24 March 2012), July 1772, trial of Robert Jones (t17720715-22).
11. Quoted in Rictor Norton, ed., "The First Public Debate about Homosexuality in England: Letters and Editorials in the *Morning Chronicle* concerning the Case of Captain Jones, 1772," *Homosexuality in Eighteenth-Century England*. See also Louis Crompton, *Byron and Greek Love: Homophobia in 19th-Century England* (Berkeley: University of California Press, 1985), 16.
12. *The State of the Case against Captain Jones* (London: Peat, [1772]), 18–19.
13. Quoted in Rictor Norton, *Mother Clap's Molly House: The Gay Subculture in England, 1700–1830* (London: GMP, 1992), 171. See also Anna Clark, *Scandal: The Sexual Politics of the British Constitution* (Princeton: Princeton University Press, 2003), 44–45; Marilyn

Morris, *Sex, Money, and Personal Character in Eighteenth-Century British Politics* (New Haven: Yale University Press, 2014), 59–97.

14. Ernest Cassara, *The Enlightenment in America* (Lanham: University Press of America, 1988); John M. Dixon, *The Enlightenment of Cadwallader Colden: Empire, Science, and Intellectual Culture in British New York* (Ithaca: Cornell University Press, 2016); Margaret C. Jacobs, *The Secular Enlightenment* (Princeton: Princeton University Press, 2019); Daniel P. Johnson, *Making the Early Modern Metropolis: Culture and Power in Pre-Revolutionary Philadelphia* (Charlottesville: University of Virginia Press, 2022), 140, 148, 156.

15. Newburgh Defense, WO 72/7/30, pp. 22, 25–28.

16. Newburgh Defense, WO 72/7/30, p. 30.

17. Newburgh Defense, WO 72/7/30, p. 34.

18. Newburgh Defense, WO 72/7/30, p. 37.

19. Newburgh Defense, WO 72/7/30, p. 48.

20. Newburgh Defense, WO 72/7/30, pp. 48–50.

21. Newburgh Defense, WO 72/7/30, pp. 50–51.

22. Quoted in Edgar Legare Pennington, "The Anglican Clergy of Pennsylvania in the American Revolution," *Pennsylvania Magazine of History and Biography* 63 (1939): 414. See also Scott to St. Leger, October 13, 1781, FHP 21734, ff. 242–47; Charles Mampoteng, "The New England Anglican Clergy in the American Revolution," *Historical Magazine of the Protestant Episcopal Church* 9 (1940): 267–304; Howard L. Applegate, "Anglican Chaplains Serving the American Revolutionary Army, 1775–83," *Historical Magazine of the Protestant Episcopal Church* 30 (1961): 138–40; Arthur Pierce Middleton, "The Colonial Virginia Parish," *Historical Magazine of the Protestant Episcopal Church* 40 (1971): 431–46; David L. Holmes, "The Episcopal Church and the American Revolution," *Historical Magazine of the Protestant Episcopal Church* 47 (1978): 261–91; John Frederick Woolverton, *Colonial Anglicanism in North America* (Detroit: Wayne State University Press, 1984); Otto Lohrenz, "The Discord of Political and Personal Loyalties: The Experiences of the Reverend William Andrews of Revolutionary Virginia," *Southern Studies* 24 (1985): 374–95; D. G. Bell, "Charles Inglis and the Anglican Clergy of Loyalist New Brunswick," *Nova Scotia Historical Review* 7 (1987): 25–47; Otto Lohrenz, "The Life, Career, and Political Loyalties of the Reverend Thomas Hall of Revolution-

ary Virginia and Leghorn, Italy," *Fides et Historia* 31 (1998): 123–36; Nancy L. Rhoden, *Revolutionary Anglicanism: The Colonial Church of England Clergy during the American Revolution* (New York: New York University Press, 1999), 78; Katherine Carté Engel, "The SPCK and the American Revolution: The Limits of International Protestantism," *Church History* 81 (2012): 77–103; Otto Lohrenz, "Parson, Naturalist, and Loyalist: Thomas Feilde of England and Revolutionary Virginia and New York," *Southern Studies* 12 (2005): 105–28. Naboth's vineyard appears in 1 Kings 21: 1–16.

23. Newburgh Defense, WO 72/7/30, pp. 52–53.
24. Newburgh Defense, WO 72/7/30, pp. 62, 68–69.
25. Newburgh Defense, WO 72/7/30, pp. 65–66.
26. Newburgh Defense, WO 72/7/30, p. 66.
27. Newburgh Defense, WO 72/7/30, p. 71. *The Memoirs of Martinus Scriblerus* was purportedly written by a group of wits known as the Scriblerus Club in 1713–14. It was later published as part of Alexander Pope's works in 1741. See *Concise Oxford Companion to English Literature*, 3rd ed. (Oxford: Oxford University Press, 2007).
28. Newburgh Defense, WO 72/7/30, pp. 71–72.
29. Newburgh Defense, WO 72/7/30, p. 72.
30. Chapman Closing Argument, WO 72/7/31, p. 1.
31. Chapman Closing Argument, WO 72/7/31, pp. 1, 5[6].
32. Chapman Closing Argument, WO 72/7/31, pp. 11–12[12–13].
33. Chapman Closing Argument, WO 72/7/31, pp. 6–7[7–8].
34. Chapman Closing Argument, WO 72/7/31, p. 7[8].
35. Chapman Closing Argument, WO 72/7/31, p. 8[9].
36. Chapman Closing Argument, WO 72/7/31, pp. 13–15[14–15].
37. Steven M. Baule, *Protecting the Empire's Frontier: Officers of the 18th (Royal Irish) Regiment of Foot during Its North American Service, 1767–76* (Athens: Ohio University Press, 2014), 111.
38. NCM, p. 102[104]; Adye's Observations, WO 72/7/32, pp. 2–3.
39. NCM, p. 102[104].
40. Newburgh Response, WO 72/7/33, pp. 3, 4.
41. *The Comedies of Terence, Literally Translated into English Prose, with Notes,* ed. Henry Thomas Riley (New York: Harper and Brothers, 1874), 139n2. Among other places, *Homo sum, humani nihil a me alienum puto* appears in "From the *Westminster Journals* of November 30, December 7, 14, and 21, 1754," *Pennsylvania Gazette*, April 17, 1755; "To the

Printer, etc.," *Leeds Intelligencer and Yorkshire General Advertiser*, May 4, 1756; "This Day Is Published," *Jackson's Oxford Journal*, May 4, 1765; "To the Printer of the *Public Advertiser*," *Public Advertiser*, February 11, 1766; "This Day Is Published," *Public Advertiser*, February 23, 1767.

42. Charles Upchurch has made this argument better than most historians. See Charles Upchurch, "Liberal Exclusions and Sex between men in the Modern Era: Speculations on a Framework," JHS 19 (2010): 409–31. See also George L. Mosse, *Nationalism and Sexuality: Middle-Class Morality and Sexual Norms in Modern Europe* (Madison: University of Wisconsin Press, 1985), 27–28; Faramerz Dabhoiwla, *The Origins of Sex: A History of the First Sexual Revolution* (New York: Oxford University Press, 2012), 138–40. For a contrary interpretation, see Crompton, *Byron and Greek Love*, 16–30; Anna Clark, "Anne Lister's Construction of Lesbian Identity," JHS 7 (1996): 23–50; Isabel V. Hull, *Sexuality, State, and Civil Society in Germany, 1700–1815* (Ithaca: Cornell University Press, 1996), 258. On Bentham, see Norton, *Mother Clap's Molly House*, 119–22; Crompton, *Byron and Greek Love*, 38–57.

43. "On Negro Slavery," *Freeman's Journal or the North American Intelligencer* (Philadelphia), February 15, 1786. See also JADA 1: 353; TJP 1: 35; *The Papers of Benjamin Franklin*, vol. 22, ed. William B. Willcox (New Haven: Yale University Press, 1982), 46–49; *The Speeches of John Wilkes*, vol. 1 (London, 1777), 175; "The Speech of Mr. Wilkes," *Freeman's Journal* (Dublin), February 27, 1777.

44. Gordon S. Wood, *The Creation of the American Republic, 1776–1789* (Chapel Hill: University of North Carolina Press, 1969); Marc W. Kruman, *Between Authority and Liberty: State Constitution Making in Revolutionary America* (Chapel Hill: University of North Carolina Press, 1997).

45. Pauline Maier, *American Scripture: Making the Declaration of Independence* (New York: Knopf, 1997), 197–98; Gordon S. Wood, *The Radicalism of the American Revolution* (New York: Knopf, 1992); Gordon S. Wood, *Power and Liberty: Constitutionalism in the American Revolution* (New York: Oxford University Press, 2021). On religious freedom, see Daniel L. Dreisbach, *Thomas Jefferson and the Wall of Separation between Church and State* (New York: New York University Press, 2002). On abolitionism, see Ira Berlin, *Many Thousands Gone: The First Two Centuries of Slavery in North America* (Cambridge: Harvard University Press, 1998), 228–55, 259; Sean Wilenz, *No Man in*

Property: Slavery and Antislavery at the Nation's Founding (Cambridge: Harvard University Press, 2018).

46. On homosexuality in Revolutionary America, see Richard Godbeer, *Sexual Revolution in Early America* (Baltimore: Johns Hopkins University Press, 2002); Clare A. Lyons, "Mapping an Atlantic Sexual Culture: Homoeroticism in Eighteenth-Century Philadelphia," WMQ 60 (2003): 119–154; Thomas A. Foster, *Sex and the Eighteenth-Century Man: Massachusetts and the History of Sexuality in America* (Boston: Beacon Press, 2006); William Benemann, *Male-Male Intimacy in Early America: Beyond Romantic Friendships* (New York: Harrington Park Press, 2006), 16–22, 245–260; Richard Godbeer, *The Overflowing of Friendship: Love between Men and the Creation of the American Republic* (Baltimore: Johns Hopkins University Press, 2009). The Revolution is conspicuously absent from pioneering works on the history of sexuality. See Jonathan Ned Katz, *Gay/Lesbian Almanac: A New Documentary* (New York: Carroll and Graf, 1983); John D'Emilio and Estelle B. Freedman, *Intimate Matters: A History of Sexuality in America*, 2nd ed. (Chicago: University of Chicago Press, 1997). On comparative accounts of revolutions, see R. R. Palmer, *The Age of Democratic Revolutions: A Political History*, 2 vols. (Princeton: Princeton University Press, 1959); Susan Dunn, *Sister Revolutions: French Lightning, American Light* (New York: Faber and Faber, 1999); Alan Gibson, *Interpreting the Founding: Guide to the Enduring Debates over the Origins and Foundations of the American Republic* (Lawrence: University Press, of Kansas, 2006).

47. Michael Bronski, *A Queer History of the United States* (Boston: Beacon Press, 2011), 26–32; Woody Holton, *Liberty Is Sweet: The Hidden History of the American Revolution* (New York: Simon and Schuster, 2021); Kate Masur, *Until Justice Be Done: America's First Civil Rights Movement, from the Revolution to Reconstruction* (New York: Norton, 2021).

48. James Kirchick, *Secret City: The Hidden History of Gay Washington* (New York: Holt, 2022).

49. NCM, p. 102–3[104–5].

50. Haldimand to Gage, August 28, 1774, FHP 21665, f. 302.

Chapter Ten: Many Circumstances Have Happened

1. Haldimand to Gage, August 28, 1774, FHP 21665, f. 302.

2. *Letters and Diary of John Rowe, Boston Merchant, 1759–62, 1764–79*, ed. Anne Rowe Cunningham (Boston: Clarke, 1903), 283–85; David

Hackett Fischer, *Paul Revere's Ride* (New York: Oxford University Press, 1994), 44–64.

3. JADA 2: 103; JCC 1: 26–27, 31; Richard R. Beeman, *Our Lives, Our Fortunes, and Our Sacred Honor: The Forging of American Independence, 1774–76* (New York: Basic Books, 2013), 41–104; Mary Beth Norton, *1774: The Long Year of Revolution* (New York: Knopf, 2020), 168–206; Kevin J. Dellape, *America's First Chaplain: The Life and Times of the Reverend Jacob Duché* (Bethlehem: Lehigh University Press, 2013), 71–93.

4. JCC 1: 67, 61, 71. See also Beeman, *Our Lives*, 105–74; David Ammerman, *In the Common Cause: American Response to the Coercive Acts of 1774* (Charlottesville: University of Virginia Press, 1974).

5. Newburgh to Gage, October 16, 1774, TGP-AS 124. See also Gage Orderly Books, New-York Historical Society, New York, N.Y., September 10, 1774; NCM, p. 103[105].

6. FCM, exhibit 3, p. 32[34].

7. Newburgh to Wilkins, September 1, 1774, enclosure in Wilkins to Gage, November 2, 1774, TGP-AS 124.

8. Wilkins to Gage, November 2, 1774, TGP-AS 124.

9. Fowler to Gage, February 2, 1775, TGP-AS 125; PCM, exhibit 18, p. 2. See also Gage to Hamilton, December 28, 1774, TGP-AS 125; Fowler to Gage, January 12, 1775, TGP-AS 125; Gage to Hamilton, February 25, 1775, TGP-AS 126; Steven M. Baule, *Protecting the Empire's Frontier: Officers of the 18th (Royal Irish) Regiment of Foot during Its North American Service, 1767–76* (Athens: Ohio University Press, 2014), 24–25, 83–84, 90–91, 97–98.

10. Newburgh to Gage, October 16, 1774, TGP-AS 124.

11. Gage to Haldimand, September 1, 1774, TGP-AS 122; NJD 29: 480; "Philadelphia, September 14," *Virginia Gazette*, September 29, 1774. See also Haldimand to Gage, September 8, 1774, FHP 21665, f. 314.

12. Newburgh to Gage, October 16, 1774, TGP-AS 124; NJD 29: 481; Baule, *Protecting the Empire's Frontier*, 89, 112; Gage to Barrington, November 1, 1774, TGP-ES 26; *Letters of John Rowe*, 286; Work Done by Captain Montressor in Boston, from December 1774 to March 1775, TGP-AS 127; Distribution of His Majesty's Forces in North America, enclosure in Gage to Barrington, July 21, 1775, TGP-ES 30; Larry R. Gerlach, "Soldiers and Citizens: The British

Army in New Jersey on the Eve of the Revolution," *New Jersey History* 93 (1975): 5–36; Paul Knight, *A Very Fine Regiment: The 47th Foot during the American War of Independence, 1773–83* (Warwick: Helion, 2022), 96–100.

13. PCM, p. 135; PCM, exhibit 6, p. 9. See also PCM, pp. 11, 20–21, 32, 35–36, 38, 48, 51, 135; Baule, *Protecting the Empire's Frontier*, 208–10.

14. Fowler to Gage, June 2, 1775, TGP-AS 129.

15. *Letters of Delegates to Congress, 1774–89*, ed. Paul H. Smith, et al., 25 vols. (Washington: Library of Congress, 1976–2000), 1: 61.

16. Fowler to Gage, September 22, 1774, TGP-AS 123. See also Gage to Hamilton, August 21, 1774, TGP-AS 122; Baule, *Protecting the Empire's Frontier*, 164.

17. PCM, p. 141. See also Baule, *Protecting the Empire's Frontier*, 177–79; Gerard Gawalt, *Elizabeth House Trist: An Undaunted Woman's Journey through Jefferson's World* (North Charleston: CreateSpace, 2017), 4–6; *A List of the General and Field-Officers, as They Rank in the Army* (London: Millan, 1775), 72.

18. PCM, exhibit 4; "Case of Alexander Fowler," *General Advertiser* (Philadelphia), July 31, 1778.

19. PCM, pp. 138–39; PCM, exhibit 6, p. 11; quoted in "Case of Alexander Fowler," *General Advertiser*, June 22, 1778. On Sears and McDougall, see Patricia U. Bonomi, *A Factious People: Politics and Society in Colonial New York* (New York: Columbia University Press, 1971); Joseph S. Tiedemann, *Reluctant Revolutionaries: New York City and the Road to Independence, 1763–76* (Ithaca: Cornell University Press, 1997); Christopher F. Minty, *Unfriendly to Liberty: Loyalist Networks and the Coming of the American Revolution* (Ithaca: Cornell University Press, 2023), 89–113. On Campbell, see Alexander V. Campbell, *The Royal American Regiment: An Atlantic Microcosm, 1755–72* (Norman: University of Oklahoma Press, 2010), 53, 163, 178, 185.

20. "Case of Alexander Fowler," *General Advertiser*, June 22, 1778; PCM, Exhibit B; "Case of Alexander Fowler," *General Advertiser*, July 31, 1778. See also PCM, pp. 149–50; PCM, Exhibit A.

21. Gage to Hamilton, November 14, 1774, TGP-AS 124.

22. Newburgh to Gage, November 24, 1774, TGP-AS 124.

23. Newburgh to Gage, December 19, 1774, TGP-AS 124; Gage to Newburgh, January 2, 1775, TGP-AS 125.

24. Newburgh to Gage, March 16, 1775, TGP-AS 126.

25. "Case of Alexander Fowler," *General Advertiser*, July 30, 1778; Gage to Newburgh, April 2, 1775, TGP-AS 127. See also Gage to Hamilton, April 2, 1775, TGP-AS 127.

26. PCM, exhibit 2.

27. Fischer, *Paul Revere's Ride*, 186–201.

28. Quoted in Robert A. Gross, *The Minutemen and Their World* (New York: Hill and Wang, 1976), 131; GGCM, p. 242. See also Fischer, *Paul Revere's Ride*, 308–9, 323; Baule, *Protecting the Empire's Frontiers*, 22–23, 89–90, 112; Knight, *Very Fine Regiment*, 105–17.

29. Quoted in Baule, *Protecting the Empire's Frontier*, 106; "Case of Alexander Fowler," *General Advertiser*, July 31, 1778. See also Copy of Order of Capt. Batt & Lieut. McLean, June 7, 1775, TGP-AS 129; Gage to Batt, June 19, 1775, TGP-AS 130; Batt to Gage, June 30, 1775, TGP-AS 130; Baule, *Protecting the Empire's Frontier*, 106–8.

30. Colden to Gage, April 25, 1775, TGP-AS 128; *The Colden Letter Books*, 2 vols. (New York: New-York Historical Society, 1876–77), 2: 403; Colden to Gage, May 6, 1775, TGP-AS 128. See also Tiedemann, *Reluctant Revolutionaries*, 220–25.

31. JCC 2: 52. See also John Gilbert McCurdy, *Quarters: The Accommodation of the British Army and the Coming of the American Revolution* (Ithaca: Cornell University Press, 2019), 231–32; Michael Cecere, *United for Independence: The Revolutionary War in the Middle Colonies, 1775–1776* (Yardley, Pa.: Westholme, 2023), 4, 8.

32. Hamilton to Gage, May 25, 1775, TGP-AS 129. See also Gage to Colden, May 4, 1775, TGP-AS 128; Colden to Gage, May 31, 1775, TGP-AS 129; *Colden Letter Books*, 2: 415; PCM, pp. 74–75.

33. "Case of Alexander Fowler," *General Advertiser*, June 22, 1778.

34. Hamilton to Gage, June 8, 1775, TGP-AS 129; PCM, pp. 115–16. See also Gage to Hamilton, May 7, 1775, TGP-AS 128; PCM, pp. 91–94; *Colden Letter Books*, 2: 411, 413–18, 423–27; Tiedemann, *Reluctant Revolutionaries*, 216, 231–32; Baule, *Protecting the Empire's Frontier*, 24, 130–31, 164–65; Cecere, *United for Independence*, 17, 20–21.

35. Gage to Hamilton, June 10, 1775, TGP-AS 129; Distribution of His Majesty's Forces in North America, enclosure in Gage to Barrington, July 21, 1775, TGP-ES 30; John Clarke, *An Impartial and Authentic Narrative of the Battle Fought on the 17th of June, 1775* in *The*

Magazine of History 8 (1909): 258; Baule, *Protecting the Empire's Frontiers*, 90; Nathaniel Philbrick, *Bunker Hill: A City, a Siege, a Revolution* (New York: Viking Penguin, 2013).

36. Gage to Barrington, July 25, 1775, TGP-ES 30. See also *A List of the General and Field-Officers, as They Rank in the Army* (London: Millan, 1775), 72; Baule, *Protecting the Empire's Frontier*, 24–25, 83–84, 90–91, 97–98.

37. Dartmouth to Gage, August 2, 1775, TGP-ES 30; John Richard Alden, *General Gage in America: Being Principally a History of His Role in the American Revolution* (Baton Rouge: Louisiana State University Press, 1948), 272–86.

38. PCM, p. 2. See also PCM, pp. 14–15, 68–70.

39. Fowler to Gage, June 2, 1775, TGP-AS 129; PCM, pp. 38, 60.

40. PCM, p. 152; FCM, exhibit 7, p. 1.

41. FCM, exhibit 2, p. 1. See also Snell to Gage, September 23, 1775, WO 71/146; Baule, *Protecting the Empire's Frontiers*, 165.

42. Quoted in Richard Frothingham, *History of the Siege of Boston, and of the Battles of Lexington and Concord, and Bunker Hill*, 3rd ed. (Boston: Little, Brown, 1872), 197n2. See also Frothingham, *History of the Siege*, 280–81n2; Baule, *Protecting the Empire's Frontier*, 25.

43. Richard Cannon, *Historical Record of the Eighteenth or the Royal Irish Regiment of Foot* (London: Parker, Furnivall, and Parker, 1848); G. le M. Gretton, *The Campaigns and History of the Royal Irish Regiment from 1684 to 1902* (Edinburgh: Blackwood and Sons, 1911); R. G. Harris, *The Irish Regiments, 1683–1999*, revised by H. R. G. Wilson (Staplehurst: Spellmount, 1999), 107–19; "The Royal Irish Regiment," *Corps, Regiments, and Units*, The British Army, <www.army.mod.uk /who-we-are/corps-regiments-and-units/infantry/royal-irish -regiment/>.

44. Batt to Haldimand, April 18, 1780, FHP 21733, ff. 112–13; Batt to Haldimand, May 16, 1780, FHP 21733, f. 128; Baule, *Protecting the Empire's Frontier*, 106–8.

45. Baule, *Protecting the Empire's Frontier*, 112–13, 131–35.

46. Baule, *Protecting the Empire's Frontier*, 90–92, 188–91, 211–13.

47. Baule, *Protecting the Empire's Frontier*, 165–66.

48. JCC 13: 217; "Preparing for the Press, and Speedily Will Be Published, *The Republican Beacon*," *Pittsburgh Weekly Gazette*, November 6, 1801. See also JCC 13: 392, 433; 15: 1242, 1252; 21: 571;

25: 745–46; 28: 163; 29: 619, 779, 813–15; 30: 85–86; TJP 35: 183–84; 39: 99–103; Baule, *Protecting the Empire's Frontier*, 166–69.

49. Gawalt, *Elizabeth House Trist*, 11–53; Baule, *Protecting the Empire's Frontier*, 179–81; Wallace Ohrt, *Defiant Peacemaker: Nicholas Trist in the Mexican War* (College Station: Texas A&M Press, 1997).

50. TJP 35: 499–500; 39: 99–103.

51. *A List of the General and Field-Officers, as They Rank in the Army* (London: Millan, 1780), 323; *A List of the General and Field-Officers, as They Rank in the Army* (London: Millan, 1781), 279.

52. Quoted in Norris Stanley Barratt, *Outline of Old St. Paul's Church, Philadelphia, Pennsylvania* (Philadelphia: Colonial Society of Pennsylvania, 1917), 93. See also Dellape, *America's First Chaplain*, 117–35, 171–79; Deborah Mathias Gough, *Christ Church, Philadelphia: The Nation's Church in a Changing City* (Philadelphia: University of Pennsylvania Press, 1995), 141, 144, 153–60.

53. 15th Foot 1st Battalion, 1774–86, WO 12/3229, NAK; *A List of the General and Field-Officers, as They Rank in the Army* (London: Millan, 1776), 69; Richard Cannon, *Historical Record of the Fifteenth, or the Yorkshire East Riding, Regiment of Foot* (London: Parker, Furnivall, and Parker, 1848), 46–54.

54. *A List of the General and Field-Officers, as They Rank in the Army* (London: Millan, 1779), 79; M. Chasle de la Touche, *Histoire de Belle-Ile-en-Mer* (Nantes: Forest, 1852); Lawrence Henry Gipson, *The Great War for the Empire: The Culmination, 1760–63* (New York: Knopf, 1954), 180–85.

55. Newburgh to Canning, September 28, 1822, George Canning Papers, Add MS 89143/1/2/23, BL. See also Bonds for Various Amounts Lent by Abraham Creighton, Merchant Tailor of Dublin, to Neal Kenny, Broghill and Arthur Robert Camac Newburgh, George Montgomery, and Others, of County Cavan, MS 39,917, NLI.

56. *The Edinburgh Magazine, and Literary Miscellany; A New Series of the Scots Magazine*, vol. 18 (Edinburgh: Constable, 1826): 503.

Epilogue: I Imagined All These Old Prejudices Were Exploded

1. Quoted in Rictor Norton, *Mother Clap's Molly House: The Gay Subculture in England, 1700–1830* (London: GMP, 1992), 120. See also Jeremy Bentham, "Offences Against One's Self: Paederesty," ed. Louis Crompton, *Journal of Homosexuality* 3 (1977): 389–406;

Charles Upchurch, *Before Wilde: Sex between Men in Britain's Age of Reform* (Berkeley: University of California Press, 2009), 103; Theo van der Meer, "Sodomy and Its Discontents: Discourse, Desire, and the Rise of a Same-Sex Proto-Something in the Early Modern Dutch Republic," *Historical Reflections / Réflexions Historiques* 33 (2007): 41–67.

2. Jonathan Ned Katz, *The Invention of Heterosexuality* (New York: Dutton, 1995).

3. George L. Mosse, *Nationalism and Sexuality: Middle-Class Morality and Sexual Norms in Modern Europe* (Madison: University of Wisconsin Press, 1985).

4. Douglas R. Egerton, *Death or Liberty: African Americans and Revolutionary America* (New York: Oxford University Press, 2009).

5. H. G. Cocks, *Nameless Offences: Homosexual Desire in the Nineteenth Century* (London: Tauris, 2010), 7–8; A. D. Harvey, *Sex in Georgian England: Attitudes and Prejudices from the 1720s to the 1820s* (New York: St. Martin's Press, 1994), 125–26. See also Upchurch, *Before Wilde*, 83–104; Jeffrey Weeks, *Coming Out: Homosexual Politics in Britain, from the Nineteenth Century to the Present* (London: Quartet, 1977), 11–12.

6. Quoted in Upchurch, *Before Wilde*, 92. See also Weeks, *Coming Out*, 13–21.

7. Quoted in Weeks, *Coming Out*, 14. See also Alan Sinfield, *The Wilde Century: Effeminacy, Oscar Wilde and the Queer Movement* (New York: Columbia University Press, 1994); Eva Thienpont, "Visibly Wild(e): A Re-evaluation of Oscar Wilde's Homosexual Image," *Irish Studies Review* 13 (2005): 291–301; Michael S. Foldy, *The Trials of Oscar Wilde: Deviance, Morality, and Late-Victorian Society* (New Haven: Yale University Press, 1997); Merlin Holland, *The Real Trial of Oscar Wilde* (New York: HarperCollins, 2004).

8. Dror Wahrman, *The Making of the Modern Self: Identity and Culture in Eighteenth-Century England* (New Haven: Yale University Press, 2004), 251; Cocks, *Nameless Offences*, 18–19; Upchurch, *Before Wilde*, 13, 85–86, 204; Randolph Trumbach, "The Birth of the Queen: Sodomy and the Emergence of Gender Equality in Modern Culture, 1660–1750," in *Hidden from History: Reclaiming the Gay and Lesbian Past*, ed. Martin Duberman, Martha Vicinus, and George Chauncey Jr. (New York: Penguin, 1989), 129–40. See also Dominic Janes, *Picturing the Closet: Male Secrecy and Homosexual Visibility in Britain*

(Oxford: Oxford University Press, 2015); Eric O. Clarke, *Virtuous Vice: Homoeroticism and the Public Sphere* (Durham: Duke University Press, 2000).

9. Brian Lacey, *Terrible Queer Creatures: Homosexuality in Irish History* (Dublin: Wordwell, 2008), 109–16, 135–56; Norton, *Mother Clap's Molly House*, 214–21; Éibhear Walshe, *Oscar's Shadow: Wilde, Homosexuality, and Modern Ireland* (Cork: Cork University Press, 2011).

10. Averill Earls, "Unnatural Offenses of English Import: The Political Association of Englishness and Same-Sex Desire in Nineteenth-Century Irish Nationalist Media," JHS 28 (2019): 396–424; Lacey, *Terrible Queer Creatures*, 91–92.

11. For example, see Richard Godbeer, "'The Cry of Sodom': Discourse, Intercourse, and Desire in Colonial New England," WMQ 52 (1995): 259–86; Clare A. Lyons, "Mapping an Atlantic Sexual Culture: Homoeroticism in Eighteenth-Century Philadelphia," WMQ 60 (2003): 119–54.

12. GWP 14: 172. See also William Benemann, *Male-Male Intimacy in Early America: Beyond Romantic Friendships* (New York: Harrington Park Press, 2006), 71–72.

13. Quoted in Randy Shilts, *Conduct Unbecoming: Gays and Lesbians in the U.S. Military* (New York: St. Martin's Press, 1993), 8. See also Benemann, *Male-Male Intimacy*, 93–120; Paul Lockhart, *The Drillmaster of Valley Forge: The Baron de Steuben and the Making of the American Army* (New York: HarperCollins, 2008).

14. Quoted in PASL 12: 281. See also B. R. Burg, "Sodomy, Masturbation, and Courts-Martial in the Antebellum American Navy," JHS 23 (2014): 53–78; TJP 2: 497; Jen Manion, *Liberty's Prisoners: Carceral Culture in Early America* (Philadelphia: University of Pennsylvania Press, 2015), 158–60, 169–78. An ambivalence also appeared in Americans' views of cross-dressing in the Revolutionary era. See Benemann, *Male-Male Intimacy*, 245–60; Michael Bronski, *A Queer History of the United States* (Boston: Beacon, 2011), 35–39.

15. Quoted in Thomas J. Balcerski, *Boson Friends: The Intimate World of James Buchanan and William Rufus King* (New York: Oxford University Press, 2019), 96. See also John D'Emilio and Estelle B. Freedman, *Intimate Matters: A History of Sexuality in America*, 2nd ed. (Chicago: University of Chicago Press, 1997), 123, 127–29.

16. Margot Canaday, *The Straight State: Sexuality and Citizenship in Twentieth-Century America* (Princeton: Princeton University Press, 2009); David K. Johnson, *The Lavender Scare: The Cold War Persecution of Gays and Lesbians in the Federal Government* (Chicago: University of Chicago Press, 2004); Sean Brady, *Masculinity and Male Homosexuality in Britain, 1861–1913* (Houndmills: Palgrave Macmillan, 2005); George Chauncey, *Gay New York: Gender, Urban Culture, and the Making of the Gay Male World, 1890–1940* (New York: Basic Books, 1994); John D'Emilio, *Sexual Politics, Sexual Communities: The Making of a Homosexual Minority in the United States, 1940–70*, 2nd ed. (Chicago: University of Chicago Press, 1998); Michael Kirby, "The Sodomy Offence: England's Least Lovely Criminal Law Export," in *Human Rights, Sexual Orientation and Gender Identity in the Commonwealth: Struggles for Decriminalization and Change*, ed. Corinne Lennox and Matthew Waites (London: Human Rights Consortium, 2013), 71.

INDEX

abolitionism, 244–45, 276

Adams, Abigail, 156

Adams, John: and American Revolution, 71, 180, 208, 243, 255; at Congress, 248, 281; in New York, 164–65, 247

adjutant, 38, 81, 126, 144

Adventures of Roderick Random, The (Smollett), 24–25, 79

Adye, Stephen Payne: at court-martial of William McDermott, 61; on court-martial of Robert Newburgh, 162, 166, 237, 240, 246, 249; at courts-martial of Nicholas Gaffney and John Green, 117–18, 141

Africans. *See* Blacks

Albigensian Crusade, 93

alcohol: Robert Newburgh's, 20, 176–78, 195–97, 217–18, 235, 238; soldiers', 36–37, 40–41, 46–47, 121–22, 133; wives selling, 43.

American colonists: and British army, 39, 46, 51, 147, 179–80, 251; on macaroni, 207–9; in Massachusetts, 65, 160, 247; in New Jersey, 175–76; in New York, 163–64, 254, 260–61; in Philadelphia, 64–65, 88–89, 145–50, 189–90, 216, 233; sexuality of, 152–55, 209–10

American Company, 58

American Revolution, 5–6, 151–52, 244–45, 289n5, 335n46; and buggery, 93–94, 243–45, 248–49, 254–55, 263–64, 279–82; and the Enlightenment, 243–45, 281–82; and macaroni, 207–9; in Massachusetts, 51, 65, 88, 139–41, 147, 247–48, 250, 257–59, 262; in New Jersey, 175–76, 251; in New York, 88, 160, 163–65, 209, 251–55, 260–63, 271; in Philadelphia, 51, 88–89, 145–51, 247–48, 271; and seduction, 180–81; war, 257–71, 280–81

Anglicans, 18–19, 22, 26–28, 30, 191–92, 232–33; in New York, 163; in Philadelphia, 55–57, 81, 149, 160–61, 216, 233, 248, 269–70. *See also* Church of Ireland, clergy

Anglo Atlantic, **4**

Northern Liberties (Philadelphia), 48, 84, 145, 249, 273–74
North, Lord (Frederick North), 88, 139
Norton, Rictor, xiii

officers' meeting at Isaac Hamilton's room, 102–3, 106, 108, 214–15, 225, 313n20
Ó hÉoghusa, Eochaidh, 21
Old Bailey. *See* Central Criminal Court
Old Daniel, 92, 94
"On a Young BOY's being dress'd in Girl's Cloathes" (Newburgh), 9–10
Osborne, Thomas, 87, 126, 162, 171, 187, 217–18, 233, 263
outhouse. *See* necessary house
Oxford, Earl of (Robert Harley), 226
Oxford University, 14, 25, 191, 236

Pamela (Richardson), 180
Paragraph 175, 276
Parker, John, 257
Parliament of England/Great Britain, 29, 51, 65, 139, 151, 154, 226; and buggery laws, 3, 22, 24, 53, 207, 278
Parliament of Ireland, 11, 13–14, 17, 27, 157; and buggery laws, 22, 25, 76
Parr, William, 101, 104, 313n19
parsons. *See* clergy
Patrick, Saint, 21
Patriots, 71–72, 147, 260–61, 267–69

Patten, John, 79–80, 111, 171–72, 311n26
Patten, Thomas, 28
Payne, Benjamin Charnock, 42–44, 95–98, 130; in Boston, 263–64; civil suit of Robert Newburgh against, 100, 124, 130, 143; at court-martial of John Green, 115–16, 118–24, 128, 142; at court-martial of Robert Newburgh, 168–69, 219; at court of enquiry of Robert Newburgh, 109–10; at courts-martial of Nicholas Gaffney, 115, 131, 135–36; in New York, 252–57, 259, 261–62; at Issac Hamilton's suit with merchant, 148; Robert Newburgh called bougre/buggerer by, 90, 92–97, 99–102, 104, 119–23, 142, 198; Robert Newburgh criticized by, 58, 78, 87, 120, 155, 162, 218; in Philadelphia, 50, 59–60, 62, 65; retires, 266
pederasty, 60–62, 69–70, 74–75, 178, 195, 197, 227–28, 234
Pells, Lawrence, 66–67
Penitential of Columban, 21–22
Penn (ship), 51–52, 74
Penn, John, 88
Pennsylvania: assembly, 51; buggery law, 66, 281; Eighteenth Regiment in, 38–39, 150; militia, 268
Pennsylvania Provincial Congress, 146–47
Penn, William, 47
Perth Amboy, N.J., 118, 251

Philadelphia, Pa., 47–48, *49*, 273–74; American Revolution in, 51, 88, 145–51, 233; Anglican clergy in, 57, 160–61, 215–16, 233, 269–70; British occupation of, 266, 270–71; Christmas in, 81; Eighteenth Regiment in, 38, 47–52, 55–65, 83–84, 95, 134–36, 145, 251; Robert Newburgh in, 58–59. *See also* Northern Liberties

Philadelphia Barracks, 48–51, *91*, 273; Eighteenth Regiment at, 57–60, 62–64, 145, 147; guard duty at, 113–14; infirmary, 160–61, 183–84, 252; military trials at, 108, 115; Robert Newburgh at, 81–93, 124–26, 144–45, 156–62, 170, 249, 271; tailors' workroom, 83–84, 90–93, 96–97, 99, 102, 119–23, 198, 230

Pitcairn, John, 257

Pittsburgh, Pa., 40, 150, 268

Plymouth, Mass., 152

Polly (ship), 88

Pope, Alexander, 234, 333n27

Powder Alarm, 247

Presbyterians, 12, 163

Prideaux, Edmund, 90, 92, 96, 203

priests. *See* clergy

prostitutes, 50, 69

Protestant Ascendancy, 11–13, 16–17, 19, 22, 25

Protestant Episcopal Church in America, 270

provisions, 48, 81–82, 86–87, 125–26, 133, 136, 147, 170

purchase system, 29–30

Pyrah, Joseph, 82, 125–26, 238

Quakers. *See* Society of Friends

Quartering Act, 39, 51, 148

quartermaster, 38, 81–82, 126.

Quebec. *See* Canada

Quincy, Josiah, 147

rape. *See* sexual assault

ratafia, 36–37

Reed, Bowes, 175

Reed, Joseph, 175–76

Regulator Movement, 209

Republican Beacon, The (Fowler), 268

Revere, Paul, 145, 247

rhetoric, 19, 222–25, 228–36

Richardson, Samuel, 180

Richardson, William, 262

riding, 16, 62–63, 128, 199

Rigby, Edward, 25, 52–53

rights: Americans', 146, 151–52, 155–56, 165, 180, 233, 248; army's, 39, 148; buggerers', 225–28, 241–45, 277–82; individuals claim, 31; Newburgh claims, 1, 6–7, 140, 157, 165, 170–71, 202, 229–36; political, 12, 234

Revolution. *See* American Revolution

Robertson, James, 65

Robinson, John, 172–73

Ross, Elizabeth Griscom, 71

Ross, George, 71, 248

Ross, James, 194–95, 210–11

Ross, John, 71, 148, *149*, 167–68, 175